Medical Sketches of the Campaigns of 1812, 13, 14 [microform]

The copy filmed here has been reproduced thanks to the generosity of:

National Library of Canada

The images appearing here are the best quality possible considering the condition and legibility of the original copy and in keeping with the filming contract specifications.

Original copies in printed paper covers are filmed beginning with the front cover and ending on the last page with a printed or illustrated impression, or the back cover when appropriate. All other original copies are filmed beginning on the first page with a printed or illustrated impression, and ending on the last page with a printed or illustrated impression.

The last recorded frame on each microfiche shall contain the symbol ➝ (meaning "CONTINUED"), or the symbol ▽ (meaning "END"), whichever applies.

Maps, plates, charts, etc., may be filmed at different reduction ratios. Those too large to be entirely included in one exposure are filmed beginning in the upper left hand corner, left to right and top to bottom, as many frames as required. The following diagrams illustrate the method:

L'exemplaire filmé fut reproduit grâce à la générosité de:

Bibliothèque nationale du Car

Les images suivantes ont été reproduites ave plus grand soin, compte tenu de la condition de la netteté de l'exemplaire filmé, et en conformité avec les conditions du contrat de filmage.

Les exemplaires originaux dont la couverture papier est imprimée sont filmés en commenç par le premier plat et en terminant soit par la dernière page qui comporte une empreinte d'impression ou d'illustration, soit par le seco plat, selon le cas. Tous les autres exemplaire originaux sont filmés en commençant par la première page qui comporte une empreinte d'impression ou d'illustration et en terminant la dernière page qui comporte une telle empreinte.

Un des symboles suivants apparaîtra sur la dernière image de chaque microfiche, selon l cas: le symbole ➝ signifie "A SUIVRE", le symbole ▽ signifie "FIN".

Les cartes, planches, tableaux, etc., peuvent filmés à des taux de réduction différents. Lorsque le document est trop grand pour êtr reproduit en un seul cliché, il est filmé à part de l'angle supérieur gauche, de gauche à dro et de haut en bas, en prenant le nombre d'images nécessaire. Les diagrammes suivan illustrent la méthode.

1	2	3

1
2
3

1	2	3
4	5	6

MEDICAL

SKETCHES

OF THE

CAMPAIGNS OF 1812, 13, 14.

TO WHICH ARE ADDED,

SURGICAL CASES; OBSERVATIONS ON MILITARY HOSPITALS; AND FLYING
HOSPITALS ATTACHED TO A MOVING ARMY.

ALSO,

AN APPENDIX,

COMPRISING

A DISSERTATION ON DYSENTERY;

WHICH OBTAINED THE BOYLSTONIAN PRIZE MEDAL FOR THE YEAR 1806;

AND

OBSERVATIONS ON THE WINTER EPIDEMIC OF 1815-16,

DENOMINATED

PERIPNEUMONIA NOTHA;

AS IT APPEARED AT SHARON AND ROCHESTER,
State of Massachusetts.

BY JAMES MANN, M. D. A. A. S.

Hospital Surgeon of the Army, Member of the Massachusetts Medical Society, and
Corresponding Member of the Georgian Medical Society.

DEDHAM:
PRINTED BY H. MANN AND CO.
1816.

ADVERTISEMENT.

In consequence of an order from Major General BROWN, Commander in Chief of the second division of the army, to repair to Detroit, these sheets were hurried through the press. Some typographical errors have consequently escaped notice; the most essential will appear subjoined under ERRATA. No apology will be made for the work in general; that something of the kind may be better executed, is desirable. The communications from Doctors HUNT, LOVELL, FULLER, WHITRIDGE, PURCELL and MARCH, need nothing to recommend them; as upon perusal, they will be found interesting to the physician, and creditable to the authors.

To HORATIO GATES SPAFFORD, Esq. my acknowledgments are particularly due. The statistical observations comprised in the book, are abstracts from a Gazetteer of the State of New-York, written by him, and published by SOUTHWICK, in 1813; as well as a few historical facts, relative to the first settlements; which were more especially introduced, to give distant readers some idea, what dangers and difficulties the first settlers had to encounter; and the astonishing rapid increase of the North-Western district of New-York. Upon the last subjects, much might have been added, but they are more appropriate to a geographical work. For a particular description of the state of New-York at large, and especially the new settlements in the Northern and Western counties, less generally known, the reader is referred to that circumstantial and comprehensive Gazetteer, which, by competent judges, is considered most correct.

The note on the winter epidemic, at *Sharon* and *Rochester*, in the State of Massachusetts, was not contemplated in the first prospectus of the book ; the transactions at those places having occurred since it was published ; but will be no less interesting to medical readers, especially in those parts of New-England, where the epidemic made dreadful ravages. The stimulating practice in that disease, had previously, on the frontiers, been opposed with some warmth. In the last instance, it has not been treated with too much severity ; although this absurd, destructive practice, in many instances, had been adopted by gentlemen of high standing as physicians ; whose medical knowledge I respect, and friendship highly esteem.

ERRATA.

Page 14—2d line from top, for *forinacea*, read *farinacea*.
    34—10th line from bottom, for *fæcal* read *fecal*.
    36—18th line from bottom, for *enebriate* read *inebriate*.
    54—15th line from top, for *various* read *numerous*.
    59—8th line from top, for *wait* read *waited*.
    76—16th line from bottom, for *ipecacuanhas were* read *ipecacuanha was*.

TO MAJOR GENERAL DEARBORN.

———

SIR—The tried patriot, who dared to resist the oppressive
measures of a despotic government, demands our reverence. At
an early period of life, when your country required the aid of
all its citizens to secure its independence, you relinquished your
medical pursuits, and abandoned every domestic enjoyment, for
the perilous and uncertain events of war. You have beheld the
sceptre of a king broken, and his crown trodden under foot.
You have seen a despotic power crouch to rational liberty, and
the principles of the inalienable rights of man, emerging from
that thraldom, which a blind faith in hereditary power imposed
on the mind. The American revolution, in which you bore a
conspicuous part, was not merely a victory of arms, but a glorious triumph of principle.

The warm advocates of a democratic form of government,
have not been disappointed; they have rejoiced in the unexampled prosperity of the nation, under a novel regimen, while
more than thirty years of successful experiment have demonstrated, that a representative government, is adequate to meet every
exigency of the nation, and under the most threatening dangers,
to call forth her resources to oppose them.

After a long period of prosperous peace, war was again provoked. To avenge the insults and aggressions of an imperious and haughty enemy, arms were resorted to. From what class of citizens was it to have been expected, the government would select a leader for its army? But from the few existing veterans, whose military talents and prowess, had been already proved on the tented field, and in the day of battle. A few only of that long catalogue of heroes, whose memories will always be engraven on the hearts of the nation, still lived. From this remnant, you, Sir, was selected, and promoted to the high grade of MAJOR GENERAL in the army. It belongs to those who have witnessed the perplexities and embarrassments attending the organization of an undisciplined body of men, to appreciate your merits. This rude assemblage of troops under your command, learnt the first rudiments of war, and were taught to beat the most celebrated veterans of Europe. You was a witness of the effects of eight months' discipline. Your early and rapid movements in 1813, preserved Sackett's Harbor and the fleet on Lake Ontario. The plans of attack prescribed by yourself, on Little York and Fort George, bear testimony to your military talents; and how much, under able Generals, the American soldiery were capable of accomplishing. The very brilliant victory of their arms, soon compelled the enemy to sue for peace. At the termination of a war, honorable to the nation, you retired to domestic enjoyment, accompanied with the benedictions of the army, and full approbation of your country; and with the pleasing consolation, that no officer has presumed to exhibit publicly, an allegation against you, nor by private insinuations, attempted to detract from your well deserved fame.

If at any period, the wily serpent of envy, or an enemy of government, remote from the scenes of your active services, has presumed to erect its head, to blast with its venomous poison your unsullied reputation; it soon retired from the refulgent beams of truth, appalled, to its native dark cell, there to expend its malignancy, while it secretly broods over its own disappointment.

The brave and virtuous call forth our esteem and awaken our affections. Honors are not the exclusive inheritance of any order of men. Integrity is found in the private walks of life. The high offices of government accessible to all, are beheld as public stations, in which the citizens in succession, perform their tours of duty. Those who have executed their task with integrity, claim our first respects, and possess our unfeigned regards. Many of these most important trusts have been committed to your charge, in which your faithfulness has been tried and proved.

In your retirement, you have an opportunity to take a retrospective view of the various scenes you have passed, possessing the conscious satisfaction, it has been your peculiar good fortune to have performed your routine of duty, to the general acceptance of the nation.

It still remains for me to express my own acknowledgments for your assistance, while I had the honor to perform duty under your command. Your knowledge of medical science, enabled you duly to estimate the importance of the hospital department of the army. In the organization of which, no small benefits were derived from your advice and judicious counsels.

May you long live to enjoy the supreme satisfaction resulting from the retrospection of a life devoted to your country, well spent in her service; while it is with peculiar pleasure, these sheets, expressive of my high respects, and wishes for the continuance of your happiness in this, as well as that life which is anticipated by all christians, are to you inscribed by

your most obedient servant,

JAMES MANN.

ting
well
hese
con-
:h is

PRELIMINARY OBSERVATIONS.

~~~~~~~~~

TO trace the various causes, which involved the United States in the late war with Great Britain, is the province of the political historian. It has been a question, whether it was good policy, to oppose with menacing attitude, the aggressions of an enemy previous to maturing warlike preparations for defence. There are periods when the most important concerns of a nation, under all governments, will be controled by public opinion. Such was the state of affairs, at that ever memorable epocha, when the war, which terminated in the independence of the United States, was commenced. Under a republican government, the voice of the people will dictate the measures to be pursued. Provocations, similar in their consequences to those, which excited the revolutionary war, existed in 1812. A state of war was demanded by the nation, at a period, when no preparations for even defensive operations had been made; when military equipments were to be furnished, and an army to be recruited. To systematize the various departments of which, was an employment which required months to accomplish. That military character, which had been acquired by the nation, during a war of seven years to establish its independence, was lost. An uninterrupted peace of thirty years had obliterated almost every vestige of military knowledge. The art of war slumbered with the heroes of the revolution. Martial renown was unknown, except on the pages of the impartial and faithful historian; while the records of military deeds and glory, in the United States, like fancied tales, excited wonder and pleasure, rather than elicited that patriotic fire, which warms the breast of the soldier, and glows in the soul of the hero, destined to protect the r   is and avenge the wrongs done his country.

Habits of subordination cannot be immediately acquired by men taken into the field from domestic employment. Recruits,

2

assembled from districts remote from each other, possessing local prejudices, and dissimilar manners, could not in a moment be
well disciplined. To organize an army, composed of such heter-
ogeneous materials, with officers, who had yet to learn the duties
of the camp and field, was a laborious task. It was an employment, which called into requisition much patience and perseverance. In the execution of these duties, through the campaign,
profound wisdom and judicious management were displayed by
the Commanding General.

The medical, with other departments of the army, at the commencement of the war, wanted a system. Military hospitals
were to be founded by gentlemen, little versed in hospital establishments, for an army. These were evils, the necessary consequence of our civil polity, and long period of peace; and
which, all new military establishments have to encounter.

The acceptance of an appointment of hospital surgeon in the
army, placed me in a novel situation. An order from Major
General Dearborn was received, to repair to Greenbush, State
of New-York, the place assigned for the general rendezvous, and
superintend the medical department of the northern army. The
mere organization of hospitals was the least perplexing part of
duty. The illy defined powers, with which the hospital surgeons were invested, even in their own department, subjected
them to many disagreeable interferences of the officers of the
line. Collisions will always exist, between officers of different
departments of an army; when their several powers and duties
are not explicitly pointed out. Officers, tenacious of authority,
assume as much as may be implied by rules and regulations.

In addition to multiplied embarrassments, the various duties
attached to the office of hospital surgeon, with those merely professional, was always so pressing, that little time was allowed
to record, particularly, the diseases and medical transactions of
the army, as they occurred. It is a matter of regret, that many
interesting cases have been lost, which might have rendered the
following sketches more comprehensive, perhaps useful; for
want of which, only a general view of the diseases, which prevailed during the war will be given, with such treatments as
come under my observation.

An extensive field for investigating the causes of diseases incident to armies, their prevention and cure, was open during the revolutionary contest, but was not improved for our benefit. The physicians and surgeons of that eventful period neglected to transmit to us their experience and observations. Excepting a few remarks interspersed in works of Dr. Rush, all to us is lost. At the commencement of that war, the mortality which prevailed among the troops was greater than the last. The forms of diseases, in all probability, were similar. The medical staff of the army of 1812, possessing no documents relative to the management of military hospitals, nor the diseases to which our armies were exposed, to direct them to the most suitable means of obviating, or the most successful methods of treating them, which in many instances, assumed forms different from those which occur in domestic practice, necessarily had recourse to European treatises on military hospitals and diseases of the camp. The practice, on the eastern continent, in diseases apparently similar, is, in many instances, illy adapted to the cure of the diseases peculiar to the United States. We are led further to observe, that while we consult practical authors, some regard should be had to climates and local situations, where their observations were made. Hence, a knowledge of geography in general, and topography, are particularly important to the physician and surgeon, to become acquainted with the connection which subsists between climates and constitutions, in exploring the manner diseases are affected thereby, inasmuch as local situations and climates produce varieties in the human constitution, which diversify the forms of disease.

The medical philosopher is not ignorant that the diseases of different climates assume forms which are peculiar to their local position; that the treatment of the diseases of one climate, is not always applicable to those of a different; also, the diseases of the same climate in different years, and during the varying seasons of the year, are not always to be treated in a similar manner.

The last observations are particularly applicable to the United States, whose extensive territories and districts embrace within their limits, a vast variety of climates; interspersed with large improved tracts, vast forests in the wildest condition, and extensive territories in intermediate states, from nature in her rudest attire, to the highest grades of cultivation.

Sydenham, an accurate observer of the nature of diseases, while noticing the changes produced in their forms by transitions of seasons and weather, observed that the fevers of his time, year succeeding year, required different methods of practice. He, likewise, cured dysentery at one period, by cathartics, at another by opium. Our own practice confirms the justness of the above observations. Intermittent fever among the soldiers we shall select as one disease; which at Gre~ bush in 1812, at Lewistown on the Niagara in 1813, at Burlington in 1814, required different methods of treatment.

Experience has taught us, the health of men is more or less affected by change of climate. Soldiers, ordered on service to a district whose temperature differs from that to which they had, from early life, been habituated, are more subject to its endemic diseases, and have severer attacks from them, than the natives. The winter epidemics on the northern frontiers, it was remarked, were more mortal among the troops from South of Delaware river, than those from the New-England states. This fact was most evident, during the winter epidemic 1813–14, in the 10th Regiment, at Plattsburgh. In the distribution of troops, it is important that regard be had to their habits, and the climates to which they may be ordered for duty. "Diseases are so modified and varied by different situations and local positions, habits of life, constitution, age and temperament, as well as transitions of climate and weather, their various forms are almost infinite."

An epidemic, which takes its general features from a pestilential state of atmosphere, when it invades a vast extent of country, assumes a variety of forms; whence originate among physicians scisms, varient opinions, and opposite, as well as indecisive methods of practice. When these disagreements exist in the same district, incalculable evils are often the consequence. But so far as they are applicable to the several districts, where they exist, the apparent difference of treating the disease may be correct. The winter epidemic of 1812–13, was ample proof of the above remark. On the northern frontiers, it assumed forms highly inflammatory, accompanied not only with strong arterial action, but higher degrees of *stenic diathesis*, in which the lungs were so gorged with blood, that the heart and arteries almost ceased to act, inducing at the extremities and on the surface of the body, torpidity and coldness; symptoms, bearing the semblance of a typhoid state of disease. In the vicinity of New-York city, the disease supervened with symptoms less inflammatory. At Washington city, the disease exhibi.. few or little symptoms of inflammation, and was considered a form of typhus fever. This epidemic most generally obtained the same nosological appellation; but in different districts of the country was qualified by some specific name, which was supposed to be applicable to its existent form. In addition to its generic denomination, *pneumonia*; it was called at one place, *pneumonia notha*; at another, *pneumonia typhoides*; *malignant pleurisy* at a third; and at a fourth, bilious pneumonia. It was also denominated a highly malignant bilious fever, from a persuasion that the organs, subservient to the secretion of the bile, or a redundance of that fluid, was a cause of the derangement. These varient opinions may be seen in communications upon the epidemic 1812, 13, 14, published in the MEDICAL REPOSITORY, New-York.

This epidemic, when it first appeared on the northern frontiers, was accompanied with symptoms so uncommon, that some physicians were induced to consider it a new or anomalous disease. It was not correctly understood by the surgeons of the army, until its nature was ascertained by dissections of those who were its victims. After the morbid states of the viscera were demonstrated, the physicians adopted a practice more successful; while these examinations were proofs convincing, that this mortal disease had, heretofore, been known in Europe; a most accurate description of which, JOHN BELL has given in his anatomy of the human body, which may be found in his 1st vol. New-York edition, page 136.

A correct history of an extensive epidemic cannot be obtained, except from collected statements from the various sections of a country where it has prevailed. How important then, that the forms of disease, with their treatment, be reported in every territory, that they, severally, may be furnished with a method of practice best adapted to its climate or local position! Such medical documents may be highly useful, so far as they may be particularly applicable to the various climates of an extensive country.

The surgeons, attached to the army, the last war, would be well employed to improve the present time to commence a history of the diseases attendant on a military life. A fund of useful observations might with little industry be collected, and preserved for the benefit of future generations. Its value would be enhanced proportionate to the additions which may be made to the general stock; in which every surgeon of the army should feel he has an interest.

The Sketches are a partial exhibition of the diseases on the northern frontiers, to which district the author was attached during the war; being abstracts of medical observations made at those points only, where he was a witness of them, with reports from a few gentlemen of the medical department, who were conversant with the diseases as they appeared in camp and the military hospitals; to whom particular acknowledgments will be made, in due place, for their aid and matter furnished for this compilation.

Although the sketches may be considered as comprising a small portion compared with the great body of facts which may be adduced; yet, however small, they may prove of some benefit to medical science. A record of incorrect practice, faithfully detailed, may be improved, like a beacon to a mariner, to avoid dangers and erroneous tracks.

These sketches may be further useful to the science of medicine, to excite others, who were attached to the medical department of the army, possessing matter of greater importance, and more leisure and talents, to appropriate them to this highly important subject—the preservation from disease and death, of that valuable and most necessary class of citizens, who are employed to protect the rights of the nation, and support its independence.

n, that
every
method
Such
may be
ensive

uld be
a his-
of use-
d pre-
uld be
ade to
should

on the
d dur-
ade at
eports
e con-
e mil-
ill be
or this

sing a
a may
bene-
hfully
avoid

medi-
al de-
tance,
ighly
th, of
e em-
inde-

MEDICAL SKETCHES.

CAMPAIGN OF 1812.

SOME preliminary remarks upon the state of weather prior, and at the time the army was forming at Greenbush, will be made; also, a concise topographical description of the cantonment at this post will be given, by which an opinion may be formed, to what extent the diseases, to which the troops were subjected, may have been produced by local causes, or their health affected by atmospheric influences, which depended merely on local situation.

The vernal months of the year 1812 were unusually wet, with few warm days. July was dry and hot, succeeded by floods of rain in the month of August; when the weather was uncommonly cool for the season. The month of September was pleasant to men in tents. October was wet and cold. The men, during this month, suffered in their healths, by sudden transitions of weather. Vegetation was later this spring, by two or three weeks, than usual. Indian corn was not planted, in the eastern states, until the last week in May, and the first weeks in June. Other grains were put into the ground later this season than was usual; nevertheless, the productions of the earth, although retarded by cold, were generally luxuriant. The summer grains were damaged during the time of harvest by rains. Wheat vegetated in the fields after it was ripe. Indian corn, for want of sufficient heat, did not generally mature. This was noticed throughout the eastern states, and the northern district of New-York; the crops of which were diminished one half by the early frosts in autumn.

Rains fell in such abundance, during the month of August, that the earth, even on declivities, was soft and miry. This was the state of clay grounds at Greenbush, upon which the army encamped, although an elevated plain. To remedy the evils of a wet encampment, the floorings of the tents were raised four or five inches above the surface of the earth, and the encampment frequently changed to fresh ground. Many of the men, at this time, were nevertheless, attacked with dysentery and diarrhœa. Hospitals were not prepared to receive the sick; consequently, they were attended in tents. There were detachments of several regiments in August, at this cantonment, amounting to about 1500 men. From the first week in September, to the first of November, regiments and detachments, week after week, marched to and from this post; during which time, the number of men varied between 1500, and 3000: while surgeons of regiments had full employment in their duty; and the weekly reports of the general hospital counted between 100 and 130, until the the first of November; at which time, the most of the troops had marched to the frontiers; when about 200 men, unable to accompany their regiments, on account of diseases and infirmities, remained in the hospital.

The most prominent diseases, among the troops at Greenbush, during the months of July, August, and September, were disorders of the bowels, under the forms of dysentery and diarrhœa. To these diseases, recruits when they take the field, are generally subjected; especially, where their rations for diet are not prepared in the most suitable manner. These diseases may, in some measure, be obviated by obliging the men to cook their food in the form of soups. This regulation should be ever enforced upon men in the field. To which, they will cheerfully submit, when experience has taught them the benefit resulting therefrom. The science of preserving health is too little known to new recruits; a knowledge of which, young officers unaccustomed to the police of a camp, do not impress upon them the importance of acquiring. An inattention to a proper dietetic management was among the causes of diseases and mortality, incident to our troops; to which may be added, filthiness, and an intemperate use of ardent spirits. These sources of disease we shall have repeated occasion to notice; as frequent causes of the failure of important expeditions, and ruin of armies; by which, the highest expectations of a nation are often disappointed.

The dysentery of this campaign was not accompanied with uncommon symptoms. A detailed description of which is unimportant, as it supervened under forms most generally described by medical authors. It was observed, that this disease at its commencement during the campaign, was attended in most cases with a fever of the synochal type, accelerated action of the arteries, and heat increased considerably above the healthy standard. With these symptoms, blood-letting was advantageously employed. One bleeding of sixteen ounces was, in most cases, necessary. This was followed by a full cathartic of calomel and jalap; which mitigated all the urgent symptoms of the disease. A repetition of a cathartic was sometimes requisite. Anodines became an appropriate medicine after the intestines were well evacuated. In cases more obstinate, emetics of tartrite of antimony, or ipecacuanha were indicated; or an emetico-cathartic composed of calomel and tartrite of antimony. There were cases, when calomel and opium, in small doses, at intervals of four or six hours, were found beneficial.

Dysentery assumed a typhoid form, in some instances, when the patient, at its first appearance was destitute of medical aid. Some of this description were admitted into the general hospital, at Greenbush; having been attacked with the disease, during a long passage from Rhode-Island to Albany, crowded in vessels, exposed during the heat of the day, and fogs of the night on deck, to avoid the suffocating state of air in the hold. Some of whom, when received into the hospital, were in a bad condition. For these patients were prescribed cathartics of sulphate of soda; super-tartrite of potash and manna; many of whom required stimulants, diluted brandy, wine. To one were administered from one to two pints of wine daily, for two weeks; and by this stimulus only was supported, and apparently from a dying state, was eventually restored to health. In all cases of this disease,

3

animal nutriment, even in the form of soups, was prohibited. Preparations of the farinacea and milk were experienced the most appropriate regimen. A milk diet was the most suitable during the state of convalescence, from this disease. There were cases where relapses followed the employment of animal food, where the patients were indulged, before the stomach and bowels had recovered their healthy tone.

An opinion prevailed among the soldiers, that ardent spirits was a sovereign remedy for these complaints of the bowels. This persuasion, added to an habitual propensity for these liquors, induced many to have recourse to their intemperate use. It was not unfrequent to find a patient, on the first visit, highly excited, even to the point of intoxication, by these inebriating draughts. This fact may account for the more frequent necessity of employing the lancet among soldiers, than citizens; not only in this, but all forms of disease.

Diseases of the bowels, among the troops, appeared most frequent under the form of diarrhœa. In which, cathartics were also employed; calomel and rhubarb; sulphate of soda. When the disease was accompanied with nausea, and anorexia, emetics of ipecacuanha likewise were administered.

Intermittent fevers of the tertian type, were sometimes connected with these complaints of the bowels. This form of disease was noticed at Greenbush hospital, only among the recruits from south of Hudson river; who, previous to leaving their first rendezvous, to join the army, had been seized with the disease, and had recovered; but relapsed, while on their long passage up the Hudson, in crowded vessels; where the sick were necessarily confined below deck. Their condition had become bad; the type of the fever, changing from an intermittent, to a continued form. Some of these men died, soon after admittance into the hospital.

When the paroxisms of these intermittents recurred, at regular periods, the cold stage of the fever was anticipated by an emetic; which seldom failed to interrupt the diseased associations, and thus counteracted the hot stage. After the first passages were evacuated by emetics, and cathartics, and during the intermissions, bark and wine were directed. These intermittents did not prove obstinate. They were readily subdued, when the above means were judiciously managed.

The change of weather was great and sudden in the month of October. Frosts commenced earlier than usual this autumn. This transition introduced, among the soldiers in tents, additional forms of disease. Among these, were acute and chronic rheumatism. Those who were subjected to their attacks were over forty years of age; who, previous to their enlistment, had been broken down by either hardships or intemperance, or both combined. Of this description of soldiers, many remained at Greenbush hospital, at the time their regiments received orders to march to the frontiers; whose services in the army here terminated, and whose only tours of duty were short marches, during the most pleasant season of the year, from their first rendezvous, to this cantonment. (See note A.)

The bad policy of government was now most evident. The experiment demonstrated, that an efficient army on the war establishment, could not be raised by the small encouragement offered the soldiers. The army was composed of that description of men, who were habitually indolent, or who could find no other employment. Few of these classes are found in the United States. Idleness is not a characteristic feature of their inhabitants; who, with adequate compensation, will always prove the most firm supporters of the nation's rights; and who will never be made the instruments of ambition to subvert its government, nor countervail its salutary laws. A young healthy man disdained to enrol himself in the army, for a compensation less than he could obtain for his services in domestic employment. The industrious yeomanry of the country, of whom our efficient armies must be composed, and who will fight its enemies, calculate upon adequate pay, with as much exactness, as a merchant calculates upon the profits of a trading voyage.

Acute rheumatism required the use of the lancet; the chronic form seldom demanded bleeding. These forms of disease generally yielded to calomel, opium, blisters and warm lodgings. The tepid bath would have proved a pleasant remedy. The

unorganized state of the hospital, at this period, did not admit of
its employment. After recovery, the patients were not secured
from the disease. Exposures to wet and cold, subjected them to
renewed attacks. The following prescriptions under different
circumstances were administered. (See note B.)

Measles shewed themselves among the soldiers, in a few instances, at Greenbush. The disease was mild, and generally
little or no medical aid was required. Bleeding in two or three
instances was necessary; so was a cathartic of calomel and
jalap, or sulphate of soda. Where a cough was troublesome, a
tea-spoonful of equal parts of antimonial wine, and compound
tincture of opium, was beneficial to remove the irritation on the
lungs, after fever had subsided.

It has been already observed, the sudden change of weather
in October introduced additional forms of disease among the
men. We have to notice one of more formidable and more
questionable symptoms; PNEUMONIA, or inflammation within the
breast. This disease was, in some instances, accompanied with
diarrhœa; or supervened where diarrhœa previously existed;
which last disease had not entirely disappeared. The above
combination of morbid actions, never, or seldom occurs in domestic practice, in the New-England states. The following
were the most prominent symptoms; pain in the chest; in some
cases one side, in others both were affected; short and difficult
respiration; dry cough; the pulse of those, whose condition was
most alarming, was small and hard; the heat of the body and
extremities not above the standard of health, sometimes below.
The above symptoms, with diarrhœa, which, in a few instances,
attended, seemed to forbid the employment of the lancet; but
subsequent practice justified its use. When this remedy was
omitted, other auxiliaries were of little or no benefit. A question at this period was made, whether there can be a state of
inflammation, where the heat of the body and extremities, at the
early onset of the disease, is below that of health, and the pulse
small. The success which followed eleven successive bleedings of four ounces each, in a case of the above description, demonstrated the affirmative. This was a soldier of the 25th regi-

ment, who was admitted into the hospital, after having been bled sixteen ounces at one time, by his own surgeon of regiment; and who, when he accompanied the man into the hospital, observed, that bleeding had been employed, as far as the condition of the man would justify. This was also my opinion, upon first examination of the case; but, after all other means had failed to procure relief, and the oppression still continuing upon the breast, bleeding was again employed, and repeated. Arterial action in this instance was not increased, as the vessels were unloaded by blood-letting, as was often the case. The pulse however, did not sink, but remained stationary. Encouragement was therefore given, to pursue depletion with caution; until difficult respiration was removed. This practice was at first adopted as a justifiable experiment, in a most desperate case. Calomel, antimonials, and blisters were freely employed through the course of the disease.

This disease, when it first appeared at Greenbush, was not considered as being connected with an epidemic state of atmosphere. The following theory was suggested by the extraordinary symptoms, under which the disease appeared. Long and unremitted exposures to cold in tents overcame the action of the arteries, at their minute extremities. The caloric upon the surface of the body was expended more rapidly, than it was evolved by the vital powers; while the pulmonic vessels became crowded with blood, and extravasated blood mixed with mucus formed congestions within the bronchiæ. The heart gorged with blood, struggled with diminished efforts to remove its load, and the whole system was pervaded with torpor. Was this a state of inflammation? The symptoms did not correspond with those, common to inflammation; while dissections demonstrated similar morbid appearances, on the important organs of life, which are connected with well known symptoms of inflammation. (See note c.)

What is inflammation, but a repletion of the sanguiferous vessels of some animated organ; and, in some instances, an elongation of its component vessels, having the appearance of being new formed. This repletion commences at a point of resistance to the circulation in the minute arteries, produced on the first attack, by abstraction of caloric. This is most evident, by the gradual enlargement of the diseased parts, with pain and higher degrees of heat, which usually accompany the local disease. The pain of distension is a stimulus, which, in common cases, excites by association the heart and arteries to increased action; these are the most common phenomena.

To talk of inflammation where there is no increased heat, is considered paradoxical. Is it difficult to understand, that where the blood vessels are greatly surcharged, or gorged, the nervous filaments, immediately connected with the gorged vessels, might by their compression, be deprived of their inherent powers of communicating sensation, and become insusceptible of pain; and that a torpor, accompanied with coldness, or death of the part, may follow? By depletion, the compression is removed, the vessels resume their action, the pulse becomes more full, pain is increased, and a glow of heat is gradually diffused through-out the whole system. This state is unquestionably inflammation. Will that state, which preceded depletion, be considered less inflammatory, or less disposed to inflammation? When there is compression on the brain, the source of sensorial power is impaired, and the mental faculty, immediately connected with it, suspended. Whereas, when the compression is upon the nervous filaments of an organ, less connected with life, as the lungs or liver, the mental faculty does not immediately suffer, and may not be impaired, even at the point of death. Those, who fell victims to this most violent form of pneumonia, retained their senses to the last moment. How is torpor, the consequence of a gorged state of the lungs, to be overcome? Not by stimulants, while the engorgement exists; because, if the nervous filaments are susceptible of the least sensation, and the gorged blood vessels connected with them capable of being excited, their state of engorgement will thereby be confirmed; while a disease, already most dangerous, will become irremediable. But, by removing the compression by bleeding, the nervous filaments may recover their powers of sensation, if those powers have not been too long interrupted; while excited arterial action, and increased pain which ensue, are evidence that one point is gained; and by further depletions cautiously employed, difficult respiration is overcome; so as the system may be restored to a state, in which more obvious remedies are indicated. The subject matter of the above form of disease will be more fully considered, when its most violent forms, as they appeared the following winter, shall be more particularly described.

A particular history of the states of disease among the troops on the frontiers, from September to the last of December, cannot be given in detail. It was reported[1] by the surgeons attached to regiments, that dysentery, diarrhœa and fever, continued to attack the men. The most prevailing disease, with which the right wing of the army was afflicted, when it was encamped at Plattsburgh, and Champlain, was the measles. It was stated, nearly one third of the troops were seized with this disease. It was accompanied with symptoms more severe, as the weather became colder, in the month of November: while the convalescents from it were predisposed to the reception of a disease, under the form of PNEUMONIA; and, in conjunction with an epidemic state of atmosphere, and other more obvious exciting causes, the army, generally, were subjected to its most violent forms. A catarrhal affection at that time, (January 1st, 1813,) was universal among the men. This epidemic was first noticed at Greenbush cantonment, the last of October, as has been before observed. In proportion to increase of cold, this disease became more frequent and severe.

It may be necessary to observe, the winter epidemic of 1812, 13, was a form of disease, distinct from that, which, in the northern districts of the eastern states, the preceding winters, had been known by the name of *spotted fever;* although the exciting causes may have been similar. In the *spotted fever,* mental derangement was an almost general concomitant of the disease. In many instances, this affection of the brain was the first symptom of morbid action. Whereas, PNEUMONIA, especially among the troops, was never accompanied with mental derangement, at its first attack, and but seldom in its more advanced stages; nor until the laborious respiration, which was a most prominent

symptom, at the first attack had somewhat subsided, or the patient at the point of death.

This epidemic appeared under the forms of both sthenic and
asthenic diathesis; although under the last, it was often, if not always, deceptive; which led the physicians, in many instances,
to a most incorrect practice; a practice which never mitigated
the symptoms, but always precipitated the patient into an incurable state. The varieties of this disease induced, depended on
prior habits and temperaments. In many of the first cases at
Burlington, where General Chandler's brigade had taken quarters for the winter, (where I was a spectator of its ravages) the
disease proved fatal, in two, three, and four days, by the violence of the first attack; in some instances, in less than twenty-
four hours, after the first symptoms of indisposition supervened.
A soldier, attached to the hospital as a nurse, complained that
he had taken cold, and that he felt an oppression at his breast;
so little was his indisposition, that he went to the lake shore,
distant sixty rods, returned with two buckets of water, flung
himself on his bed, and died in six minutes, apparently in a state
of suffocation. There were other instances of deaths, almost
as sudden.

The following were the most conspicuous features of the disease, under its most deadly form. At the first attack, the heat
of the body and extremities, were below the standard of health;
the pulse contracted and hard; sometimes scarcely perceptible;
respiration extremely laborious; not apparently so much from
sharp pains through the sides and breast, as from a sense of suffocation. The patients say, upon enquiry, that they do not suffer from extreme pain, but a weight upon the chest; an oppression from inability to inhale the air; a sensation, one might im-
agine, similar to that which might be produced by breathing air
deprived of its *oxygene.* The suffocation on the first attack may
be accounted for, by supposing the lungs in a condition which
rendered this organ incapable of absorbing, or transmitting
through its membranes, the vital principle of the atmospheric air;
or, in consequence of the engorgement of the bronchiæ, the air
was excluded from their smaller ramifications. This state of

the lungs was made most evident, by many dissections of those, who had died by the disease. The appearances were engorgements, congestions, and inflammations; even, where there was previous to death no increase of heat. The bronchiæ were charged with a mixture of blood, and mucus. Where the disease had been of some duration, adhesions of the lungs to the circumjacent parts were noticed. The spongy texture of this viscus was lost; while it assumed in some measure, the solid and compact state of the liver. It was sometimes covered with a yellowish, glutinous, extravasate. fluid, which adhered with some force to its surface.

JOHN BELL has given a description of a similar disease, which appeared in Europe. The appearances of the viscera, as delineated by him, so exactly correspond with those which fell under our observation, during the prevalence of the winter epidemic of 1812-13, that his account of it will be here subjoined. It may convince those of their error, who believed that the epidemic was a new, or an anomalous disease.

"In the peripneumonia notha," Bell observes, "there is not merely an inflammation of the pleura, as the name expresses, but of the lungs themselves; and it is not from inflammation, pain, fever or acute suffering that they die, but because the lungs are entirely crammed with blood; the heart can no longer move; they (the patients,) are not sensible of their dangerous state, but are suffocated in a moment, and die without a groan. It seems more frequent in other countries, than in this, (Great Britain,) although no country is exempted. When this disease comes upon a place, it comes with all the frequency and destruction of an epidemic disease; and the sudden and unexpected deaths are terrible." In like form, it appeared in the army on the frontiers; and with no less violence were its attacks made upon the inhabitants scattered over a very extensive district of country, from lake Erie down to lake Champlain; over Vermont, the northern counties of Connecticut, Massachusetts, and New-Hampshire.

"The pulse is weak," continues Bell; "the cough is slight; the difficulty of breathing more anxious than painful, arising

4

from inability to inhale the air; the face sunk in the features, and flushed, or rather of a lurid colour, except when cadaverous, pale and sallow; the suffocation is sudden; the lungs have a liver-like solid consistence; they have no longer the cellular appearance of lungs; for their bronchiæ are crammed with blood; their common cellular texture is also full of exuded blood; they are dense, solid and heavy, and they sink in water. The heart is so curbed in its action, that it gives but a small, feeble, trembling pulse; and even in a few days, the heart is wonderfully dilated and enlarged, and filled with fluid and grumous blood."

The physician, in these cases, hesitated, and cautiously employed the lancet. Here however, it may be necessary to observe, that there were two states of this most dangerous form of disease, which were somewhat similar, as regards the pulse, but which were essentially different. In one, with its apparent weakness, there was a hardness; it was called a contracted hard pulse, by some a stifled pulse, and should be distinguished from the other, which was weak and soft; in both, the pulse was small.

In the first state, accompanied with most laborious and suffocated respiration, there was no expectoration, nor much pain in the chest. Here a cautious use of the lancet was required. Here, not only the pulmonic vessels were crowded with blood, but the bronchiæ were loaded with bloody mucus; the heart and arteries ceased to act, not because they were debilitated, but because they were surcharged with blood. This state was attended with coldness and torpor. Heat could not be permanently restored by any means, but by the abstraction of blood, at the commencement of the disease. Blood however, should be taken away with caution. When bleeding was employed to the quantity of four or six ounces, at short intervals of four, six, or eight hours, it gave the gorged vessels opportunity to free themselves from the oppressive load; and, more certainly, when warm applications had been previously made and continued upon the surface and extremities of the body. By the above means, the pulse became fuller and heat was restored; when a full bleeding might, in some cases be employed, not only with safety, but with benefit. As soon as warmth and the circulation of the blood were restored to the surface and extremities, the patient was considered in a curable condition; wherein, appropriate remedies might be administered; being such as are usually employed in pneumonic affections with fever.

In cases where death had immediately followed the above symptoms of contracted hard pulse, torpor, and general coldness, various dissections have demonstrated the highest state of distention of the pulmonic vessels, with blood; and of ' chial engorgement with bloody mucus. The lungs assu the appearance of inflammation. By what means may these formidable congestions within that congeries of air and blood vessels, of which the lungs are composed, be resolved, except by bleeding? Without the employment of the lancet, other auxiliary remedies proved ineffectual. The bleeding should be small and repeated, until the pulse becomes fuller, and the heat of the body is increased above the healthy standard; when the patient may bear a larger quantity. The patient sometimes fainted with the loss of eight ounces of blood at first; who, subsequently, was bled sixteen ounces, without any collapse of the vessels. The number taken down with this most formidable state of disease was few, compared with the multitude seized. A fortunate administration of stimulants, in a solitary instance only, within my knowledge, proved successful; while their indiscriminate use induced a most deadly practice. Such was the practice in the army, for a short period. Brandy, wine, and soups were the remedies administered, in every form of these pneumonic affections. Prior to these potent stimulants, emetics, cathartics, and blisters were employed. The lancet was prohibited under every form of this epidemic.

It has been observed, the physicians, at the first appearance of this epidemic, doubted the propriety of bleeding. Their doubts were removed by the superior success which followed the use of the lancet; while stimulants proved fatal. It is worthy of notice, in two cases, which came under my observation, where blood-letting was cautiously employed, the providential opening of the orifice, during a restless night, produced so much relief, (even the removal of every alarming symptom) as led to a persuasion, that, in some instances, where the disease had proved fatal, bleeding, from too great timidity, had been improperly neglected; and, in others, employed with too much caution.

The above form of this epidemic was considered by some, typhoid, or asthenic. A typhous fever is always accompanied with a prostration of strength, and low delirium. Will a disease be considered typhous, where the patient is able to walk the room, and continue this exercise, even a few minutes previous to death? Is that disease typhous, which is relieved by bleeding? This form of the disease, in some cases, demanded as many ounces of blood, in the course of the treatment, as is often drawn from a person in severe pneumonia, accompanied with high degrees of heat, strong arterial action, and acute pain. Yet, in this uncommon form of disease, it was inexpedient to take more than two, four, six, or eight ounces at once. The above quantities were taken away, every two, four, or six hours, *pro re nata ;* until permanent relief was procured. Sometimes after the first bleeding, the pulse became fuller, and the heat of the body increased. This favourable circumstance, however, did not usually follow, until after the third, or fourth bleeding. It was not arterial action, but the state of respiration which governed the employment of the lancet in this form of disease. Whenever the tepid bath could be employed, it proved beneficial, in the cold and torpid state of the system, to restore warmth to the surface of the body, and action to the extreme vessels.

The progress of this form of the disease, was most rapid. It assumed in a few hours the strongest marked symptoms of dissolution. It may be added, that even when suffocation and rattling supervened, and, at the moment death was closing the scene, and the heart and arteries ceased to perform their offices, that muscular strength was not remarkably impaired ; nor was the mind deranged. The conflict, exhibited in some instances by the patient, was most distressing. Several have been seen to walk the room a few hours, and even a few minutes previous to death ; possessing a keen sense of their irremediable state, and inevitable dissolution.

ed to
had
prop-
cau-

ome,
nied
sease
; the
vious
leed-
ma-
often
with
Yet,
take
bove
, pro
after
f the
, did
. It
gov-
ease.
nefi-
rmth
.

. It
dis-
rat-
the
ices,
was
nces
seen
ious
and

The number taken down with this most formidable state of the epidemic were few, compared with the multitude seized.

In the second state of the disease, and where there was a weak soft pulse, bleeding was injurious; yet the antiphlogistic regimen was necessary. Here the respiration was difficult, but not suffocated; accompanied with pain in the side, and expectoration of bloody mucus; the bronchiæ were not so crowded, as to be incapacitated to free themselves from the load with which they were oppressed; the heat of the body was never much above the common standard of health. This form of the disease was frequently accompanied with diarrhœa; where drastic purges were prohibited, and milder cathartics administered with great caution. The diarrhœa, at times, was so profuse, that cathartics were injurious; while it was necessary to check these alvine discharges by opium. The diarrhœa, which accompanied the disease, was not critical; nor was it checked, as the fever abated, except by opium; continuing obstinate, in some instances, after return of appetite. This perverse diarrhœa, according to the report of Doctor LOVELL, yielded to lime-water. Emetics of ipecacuanha, were beneficial to promote expectoration; and repeated blisters of the highest importance to counteract pain. Stimulants were improper, until difficult respiration was removed, and expectoration became copious. During convalescency, wine in small quantity, was an appropriate remedy, and grateful to the patient.

The above forms of the disease were similar to the *pneumonia notha* of the ancients. It is not unworthy of notice, that its attacks were most severe upon those, who were in habits of intemperate potations of spirituous liquors.

The third form of this disease shewed itself with less questionable symptoms. At the first onset of the disease, there were strong rigors, with acute pain through the chest. The rigors were soon followed by much heat, strong pulse, cough, and no expectoration. The efforts of coughing always increased the pain in the breast. The above symptoms promptly demanded blood-letting from sixteen, to thirty-two ounces. If any mitigation was procured by this operation, some expectoration of mu-

cus streaked with blood followed. Evening exacerbations frequently required a repetition of the lancet. In a few instances,
two quarts were drawn from the arm of the patient, in forty-
eight hours, with t' best effect—the removal of every alarming symptom.

But, when this most important remedy, bleeding was omitted,
the patient most generally died in the first stage of the disease,
with an abscess within the lungs; or, if he survived the bursting
of the abscess, life was protracted, possibly, some weeks; when
he died with hectic emaciation.

The following case is interesting. A physician, who joined
the army, at a late period of the epidemic, observed, that by the
aid of emetics, cathartics, blisters, and calomel, in large and
small doses, without blood-letting, he was able to cure the fever.
The importance and necessity of this evacuation was forcibly
urged. Notwithstanding, he obstinately persisted in his own
plan of practice, until four of his first patients had succumbed
under his prescriptions. The fifth was an interesting young
man, who had, during a former sickness, been attended by myself. The fourth day after he was taken down, and when recovery was despaired of by his physician, I was called in consultation. The case, at this period, was most desperate; when my
opinion was unreservedly given, that bleeding, at an earlier
stage, would have saved his patient. If so, why will you not
bleed him now, replied his physician. Because bleeding, under
his circumstances, had become an uncertain remedy; and, in as
much as the reputation of this evacuation was but recently established, as a remedy in this disease, it would be reluctantly
employed by myself, in a case, where it was my strong apprehension, it would not succeed. In this case, as the disease had
been of four days duration, with a full soft pulse, laborious respiration, and a hectic flush on the countenance, my persuasion
was, that suppuration had supervened on the lungs. Upon the
point of retiring without making a prescription, the patient, with
wild emotions, feebly articulated, will you leave me thus? Bleed
me, or death is my fate! Yes, you shall be bled, was my reply.
The anxious looks, with mixed expression of anguish and re-

proof, and tone of despair, sunk deep into my heart; it was like an electric shock to my frame. The feelings of responsibility no longer opposed the emotions of sensibility, all active for the fate of the amiable young man. He was immediately bled sixteen ounces. The following day sixteen ounces were again taken away. Bleeding was repeated to the amount of seventy ounces in four days; when he convalesced, was able to leave his bed some hours in the day, and walk his room, with a returning appetite. Orders at this time, to march to a distant post, precluded me from knowing, whether his health was fully reinstated, or whether it deteriorated to a hectic decline; which might have been expected, from the profuse expectorations, which succeeded the resolution of inflammation within the breast.

A cathartic of calomel and jalap, or calomel *per se* was administered, after the first bleeding, in this form of disease. This it was necessary to repeat. As soon as the fever with pain was reduced by bleeding, and cathartics, calomel, and tartrite of antimony were given, with, or without opium, to promote expectoration; and when a gentle spitting was produced, the remains of pain in the breast gradually removed; difficult respiration abated, and a gentle moisture upon the skin supervened. Equal parts of antimonial wine, and compound tincture of opium, proved an excellent medicine, in this state of the disease. When the antimony occasioned too loose a state of the bowels, Dover's powders, in small doses, were substituted. After the inflammatory state of the disease was subdued, by the above means, especially, where nausea, or anorexy existed, emetics of ipecacuanha, were advantageously administered; with intention of promoting expectoration, and determining the circulation to the extreme vessels. Blisters, in the course of the disease, were indispensable to remove stiches in the breast and sides, after bloodletting was carried to its full extent; believing with others, that there is a blistering, as well as a bleeding, and emetic period in fevers; the bounds of which being ascertained, should never be intruded upon by each other.

Where stimulants were demanded, as they never were while there was difficult respiration; a mixture of spirit. nit. dulc and aqua ammonia, six parts of the first, and one of the last, was an appropriate medicine.

Coughs, in a few instances, were obstinate, after there was a resolution of fever. These were gradually subdued by a teaspoonful of a mixture of equal parts of antimonial wine and compound tincture of opium, administered every four or six hours, *pro re nata;* or as often as the urgency of the cough required. Mucilaginous drinks sweetened with honey, or liquorice, were directed in all forms of the disease. Hectick emaciations, and gradual decay, in some instances, followed this epidemic. Some few were to be found in our hospitals, twelve months after the first attack of the disease, where death eventually closed the scene. During which period, infirm life was chequered with reviving hope, painful anxiety, and severe distress.

More dependence was placed upon a dietetic management, to restore the convalescents to health, than diffusable stimulants.

Bleeding was opposed in cases of attack of this epidemic, at the time of its first appearance, by some physicians of respectability, in the vicinity of the army. A warm interest was excited against the practice, at Albany; where the epidemic was considered by some, as a malignant, bilious fever.

The first case, which was reported by a physician at that place, was of a citizen, who was taken ill at Greenbush encampment. This was represented as a bilious fever, of a malignant type. This case was examined by some of the medical gentlemen of the hospital, previous to his removal to Albany; who stated to me, that he did not labour under all the symptoms, which, in the hospital, were denominated PNEUMONIA; under which, without the use of the lancet, few, if any recovered. The above man was bled, and died under the hands of his physician, who adduced this, as a case where bleeding did not succeed. Incorrect, or not, the above case proved nothing against bleeding. As it was well understood, that many, attacked with the real epidemic, died under the prescription of the same physician, who were not bled.

That an epidemic should have assumed an appearance somewhat different in form, among citizens in a city, with an extensive population, from that in camp, produced by the same remote and predisposing causes, may be readily accounted for, from the circumstance, that epidemic diseases are, generally, most prevalent among that class of citizens of every age, sex, and constitution, whose circumstances in life do not admit them to the enjoyment of all the necessaries and comforts, for healthy support. Cold lodgings, coarse and spare diet, and dirty houses, predispose the body to a form of disease, somewhat different from that which appears among men fed with a full ration of animal food, and superabundance of ardent spirits.

It was a fortunate circumstance, that there was no essential difference of opinion, as to the nature of the disease, and method of practice among the physicians of the army, after it was well understood. Its nature had been anticipated, before demonstrations were made by dissections; so that the daily employment of bleeding, and its attendant success warranted a continuance of the practice, in opposition to preconceived opinion, founded merely on theoretic doctrines.

The predisposing causes of extensive endemic diseases, are involved in obscurity. They are not confined to any season. An epidemic state of atmosphere, is known by effects produced. When no obvious causes can be assigned for epidemic diseases, astronomical influences, unsatisfactory as they are, have been resorted to as causes, by the poets of antiquity, and more modern philosophers. Hence comets, in all ages, have been viewed as portentous signs, which forebode both natural and moral evils. The varying aspects of the planets, have, from time immemorial, been consulted upon the most trivial, as well as the more important affairs of men. Those remotely revolving orbs, even at this day, are considered as powerful agents, operating upon our globe, and through the medium of its atmosphere, diffusing pestiferous influences on animate and inanimate nature. These vagaries and more elaborated theories are inoffensive and pleasantly amusing; but do not obviate one evil, nor bestow one blessing upon the human race, even if they were demonstrated truths. The more obvious exciting causes, which are more under our control, are to be explored; that when

5

known, they may be obviated; these several causes will be noticed hereafter.

The substance of the above sketches of the epidemic was published in the New-York Repository in 1813; more precision has been here observed in pointing out the several forms of the epidemic, as it appeared among the troops.

A remarkable coincidence of opinion, respecting the nature and treatment of this epidemic, is exhibited in the following communication of Doctor SILAS FULLER, of the 3d Regiment, when on the Niagara frontier. It was first published in the ARGUS at Albany, and republished in the MEDICAL REPOSITORY at New-York. It is here introduced to shew, that this disease was viewed in the same light, and treated in a similar manner by him, at the distance of three hundred miles, as it was, at the same period, viewed and treated by myself.

"This sickness," observes Doctor FULLER, " is not, as has been represented, confined wholly to the army. The soldiers have only shared in a wide spreading and alarming epidemic, pervading a vast extent of country; the mortality of which is without example in this part of the state. The disease appears evidently to depend on some peculiar state of atmosphere, as a remote cause ; and an exposure to wet, cold, and fatigue, as an exciting cause. In proportion as these causes have taken place, a more or less violent form of the disease is produced. The most common form under which it has presented itself, is that of *sthenic pneumonia ;* the most fatal and unmanageable of the *pneumonia notha* of the old books.

" Under this last form, it has but seldom appeared ; and notwithstanding, it is evidently produced by the same remote and exciting causes, there is a strongly marked difference in the phenomena of them.

" Those advanced in years, and in a particular manner, those, who have weakened, or broken down their constitutions by an intemperate use of spirits, are subjects of this asthenic form of this epidemic.

" The asthenic form, most commonly commences with cold shivering. After some time, there is a sense of heat. In some l be no-

nic was
recision
as of the

e nature
ollowing
egiment,
l in the
crosito-
this dis-
lar man-
was, at

t, as has
soldiers
pidemic,
which is
appears
ere, as a
ue, as an
en place,
d. The
lf, is that
le of the

and not-
mote and
e in the

er, those,
ns by au
c form of

with cold
In some

instances, the common symptoms of PYREXIA are noticed. The pulse, however, for the most part is small, and the heat not higher in degree than natural. During the course of the disease, respiration is extremely laborious. with slight erratic pains through the chest.

" A sense of weight, and fullness is felt through the whole extent of the thorax, which are increased in an insupportable degree, while the patient is in a horizontal position. There is a peculiar paleness and wildness of aspect not easily described. In some cases, a diarrhœa adds to the list of morbid phenomena. Some have expired while sitting and walking, apparently from suffocation.

" In the above described cases, the lancet has been employed with caution. Bleeding, however, has been attended with advantage. The pulse has become fuller, after the first bleeding, while its repetition with other remedies has completed the cure.

" An attentive scheme, by the use of calomel, nauseating doses of emetic tartar, epispastics, fomentation of the extremities and the lungs, in the form of vapour, has been generally pursued, and in some instances with success. It is, however, to be regretted, that notwithstanding every exertion, a very considerable number of cases have put on formidable symptoms in a few hours, such as rattling in the throat, a greatly altered countenance, and, finally, have terminated in death, in the course of one day.

" Upon laying open the chest of some who died under this form of disease, congestions, inflammation, and adhesions have presented themselves.

" The above cases, when compared with the sthenic form of the disease, so far as my observation extends, have appeared only, in the proportion of one to fifty. This epidemic, in its sthenic form, is not always a pneumonia. The fever has sometimes appeared without any local affection, under the type of SYNOCHA. In a few instances, the inflammation has attacked the brain and its meninges, producing PHRENITIS. Inflammation followed with suppuration in the throat, and frontal sinuses are varieties of the disease. Distinctions, however, like these,

are of little practical utility, as local inflammations are invariably removed by the same course of remedies. The only
practical distinctions found necessary, are of its several stages,
which present themselves in the order of cold, hot, and low
stage.

"The sthenic form of this disease, is ushered in by a cold
and shivering fit, rather remarkable in force and duration, which,
if followed by increased heat, frequency and strength of pulse,
pain in the side, difficult respiration, cough and expectoration,
for the most part streaked with blood, a more or less violent
form of the disease may be expected.

"The first intention is to remove the cold stage; this is effected by bathing the feet in warm water, by placing the patient
in bed, and by the frequent use of vinegar whey for drink. This
last is a simple, safe, but powerful sudorific, producing its effects
without danger from its stimulating quality. These means
properly applied, shorten the duration of the cold stage, of
course, lessen the hot and febrile stage, which succeeds; and
mitigate inflammation and pain wherever seated. Stimulants,
especially astringents, as the patient's life is endangered thereby, should here be avoided. These last, when employed in any
considerable degree, increase inflammation and render the effects of suitable remedies uncertain. As soon as the cold stage
is removed, and re-action upon the surface takes place, accompanied with heat higher in degree than natural—flushed countenance—hardness, fullness, and frequency of the pulse—cough,
difficulty of respiration—pain in the head or side—or even when
the disease shews itself only by an increase of arterial action,
immediate recourse must be had to the lancet. The bleeding
must be repeated *pro re nata.* After venesection, should there
be much heat, sulphate of soda, (glaubers salts) may be administered for a cathartic; after which, calomel may be employed
either as a purgative, or an alterative, as the case indicates,
with antimonials in nauseating doses. Full vomits should not
be given until proper evacuations have been made. Puking,
previous to any evacuation, while the vessels are distended, and
highly excited, may be productive of fatal consequences, by

rupturing the blood vessels of the brain or lungs. Nitre, cream tartar, demulcent drinks, and diluents should not be overlooked in this stage of the disease.

"When expectoration is difficult, and the lungs loaded with viscid phlegm, the steams of equal parts of vinegar and water may be inhaled with advantage.

"As soon as the violence of inflammation is, in some measure abated, epispastics should be applied to the pained part. These it may be necessary to repeat, as the nature of the case may require. If we can place any reliance upon our own knowledge, or have the least confidence in medical science, it must be conceded that this form of epidemic is of an inflammatory character, requiring depletion and the antiphlogistic treatment for its cure. In this state, we have not been governed in the employment of the lancet, wholly by the pulse, which, in some instances, is rendered small by the obstruction of the capillary circulation, by congestions, and general torpor. When a resolution of the inflammation is not obtained by the employment of the above means, the disease terminates fatally, in eight or nine days.

"The sinking stage of the disease is known by the smallness of the pulse, coldness of the extremities, dark or shining appearance of the tongue, extreme debility, with some degree of delirium, and subsultus tendinum. Here the patient should be supported with wine whey, wine and water, &c. carefully avoiding the extremes of too high, or too low excitement.

"An over proportion of excitement will increase the local affection, which is supposed still to exist in a degree, while the want of it will leave the patient to languish, and sink under a general debility. Calomel, in small doses, so as to produce some degree of ptyalism, gentle emetics of ipecacuanha, epispastics, laudanum and eccoprotics, properly timed prove serviceable in this stage and are, in a great proportion of cases, attended with success. In the cure of this disease, much depends on judiciously timing the remedies.

"This disease has prevailed in camp among the soldiers, and in our towns and villages among citizens under similar symptoms; and it is a well known fact, that more of the latter, in proportion to the number sick in this vicinity, have fallen victims to this disease than the former."

Jaundice was a common complaint, during the convalescent state of this epidemic. The *tunica adnata* of the eyes, and the skin were yellow; even where calomel had been employed, during the course of the disease. Its continuance in small doses, was experienced beneficial; as were emetics of ipecacuanha, occasionally repeated. Obstructions in the *ductus communis choledocus*, were the cause of this regurgitation of bile; which exhibited itself throughout the lymphatic vessels, upon the surface. This is one evidence, among others, which may be adduced, that during the disease, there was a want, instead of redundance of bile in the intestinal tube. The yellowness did not supervene, until a resolution of fever was effected; and the liver with the other secretory organs resumed its proper office. In consequence of concretions, or inspissations, which existed in the common biliary duct, the cause of the disease, the bile was refused a passage to the duodenum; and accumulating in its proper reservoir, was reverted into the general circulation; whence, was absorbed into the lymphatics. This secondary complaint, readily yielded to remedies, commonly employed in this disease. The most efficient of which, were emetics of ipecacuanha.

Jaundice is a symtomatic disease, the effect of concretions, or canculi lodged or formed in the common biliary duct. The bile which shews itself upon the surface, is not absorbed into the lymphatics from the intestines. During the yellowness, the fæcal evacuations are generally white or clay-coloured.

Cases of disease occur, where the intestinal evacuations are dark, brown, or greenish, or these combined. These appearances accompany indigestion, and deficient secretion of gastric and intestinal liquors, as in febrile diseases. These morbid evacuations have been supposed to be vitiated bile; whereas, they exist where there is deficiency of this fluid. When there are high grades of febrile disease, all the secretory glands are deranged, and cease to perform their offices, and become torpid.

latter, in
llen vic-

alescent
and the
iployed,
iall dos-
cuanha,
mmunis
; which
the sur-
y be ad-
id of re-
ess did
and the
' office.
existed
he bile
iulating
circula-
econda-
iployed
etics of

'etions,
The
nto the
he fæ-

ins are
ippear-
gastric
norbid
iereas,
there
ds are
orpid.

One of the most important, in the economy of the living body, is the liver. A deficiency of bile, is not only a symptom of diseased action, but becomes also, a concomitant cause of fever. Whenever the intestinal evacuations, under this state of disease, exhibit a shew of bile, a resolution of the disease may be expected.

Hemorrhagia from the intestines indicates a torpid state of the liver, when the blood passes from that viscus, without resistance. It occurs sometimes, in the last stage of typhous fever; wherein, from one to four pounds of blood have been evacuated in forty-eight hours. From two to four grains of acetite of lead, with one grain of opium, have been experienced an excellent remedy. Then a blister, on the region of the liver; bark and wine.

The liver of inebriates becomes torpid. Having lost its secreting powers, the blood sometimes pours in torrents, through the *ductus communis choledocus* into the duodenum; thence, evacuated *per anum*. In these cases, hemorrhagia may prove salutary, by obviating a more formidable disease—apoplexy. An enebriate, after large potations of ardent spirits, was found apoplectic in his bed. Intestinal hemorrhagia soon succeeded, and removed the effects of the spiritous excitement on the brain.

Of the *causes* of diseases, as they appeared in the army, the following observations suggest themselves. It cannot be too often repeated, an intemperate use of ardent spirits, is among the exciting causes of violent disease. A disease, which might have been mild, generated only by unavoidable causes, became severe, by alcoholic excitement. A man in a convalescent state from the epidemic of the winter left the hospital without permission, and returned to his quarters, where he drank half a pint of whiskey. A recurrence of fever was excited, with the most formidable symptoms. He was sent back to the hospital, where in twelve hours he died—a victim to folly and imprudence.

Immoderate potations of spirits, by weakening the sensorial powers, and inducing general debility, become a predisponent cause of disease. They are likewise an exciting cause, at the time they are taken into the stomach, by excess of stimulation; and when superadded to remote atmospheric, and more obvious causes, induce, where there is morbid action, a most violent disease. Not a few, who were subjected to the epidemic of the winter 1812–13, fell victims to that disease, from this exciting cause.

An irregularity must not be passed by without notice. It was observed at times during the war, that non-commissioned officers, whose duty it was to issue the ration of spirits to the men, performed it by obliging them to drink the whole at once, rather than submit to the more slow task of pouring it into their canteens. This was performed in the morning before breakfast. This disorderly practice was not countenanced by officers, who regarded the health of the men under their immediate command; consequently, the practice was not general.

My opinion long has been, that ardent spirits are an unnecessary part of a ration. This allowance, as a part of a ration, is not however, the evil which demands a remedy. It is the abuse of spirits. Sutlers unrestrained, as they frequently are, destroy more lives by these liquors, than are lost by other causes to which soldiers are exposed; and, so long as ardent spirits are permitted to be publicly sold in the vicinity of a cantonment, these evils cannot be remedied by any restrictions, under which sutlers may be placed. A soldier habitually intemperate, is always industrious to procure the means of indulging his appetite. All his cunning and every artifice are put into requisition to obtain the inebriating draught. Reputation, honour, health, and even life are sacrificed to his gratification.

Examples may be furnished to demonstrate, that ardent spirits are a useless part of a soldier's ration. At those periods, during the revolutionary war, when the army received no pay for their services, and possessed not the means to procure spirits, it was healthy. The 4th Massachusetts regiment at that eventful period, of which I was the surgeon, lost in three years, by sickness, not more than 5 or 6 men. It was at a time when the army was destitute of money. During the winter of 79, 80, there was only one occurrence of fever in the regiment; and that was a pneumonia of a mild form. It was observable the last war, from December 1814, to April 1815, the soldiers at Plattsburgh were not attacked with fevers as they had been the preceding winters. The troops, during this period, were not paid; a fortunate circumstance to the army; arising from a want of funds. This embarrassment, which was considered a national calamity, proved a blessing to the soldier. When he is found poor in money, it is always the case that he abounds in health. A fact worth recording!

Deserters from the British army, of whom some hundreds came to our posts, exhibited marks of high health; while those of our soldiers were pallid and emaciated. The difference was too obvious to have escaped the observation of the officers of the army. It led me to seek the cause. Upon enquiry it was learnt, that spirits were no part of the ration of the British soldier; that these liquors could not be procured in the upper province of Canada for money. While, in addition to their daily rations, our soldiers, when they had money in their pockets, had free access to spirits at the stores of the sutlers. Diseases and mortality generally, but not necessarily, followed the pay-masters of the army. With means to make themselves comfortable, soldiers frequently render their lives wretched.

It may be esteemed medical heresy by some, to declare it is my opinion, that ardent spirits should not be used as a common beverage, diluted or not. Habits are unconquerably stubborn. Long established propensities will not yield to the voice of reason. Temperance is one of the precepts inculcated by our divine master; and the doctrine has been preached by his disciples. Still, with all the heavy denunciations of heaven against the sin of inebriation, but few reform. This vice is a growing evil.

The time was when ardent spirits were not known. Then the salubrious fountains of water were resorted to by the healthy and athletic to satiate their thirst. The early productions of the still, it is highly probable, were employed as medicine. They now hold a distinguished place in the *materia medica*, and

6

were they confined to the store-houses of druggists, and the dispensaries of physicians, the sphere of their utility would be vastly enlarged.

Cleanliness is the life of an army; while filth and dirt are among its disease-generating causes. The observance of cleanliness in domestic life is of the highest importance to secure the body in health. It is no less valuable as a mean of supporting the strength and efficient force of an army in actual service. Filth and dirt become more active destroyers of life when they cooperate with pestilential states of atmosphere, or insalubrious gasses, the production of unhealthy climates or noxious situations. Cleanliness should be enforced upon soldiers with most rigid laws. That code under the Jewish dispensation, enjoining ablutions and purifications, was obeyed as a religious rite; it has been quoted as a system well adapted to a camp. It has been observed, that those regiments which have been subjected to rigid discipline, and where cleanliness has been strongly enforced, have enjoyed higher states of health than those who have been inattentive to this duty. A man cannot be made a good soldier unless he is made to keep himself clean. This is better effected by infusing into his soul a pride for neatness of dress and appearance, than by punishment for neglect; though the last is sometimes necessary. Good discipline is better maintained among a body of men by what is termed *l'esprit du corps*, than by austerity and severity. *A good soldier* will be ambitious to execute his duty with fidelity; he will feel that he has not degraded himself by assuming the profession of arms. To form within him this state of mind, he should be taught to obey the civil laws of his country, and to respect the interests of the citizen; and to violate either is not only criminal, but extremely *dishonorable*. He should realize, that his country beholds him as an *honorable protector* of its *rights*, and a *just avenger* of its *wrongs*.

A treatment, which is due to a rational being, not such as a slave or a servile subject of a tyrant receives, will impress upon a soldier exalted sentiments of honor and justice, so necessary to secure his warmest attachment, and faithful services to the state.

The regiments of heavy and light artillery suffered less by disease during the war, than any other regiments on the northern frontiers. It is unnecessary to observe, these regiments have been always subject to correct discipline; and their better health may be much imputed to cleanliness. Their quarters and encampments were generally in the best state; the men were, mostly, neat and clean in their dress and appearance.

There was one regiment on the frontiers, which at one time counted nine hundred strong, but was reduced by a total want of good police to less than two hundred fit for duty in the course of two months. This regiment, in its appearance, was at that time dirty in the extreme. To save the remnant, if possible, General Dearborn found it necessary to place it under the command of Colonel Miller (now General) by annexing it to his regiment. At one period more than three hundred and forty of this regiment were in hospitals; in addition to these, a large number were reported sick in camp. At the close of the war, this regiment had established a high reputation. Its good discipline and bravery, were excelled by none.

Health is impaired, and fatal diseases are the consequence of unequal and variable excitements in the system, produced by any cause; either acting as a preternatural stimulus on the stomach, the skin, or the lungs. Such are large potations of spirits. Such are accumulations of filth and dirt, when in contact with the skin. Such are those emanations which proceed from substances in a state of putrefaction, when received into the lungs. Under the above circumstances, cold, in an especial manner, produces its deleterious effects.

Unequal excitements in the animal system are induced by transition of seasons, as well as weather. These transitions, with the cooperation of pestilential states of atmosphere and other causes better understood, produce diseased actions, destroy health, and accelerate death. These fatal evils, the cause of a part of which being cold, may in some degree be obviated by warm cloathing.

More especially the sudden changes of weather to which soldiers are unavoidably exposed in the field, and the formidable diseases which are the consequence, might be an inducement to government, as it is for the highest interest of the nation, to guard the health of the army, and preserve the services of the men in the field, to furnish them annually with a pair of woollen shirts. A garment of wool next the skin would secure the body from cold more effectually than three garments of the same thickness worn over linen. Wool is not a good conductor of heat; consequently, under all circumstances of cold and wet, it retains the natural heat of the body.

The additional expense of woollen shirts to the nation would be but small, which would be remunerated by this improvement; not only in the saving of bounties paid to necessary recruits to supply the loss occasioned by sickness and its consequences; but more especially in obviating the wounds too frequently inflicted by death of a friend or connection.

The substance of the last observation was published in the MEDICAL REPOSITORY, at New-York, in connection with communications upon the winter epidemic of 1812, 13. The sentiments herein adduced had been previously communicated to officers of high grade in the army. What influence the suggestion had at that time to effect the proposed improvement, is to me unknown. The winter following, however, with much gratification, it was understood that a pair of woollen shirts, in conformity to the proposition, was made by government a part of cloathing allowed the soldier. This garment was worn by officers also, even during the summer months, while in tents.

Having experienced from woollen garments next the skin the greatest benefits, while exposed in my tent on the northern frontiers, during every campaign, and witnessed its salutary effects in others while in the field, an additional improvement is urged, for the consideration of government. That the soldiers destined to perform duty on the northern and western frontiers be entirely furnished with woollen garments. There are a few days only, during a campaign, that men would be incommoded by the increased heat of woollen garments; then only a few hours in the day.

Men in tents during the hot seasons experience little inconvenience from these garments of wool next the skin, which is overbalanced by their advantageous effects, while exposed to cold and rain on necessary duty. Checks of perspiration, or an abstraction of heat from the surface of the body, cooperate with a variety of other causes to produce diseases, which these garments would obviate. Woollen garments are most important and necessary for men employed on expeditions, in the wilderderness, when at war with hostile savages ; where, destitute of tents, they are unavoidably exposed to weather, both wet and cold. Clothed in wool, during all seasons, soldiers would enjoy higher degrees of health. We should behold them more hardy and robust, enduring the severest hardships, the most fatiguing marches, and the inclemency of seasons, without attacks of disease.

If an unequal excitement exists in the system during a state of fever, it is most evident that cold, or an abstraction of heat from the surface, is among the most hurtful agents.

It is also evident, that while the surface of the body is under a state of exhaustion by cold, an excess of stimulants taken into the stomach does not diminish, but increases the dangerous state.

The deleterious effects produced by the above hurtful agents are proportionate to the degrees of exhaustion on the surface, and the exciting powers received into the stomach.

Hence ardent spirits become more hurtful agents during the severe frosts of winter, than during the heat of summer.

The two first hurtful agents in conjunction during winter, induce the most dangerous forms of our winter epidemics.

These epidemics, therefore, are most fatal to men whose vital energies have been most frequently exhausted ; they are accompanied by engorgement of some viscus important to life, and feeble action of the arteries at their extremities.

This state is sometimes attended with a deficient venous absorption ; hence the spots which are seen in the skin.

When robust men, who have not often been exposed to those hurtful powers, become subjected to them, a dangerous fever ensues with strong arterial action. During its violence, either the brain or the lungs are endangered by its excess.

When hurtful agents operate upon a body exposed to them during the heat of summer, the excess of unequal excitements is not so great; because the degrees of hurtful powers are relatively less than during winter, yet sufficiently great to induce a dangerous fever.

This state however does not necessarily precipitate the body to a most sudden death; but a destruction of an organ important to life slowly progresses. Although death does not immediately ensue, yet it is as certain; provided the diseased state is left to its own operation.

Of this description are the fevers of summer and autumn. These last states of fever, however, are under the influence of additional hurtful agents, which depend on local causes for their existence; such as marsh miasmata, and putrid effluvia.

These last described states of fever have for causes other co-operating hurtful agents; as bad nutriment, excessive fatigues, long watchings, and mental depressions, &c.

The hurtful agents of winter above mentioned exhibit their effects immediately upon the lungs or the brain, mediately upon the muscular system by pains in greater or lesser degrees, proportionate to the powers of those agents.

The above agents during summer and autumn, exhibit their first deleterious effects most frequently upon the intestines; their second throughout the system by association.

In all states of fever the first indication is to remove the hurtful agents. The cold upon the surface and extremities is obviated by artificial heat; various modes of applying heat have been employed. Those means, by which heat is most equally diffused, are to be preferred.

The suitable application of heat, in the cold stage of fever, is the first mean to be employed to equalise excitement.

The second indication is to obviate the tendency to death, the effect of engorgement by evacuations; as cautious bleedings, in cases where arterial action is suppressed at the extremities, and by cathartics; or bold bleedings, where the arteries act with force at their extremities; and by drastic purges. These are the second means employed to equalise excitement.

The third indication is to remove the remains of unequal excitement, the consequence of hurtful agents, by means less powerful than those above mentioned, but which are adapted to particular affections, the effects of diseased action, the consequence of association of parts.

These are opium, blisters, emetics, eccoprotics, antimonials, and calomel in small doses. These are the third means employed to equalise excitement in the system.

The fourth indication is to obviate debility, the effects of the hurtful agents; or of those means, which are necessarily employed to counteract the tendency to death.

These are either natural or artificial stimulants. The first is nutriment, which is permanent. The last are vinous liquors, or spirits, which are diffusible and transient.

These stimulants require caution in their administration; and are to be adapted to the state of debility, or excitability of the system.

The following extracts of reports will shew the state of the hospitals, under my direction, during the winter 1812-13.

" The hospital department at Plattsburgh has not been destitute of the common supplies, which are usually furnished the sick of an army; while every requisition, made for hospital stores, has been promptly answered. During the month of November, ample supplies of stores, as wine, spirits, sugar, molasses, rice, tea, and chocolate, were ordered by General DEARBORN, to be forwarded to Plattsburgh, under the charge of Doctor WILSON, hospital surgeon's mate. In December, an additional quantity was, by orders, directed to the same post, and Burlington. Upon an interview with Doctor WILSON, when inspecting the hospital at Plattsburgh, in the month of January 1813, who then had the charge of the hospital at that post; information was given, that the supplies of November had not been expended. The hospital under his direction is found in the best state. The beds are amply furnished, the wards clean, the kitchen neat. No less credit is due to Doctor LOVELL, surgeon of the 9th regiment, under whose charge the hospital at Burlington is placed, on account of its good condition, and the unremitted attention bestowed on the sick."

" The hospital at Greenbush is in good order, and the patients comfortable."

At this period, in an official report, it was also stated, " that no army was ever better supplied, with hospital stores, than that on the frontiers." Therefore, a want of necessaries could not justly have been assigned a cause of the great mortality, as was rumored at a distance from the army. It might have been expected at such a period, that the number of deaths would have been vastly exaggerated; but, when it was most evident, that erroneous reports were imposed upon the public, with design to render government and its officers odious, to effect the purposes of a party, the evil required a remedy.

It was well known at the commencement of the war, that there were men in service on the frontiers, who exerted their talents to render the army disreputable; to create discontentment, and encourage insubordination among the soldiers. The officers of the regular army were not implicated in this charge. The following is a correct statement—a detachment of the New-York militia was not furnished with hospital stores, agreeably to a requisition of its surgeon. In this case, the officer commanding the regiment refused to conform to a regulation adopted for the government of the hospital department; which was, that requisitions for stores should have the signature of the commandants of corps. The surgeon of this regiment of militia, in a letter addressed to myself, feelingly, and politely regretted the "untoward disposition," of his commanding officer, which prevented him such supplies as he required. For the want of these, no one could have been made accountable, except his perverse and obstinate commanding officer.

The above recited transaction gave rise to a report, as was intended, injurious in its consequences to the public service. Exaggerated accounts of deaths in the army, with a similar view, were crowded into the public papers; when the mortality among citizens was scarcely noticed by them. From these sources, it is highly probable, that Doctor GALLUP obtained his information, respecting the ravages of the *pneumonic epidemic*, at Burlington. (See note D.)

The greatest mortality in the army was in the month of December, 1812; at a period when stimulants were employed as medicine. The evacuating and antiphlogistic practice was adopted the first week in January; during which month, mortality had nearly ceased, as the disease was generally under the control of remedies, although the number on the sick reports was not diminished. This last fact was evident, by the monthly regimental reports. The number of deaths reported in the 21st regiment, for December, 1812, was thirty-three. The number reported in the same regiment, for January, 1813, was three. If we take the reports of the 21st regiment, as the ratio for December and January, the deaths were as eleven to one. Then as the whole number of deaths, agreeably to official reports, in the month of December at Burlington, was one hundred and fifty; so in the month of January, the deaths did not exceed fourteen. It is a truth, that in a hospital, which contained one hundred men, there was not one death the two last weeks in January. The reports of deaths were less in February, than the preceding month; three only died in the same hospital, during the last month. During the month of March, there were but few cases of the epidemic.

From the preceding statements, which are the most correct, which can at this time be given, it is evident, that the number of deaths from the last week in November, 1812, to the last of February, 1813, at Burlington, did not exceed two hundred. It has been estimated, that during the above period, about two hundred died at Plattsburgh. From a correct report, made at Greenbush, of deaths from the first of August, 1812, to the last of February, 1813, the whole number was eighty-nine.

A general account of the weather, from July to November 1812, has been noticed. December was severely cold. The second week in January 1813, there was rain and thaw. From the middle of January, to the middle of February, the weather, on the border of Lake Champlain, was cold, and little variable.

The order in which the several forms of disease supervened, during the campaign 1812, is as follows: Dysentery, diarrhœa, and fever, in the month of July, August, and September. Diar-

7

rhœa and pneumonia, diarrhœa and rheumatalgia, and measles, in October and November. Pneumonia notha, and severe pneumonia, in December 1812, and January and February 1813; which were the prevailing winter epidemics.

END OF CAMPAIGN 1812.

CAMPAIGN OF 1813.

~~~~~~~~~~~~~~~~~

HAVING inspected the hospitals at Plattsburgh and Burlington, duty made it requisite for me to return on the 16th of February, 1813, to Greenbush, where the direction of the hospital employed most of my time the remainder of that month. The sick, who had been comfortably accommodated in one of the common barracks, were now removed to the new hospital. The regiment of dragoons, under the command of Col. BURNS, and a detachment of light artillery, commanded by Major (now Colonel) EUSTIS, had taken quarters for the winter at this cantonment.

The soldiers of these regiments, particularly those of the light artillery, had severely suffered by the epidemic pneumonia. After my return from Lake Champlain, there were many severe cases of the disease at this post. The surgeon, under whose charge the hospital had been placed, during my absence, exposed himself to reprehension, by inattention to duty. This was supposed, by the officers of light artillery, to have been one cause of a number of sudden deaths in that corps. It was meditated to prefer charges against the delinquent. These were suppressed, while preparations to obey orders, from the Commander in Chief to march, absorbed every other consideration of minor consequence.

The movement of the troops from Greenbush, at this season, March 2, 1813, preceded by General DEARBORN to Sackett's Harbour, on Lake Ontario, indicated that active operations would commence early the ensuing campaign. This march, a distance of nearly two hundred miles, was accomplished in five and six days. The greatest part of which was performed during a storm of snow, or weather severely cold. The direction of the line of march was on the Mohawk turnpike.

The Mohawk empties into the Hudson, six miles north of Albany, between the towns of Troy and Waterford, by several mouths. Two miles above these outlets is Cahoos falls. These falls are seen at the distance of two or three miles, and combined with the surrounding hills, the adjacent flats, and the small villages on the banks of the river, with its divided branches, winding their courses between little islands at its mouth, exhibit a landscape pleasingly picturesque. A nearer view of the uninterrupted sheet of water, two hundred yards in width, falling from a height of seventy feet, is a scene truly sublime. One mile below the falls, the river is passed over by a handsome bridge.

Schenectady, an incorporated city, is situated on the banks of the Mohawk, twelve miles above the falls. It was, originally, settled by the Dutch; and is one of the most ancient towns in the state of New-York. Its early inhabitants severely suffered by the Indian wars, and their depredations. The town, consisting of sixty-three houses, was destroyed in February 1690, by a party of French and Indians from Canada. This was a frontier post, until the conclusion of the revolutionary war. Since which, it has wonderfully increased. Its population in 1810, by the census, was 5909. The great turnpike, from Albany up the Mohawk, passes through this town, and here crosses that river, over a superb wooden bridge, 997 feet in length, roofed over throughout its extent. The lands in its vicinity are nearly level, the soil rich. On the west, the city plat is washed by the Mohawk; over which are extensive alluvial lands, under good cultivation. On the east, the lands are sandy and light loam, barren, and little cultivated for several miles, covered with yellow pines of diminished growth. The city is built on streets, regularly laid out in squares, and contains between five and six hundred houses mostly of brick; three edifices for the College, which is in an improving state, by liberal public and private endowments; from its position and increasing importance, it will become within a few years, the first literary institution in the United States. Here are four houses for divine worship. The courts for the county are held at this city.

Boat navigation up the Mohawk commences here. From this place to Albany is a portage of sixteen miles, occasioned by the Cahoos falls, which intervene between the Mohawk and Hudson.

With the aid of four short canals, boat navigation up this river is continued to Wood-Creek, through Oneida lake, and Oswego river; a distance of more than two hundred miles. The canal at Little Falls, seventy-one miles west from Albany, is one mile in length; upon which are several locks, which give a rise of more than forty feet. The canal, which connects the upper branch of the Mohawk, with the Ontario at Rome, one hundred and eight miles N. W. from Albany, is one and a half mile in length, with a lock at each end. The lift at the eastern is ten feet; that at the western, eight feet. At Wood-Creek are four other locks.

As we ascend the Mohawk, on the turnpike, a number of creeks are passed; over which are safe, durable, and handsome bridges.

The country bounding this river, until you pass Little Falls, is broken, gradually sloping from the alluvial flats, until it rises to hills and heights mountainous. These elevated lands are good for wheat and pastures. The flats and alluvials, immediately bordering the river, are rich and excellent; very productive in every species of corn and grass.

Extensive farms, fine settlements, and handsome villages, present themselves to the view of the traveller, as he advances up the Mohawk. These are interspersed with perpendicular ledges of rocks, topped with projecting fragments, threatening in their aspect; dreadful precipices, which cause the pallid chill; small streams of water spouting from the lofty clefts of rocks; and bolder cascades, rolling from rude cragged steeps, to please the eye and excite admiration.

Fifteen miles above Schenectady is Amsterdam, a handsome

village, situated on the north side of the Mohawk. Here the turnpike crosses Chuctenunda creek, a small rivulet. One hundred rods above its mouth, the stream falls one hundred and twenty feet; on which are a number of mill-seats. There are now in operation at this place, five mills for grain, four saw-mills, two fulling-mills, two oil mills, a trip-hammer, and an extensive iron manufactory. This place may accommodate an increased number of water works, to aid manufactories.

Eight miles above Amsterdam, the turnpike passes Kingsbury, a village of little note; and two miles farther, immediately on the bank of the Mohawk, Cahnawaga village of aboriginal memory, as being once the residence of a part of the Mohawk tribe of Indians; where at this day, are to be seen their orchards of apple-trees. These last villages are within the limits of Johnstown. The principal village of this town is situated four miles north of these; where the courts of the county hold their sessions. The last is a very beautiful village, a place of considerable traffic, which increases with the population of the country.

About fifty years ago, Sir WILLIAM JOHNSON conducted a few settlers to this tract, then a wilderness; who enjoyed their new habitation in peace but a short period. They were compelled, during the revolutionary war, to seek places of more security, in the older towns on the Hudson, and at Schenectady; and did not return until JOHNSON, the leader of the enemies of the revolution in the northern district of New-York, with the hostile Indians under his control, were expelled the country.

After passing some fine settlements, well built commodious houses, and farms under a good cultivation, we arrive at Little Falls, a compact settlement of fifty houses, unpleasant, surrounded with broken crags and huge rocks; a site commodious for manufactories, which require the aid of water. This is a village of the town of Herkimer, of considerable note, having a population in 1810, of nearly three thousand inhabitants, seventy-eight miles from Albany. Here the alluvial grounds, on the border of the Mohawk, are very extensive. They were known by the first settlers of this country, by the name of German flats, as were other alluvials, at different points up this river to Rome.

The general face of the country presents a rich soil, cultivated by the hands of an industrious yeomanry. This is an old settled town. The village of Herkimer is very pleasant, exhibiting considerable taste and opulence. In its vicinity, the turnpike crosses West-Canada creek, which empties itself into the Mohawk from the north.

The next most important town, through which the Mohawk turnpike passes, is the village of Utica, within the bounds of Whitestown, ninety-three miles from Albany. This village, from its first beginning, which was since the revolutionary war, has increased to a size which surpasses belief. One, knowing the state of this country thirty years ago, ignorant of its rapid improvement, might naturally suppose, that at a distance of one hundred miles west from Albany, he would find himself buried in a wilderness, where nature is beheld in its most rude and savage state. The sceneries up the Mohawk are circumscribed in all directions, by diversified broken ranges of hills, and intervening vallies. While travelling on a road up and down, and whether rising on hills, or descending to the plains below, no distant prospects are to be seen. But as we approach the head of the Mohawk, a new world, in a high state of cultivation, is displayed to the sight. Those stupendous mountains and precipices, which accompanied us from stage to stage up the Mohawk, are either left behind, or gradually sink and are lost in the vast extensive plains before us. We view the surrounding and more remote sceneries not only with delight, but with wonder and amazement. The transition, though not very sudden, is like enchantment.

Utica is situated on the south side of the Mohawk. Having passed over a level road, twelve miles or more, we enter the village over a durable roofed bridge. The surrounding country is a vast plain, open in all directions, having no intervening hills, and few tracts of wood-land, to intercept the sight. This champaign country extends to Lake Erie, two hundred miles west. Every thing is new; at the same time, taste, riches, and opulence, are generally displayed. These are proofs demonstrative of a soil highly luxuriant, and a population very industrious. The artisan, as well as the husbandman and merchant, here increase in riches. Mills, factories, and mechanic shops, are seen in all directions. In this village are two houses for divine worship.

During the revolutionary war, this was the site of Fort Schuyler, which will be long known in history. Utica contains between three and four hundred houses compact, and a population of two thousand souls. The commerce of the extensive western country concentrates at this point, about fifteen miles below the head of boat navigation on the Mohawk.

Whitesborough, the second village as to importance, within the limits of Whitestown, and situated four miles north-west of Utica, seems on account of the uninterrupted population, to be a continuation of the last village. Its first settler was HUGH WHITE, afterwards a Judge of one of the courts. He emigrated from Connecticut, in the year 1785; and was the first who had resolution to adventure into these dreary regions, unfrequented, except by savage beasts, and more savage men.

Whitesborough village is beautiful and elegant. It comprises one hundred houses, and seven hundred inhabitants.

New-Hartford, the third village, is situated west from Utica. This also, is a continuation of the last. Farms, in a state of high cultivation, here present themselves to the view of the passing traveller.

Whitestown, with its villages, Utica, Whitesborough, and New-Hartford, exhibit more important improvements in commerce, manufactories and agriculture, than any town of the same age, in the state of New-York, perhaps in the United States. The public buildings are superb, and many of the private mansions finished in a style of elegance. They are such as would be thought ornamental in the older towns of the Atlantic States. The face of the country, with its various improvements and embellishments, give the spectator some idea of its wealth and present resources, and what may be its future opulence, arising from their rapid increase. But when he reflects upon the recent date of their origin, the many dangers, hardships and privations, the first settlers had to encounter, to make themselves only comfortable, he is struck with admiration; and when he learns, that these vast improvements, from a wild state, are the produce of only ,thirty years of industrious labour, he is lost in astonishment.

Upon the ancient site of fort Stanwix stands the handsome village of Rome, thirteen miles N. W. from Utica. During the revolutionary war, it was an out-post surrounded with vast forests in the wildest state, now encircled with luxuriant fields; which amply repay the industrious husbandman with abundant harvest for his labour. Fort Stanwix was built by the British in 1758; and was evacuated at the close of the French war, after the conquest of Canada, and was suffered to fall to ruin; but during the war with Britain, was rebuilt, and maintained as a frontier garrison by the revolutionists; and with a number of posts, from fort Schuyler to Schenectady, on the Mohawk, formed a communicating line of fortifications, to prevent surprise, and protect the interior settlements from incursions and depredations of the enemy, and his savage allies.

The first settlers of Rome were Dutch. Its present population consists of emigrants from the eastern states; as do those of Whitestown and its villages. The Mohawk passes within half a mile of its village, composed of thirty houses; on which are seats for water machinery, which adds value to the position. It was in this town, that General HERKIMER was killed in an action with the Indians, during the revolutionary war. The canal, which unites the head waters of the Mohawk and Wood-Creek, passes through this town.

From Utica, the course of Sackett's Harbour is nearly N. N. West; to Otswego on Lake Ontario, is nearly west. After leaving the upper branches of the Mohawk, and passing the high lands, which separate its waters from the smaller streams of Black River, which empties into Sackett's Harbour; the country down is variously uneven, mountainous, precipitous, and rugged with rocks. The forests are variegated with several species of hard and soft woods, and evergreens. Many sceneries pass in review of the traveller, as he progresses down Black River.

This river has its sources in the high lands, north of Little Falls and the Mohawk. Its course is N. N. W ; and empties itself into a large bay, in which is Sackett's Harbour, ninety miles from Utica, and one hundred and ninety six miles N. W. from Albany.

Twelve miles north from Utica, is the town of Trenton, remarkable on account of a cataract in the vicinity of the village. The water tumbles over successive strata of rocks, from an eminence of one hundred feet. The rapids below are confined within contracted limits by rocks which rise perpendicularly one hundred feet or more, overspread with evergreens. The scene from below, although circumscribed within narrow bounds, by the surrounding broken highlands and cragged precipices, is romantic ; while the whole assemblage is truly sublime. The soil of this town is good ; the forests are variegated with various species of both hard and soft wood, and evergreens. Its principal village contains about eighty houses.

On the route down Black River from Trenton, we pass Bowen's settlements, Steuben, Boonville and Leyden ; the last is thirty three miles from Utica, and one hundred and fifteen N. W. from Albany, comprising a tract of country, with thinly scattered settlements, and inconsiderable villages.

The next town of much consequence, is Martinsburgh, forty eight miles from Utica, and one hundred and thirty N. W. from Albany ; it is in a fine state of cultivation. The face of the land is gently rising and falling. The soil is rich. The country from this to Brownville abounds with lime-stone. The village of Martinsburgh contains between thirty and forty houses, county buildings, a house of public worship, two distilleries, a saw-mill, grain-mill, paper-mill, taverns and stores.

Fifty seven miles north from Utica, we arrive at Lowville, one hundred and fifty-nine miles N. W. from Albany, one of the most improved towns on Black River. The village, laid out in squares, is beautiful, comprising fifty houses ; many built in a style of taste and elegance. Here is an academy ; the building is handsome. An elegant and spacious edifice is improved as an hotel. The lands, which lie in gentle swells and easy vales, are pleasant. The soil is of superior quality. This district conveys to the mind of the traveller, that its inhabitants enjoy not only the necessaries and conveniences of life, but possess wealth and affluence.

Six miles north of Lowville is Denmark; the settlements are thinly scattered, exhibiting a country but just beginning to emerge from its wild state. However, over an area of twenty two thousand acres, the aggregate population is considerable. On Deer creek, which empties into Black river, is a perpendicular fall of one hundred and seventy-five feet. The stream below is bounded the distance of eighty rods, by calcarious rocks, two hundred feet in height. Here, since its first settlement, (ten years) have been erected six saw-mills, two grain-mills, two carding machines, two clothiers works, three spinning-machines. Copenhagen a small village, lies above the falls. Denmark is distant one hundred and fifty-six miles N. W. from Albany.

The distance from Denmark to Watertown is about twenty miles, and one hundred and seventy-six miles N. W. from Albany. This is a pleasant growing village, situated immediately on the south side of Black River. From a wilderness, within twelve years, it has become a place of considerable importance. The courts for the county have their sessions here; where is erected a commodious court-house of wood, and an arsenal built of brick. The village also contains sixty houses, some of which are elegant; likewise a spacious and well built academy of brick, which in March, April, June and July, 1813, was improved as an hospital for the United States army. Within the limits of the village, are a paper-mill, two corn mills, three saw-mills, a carding machine, three tanneries, and a printing-office, with a number of mechanic shops. The lands in this vicinity are good; cultivation is in an improving state; the inhabitants are industrious and becoming rich. Lime-stone and other materials for building are found in abundance, from the sources of Black River to its mouth. Watertown is situated four miles from boat navigation on Lake Ontario. A considerable traffic is carried on between this place and Montreal, by the lake and river St. Lawrence.

From Watertown to Sackett's Harbour, we pass Brownville, a town of great extent, comprising within its limits, a length of twenty-four miles, and a breadth of twenty-two. It is bounded on the N. W. by St. Lawrence, S. W. by Lake Ontario, south by Black River, on the east by the town of Le Ray. The soil is rich and fertile. Within the limits of this town, there are no hills; the surface of the earth gently uneven. This town was first settled about fourteen years ago, by John Brown, from Pennsylvania; since which, its population has increased in an astonishing manner. There were by the census, in 1810, 1662 inhabitants, mostly emigrants from Pennsylvania, and the New-England States. This town is well watered, and abounds with lime-stone, as does all the country in this vicinity. Several islands in Lake Ontario and St. Lawrence, are within the limits of Brownville. The village situated on the north of Black River, contains thirty houses, a number of stores and mills, and is a place of considerable mercantile business, which is carried on with Montreal, by St. Lawrence. This is a pleasant village, and will from its situation, become in a few years, a place of great importance.

General Brown is the son of John Brown, from whom this town derived its name. From a private citizen, in the course of three years, he was elevated to the first grade in the army. The battles fought on the Niagara, by the army under his command, have given to the American soldiery, a character for patience, perseverance, and undaunted bravery, surpassed by none.

A military hospital was established at Brownville, two last years of the war. Its position was favorable to such an establishment; as there is a water communication between this place and Sacket's Harbour, the centre of active operations on the northern frontiers.

The country in this vicinity, especially those posts bordering on the bays of Lake Ontario, like all new countries, are considered unhealthy.

Sackett's Harbour was the only secure port for a navy on the lake; where Commodore Chauncey had hauled up the armed flotilla, during the cold season, waiting the breaking up of winter, to re-assume operations against the enemy. To this flotilla, was added a ship of twenty-eight guns, built entirely of green timber from the wilderness, within three months; and which was in preparation to sail, as soon as the obstructions formed by ice were removed. Sacket's Harbour was protected by two batteries, and two block-houses. This post, the preceding campaign, had been occupied by militia. The hospital, so denominated, was in a filthy condition. From information, the winter epidemic had proved very mortal among the troops. The disease at this period, (March 10, 1813,) had not disappeared. The few existing cases were attended with symptoms less formidable than at its commencement.

Information had been received, that the enemy was concentrating his disposable force, at Kingston, Upper Canada, distant thirty miles. Apprehensive of an attack from him, General Dearborn ordered a temporary hospital establishment at Watertown, twelve miles east of the harbour, on black river, where the sick would be less exposed to depredations of the enemy. This precaution was more necessary, as the sick could not be accommodated at the harbour, within the line of defence. An hospital sufficiently capacious to accommodate 100 patients, was, within ten days, established; to which the sick at the harbour were removed. Among the number were about 20 of General Pike's brigade, who, on their route from Plattsburgh, by way of Chataugay and Malone, in the month of March, had badly frozen their feet and toes; which, in almost every case, mortified, and required amputation. At this hospital two cases of the winter epidemic were admitted, when the disease was at its last stage. In both cases there were large expectorations of mucus uniformly mixed with blood. Respiration was difficult; diarrhœa accompanied the disease. A pill of one grain of calomel and opium was directed night and morning: also small doses of antimonial wine and camphorated tincture of opium, were administered at intervals of three or four hours, as an expectorant; likewise blisters and gentle emetics. Under the employment of the above means, with the addition of a soft nutritive diet, and wine, these men were restored to health. The most prevalent disease at

this period, March and April, were coughs, fevers of the synochr-
al type, diarrhœas.

On the 23d April, an order was received, to place the hospital
under the charge of surgeon's mate, MARCH, and to repair to
Sackett's Harbour; where, having arrived, information was obtained, that sixteen hundred men, destined for a secret expedition, had embarked on board the fleet, and that commodore
Chauncy waited only for a fair wind to sail. This armament, to
which I was attached, was commanded by General Dearborn,
being composed of a part of General Pike's brigade, one battalion
of Colonel RIPLEY's regiment, two companies of New-York and
Baltimore volunteers, 200 riflemen, and two companies of light
artillery. On the 25th of April, the fleet weighed anchor, with a
favourable breeze, and steered their course to the head of Lake
Ontario. On the 27th, at day-break, were in sight of the Light
House, at the entrance of the bay of Little York, in Upper Canada. At eight o'clock this morning, the fleet dropped anchor
opposite the batteries, at six hundred yards distance, when the
signal for debarkation was displayed.

Major Forsyth, with two hundred of his battalion of riflemen
in batteaus composed the advance. General Pike, who commanded the attack on shore, with three battalions of the 6th, 15th,
and 16th regiments succeeded the advance, supported by Colonel (now General) Ripley, with one battalion, composed of 21st
regiment, and two companies of Baltimore and New-York volunteers, under Colonel McClure, one company of artillery, commanded by Major (now Colonel) Eustis.

Major Forsyth, on approaching the shore, met a severe resistance from three hundred British regulars, seven hundred Canadian
militia, and a small body of Indians, who occupied the high
banks on the lake shore. Under a heavy fire from the enemy,
this corps made good its landing, and most gallantly maintained
its ground twenty minutes, unsupported, until General Pike and
Colonel Ripley gained the land, when the enemy's line in succession broke, fell back, rallied, was thrown into confusion, and
retreated with precipitation. General Pike immediately formed
his army in open column, and pursued the fugitives. During

the attack on shore, the enemy's batteries were silenced by the well-directed fire of the light armed schooners of the fleet, at which time a small magazine took fire. A ship and brig could not approach within battering distance, on accou..t of shoal water.

Our column, at the distance of four hundred yards from the enemy's batteries, halted with a view to reconnoitre their position, and wait the bringing up of two pieces of artillery, under Major Eustis, who had to encounter many obstacles from fallen timber and miry grounds. At this moment, the enemy's principal magazine exploded. By this catastrophe, General PIKE, an officer of superior merit, and held in the highest estimation by the army, received a mortal wound, which he survived a few hours. The effects of this explosion were dreadful. Sixty rank and file were found dead on the field, and one hundred and eighty wounded and mangled in a most wretched and deplorable manner, by the fall of stones which formed the magazine; to which the enemy, when he evacuated the battery, set fire, by mean of a train or slow match, prepared for the event of abandoning the works. The effect was similar to the springing of a mine.

The remnant of the British army fled with the commanding officer, the Governor of Upper Canada, who was the first to make his escape. The commanding officer of the Canadian militia, who had retreated to the town, sent a flag, with terms of capitulation, when hostilities immediately ceased. One article which was acceded to by General Dearborn, was, that private property should be respected, and all public property be given up. This article, conciliatory to the feelings of the inhabitants of Little York, and magnanimous on the part of the victorious General, was not violated in any of its parts, except in one or two instances, by a few licentious soldiers. These outrageous acts were discountenanced in forcible language, in General Orders; and on the spot satisfactory indemnification was made, as soon as the damages were ascertained by the sufferers.

A very different representation of the transaction at Little York has been given. It is not a little astonishing, that an historian should thus commit himself as the author.

It is no apology for this outrage on truth, that the substance of the abusive paragraph was extracted from *a daily newspaper* devoted to a party opposed to the war. The statement of the historian, at the time of its publication, had been repeatedly contradicted by official documents; and its falsity has since been proved by unequivocal declarations of officers of high grade and respectable standing in the army, who held commands in the armament employed on this expedition. An historian, possessing honorable motives, upon conviction of his incorrectness, which implicated any man, especially the commanding General, in disgraceful and reproachful conduct, would feel himself bound to make ample reparation for the injury. Nothing less than a full and candid acknowledgment of his error, or suppression of the publication, can wipe away the intended stigma, and place the author in a magnanimous light. The work is in circulation, with all its malignancy. Its poison is diffused. It has been, and will be read without the apologetical note, for the criminal publication of mere newspaper reports, unsupported by official documents. Besides, the note is only a partial retraction of the erroneous statement made by the author, which is, that General DEARBORN was immediately compelled to evacuate the place, with considerable loss; while the truth is, the object of the expedition, the capture of the enemy's fleet, and destruction of his stores, was effected in all its parts. (See Note E.)

The army, with the wounded and sick, after having undisturbed possession of the place four days, re-embarked. The following night a gale of wind commenced, with rain, and continued with violence, which prevented the fleet from sailing until 7th May. After a pleasant passage of twelve hours, the fleet came to anchor opposite the mouth of the Niagara; upon the 8th the wounded and sick were landed, and encamped in tents, two miles east of the fort, where they remained until after the capture of Fort George, in Upper Canada.

Previous to further movements of the army, while arrangements were making to attack Fort George, General DEARBORN had been severely seized with a fever of the synochal type, which confined him to his bed more than a fortnight; from which he was not recovered when the army was in readiness to move. Notwithstanding his bad state of health, he accompanied the expedition against Fort George in opposition to the opinion of his physicians, and against remonstrances of the officers of his army; persuaded, as they were, that the unavoidable exposure to weather and fatigue attending would, under his state of debility, produce a relapse, and endanger his life, whereby subsequent operations of the army against the enemy might be retarded.

The assault upon Fort George was commenced on the 25th, and continued the 26th, from Fort Niagara and other batteries recently erected, by a heavy cannonade under the direction of Colonel (now Brigadier General) M. PORTER. The fire was so well directed, that Fort George was silenced; the Block House and other buildings were set on fire by hot shot, and consumed. This was preparatory to the grand assault. May 27th the army crossed the strait in three divisions, under the immediate command of General LEWIS. The brigades of Generals BOYD and WINDER composed the columns of attack, preceded by a detachment of six hundred men, commanded by Colonel (now General) SCOTT. The brigade of General CHANDLER was a column of reserve.

These several brigades embarked in boats at dawn of day, four miles east of the outlet of Niagara Strait. The boats moved across the mouth of the Strait, in a line parallel with the north shore on the Canada side, at a distance of two miles from the land in a west direction, until they were opposite the point designated for debarkation. The boats then wheeled by brigades to the south, and approached the shore in good order. This point was one mile north of the village of Newark. The movement of the troops, exposed to the full view of the enemy, gave him time to form his line most advantageously to oppose, from the high bank of the lake shore, their landing. The enemy's line was supported on his right flank by a battery; opposed to which was an armed schooner, while four armed schooners covered the landing of the army.

9

Colonel (now General) Scott, with the light troops, effected his landing under a blaze of musketry from two thousand British regulars and Canadian militia ; and twice attempted to rise the bank, but fell back, and waited for the first brigade under General Boyd ; when the enemy, repulsed at every point, retreated in disorder.   The enemy was pursued through the village of Newark, to within three miles of Queenstown, when the pursuing troops were ordered to retire, by the orders of General Lewis. After the action there were found on the field of battle, of the United States' troops 27 killed, and 87 wounded; of the British 102 killed, and 175 wounded.   The enemy halted the following night at Queenstown ; whence, after collecting his scattered troops, the next morning at dawn of day, he took up his line of march to Burlington Heights, at the head of the lake.   On the 28th two brigades under the command of General Chandler were ordered to pursue the retreating enemy.   At Stony Creek a subsequent battle ensued, unfortunate in the result, although the enemy was beaten.   Generals Chandler and Winder were made prisoners.

These several actions gave us an additional number of wounded men.   Many capital operations were performed, both upon the Americans and British, after these several actions.

The lands in the vicinity of Niagara were wet at this season of the year.   Upon this wet ground the flying hospital was encamped, for want of better accommodations.   Many of those wounded at Little York died with typhous fever, accompanied with diarrhœa.   The condition of the wounds generally was bad.

Having experienced in the short period of four weeks, that our present encampment was unsuitable for a hospital, and its unhealthy position having been reported to the Commander in Chief, an order was received subsequent to the last battles, which had vastly increased the list of sick and wounded, to explore a situation more healthy.   Lewistown, eight miles up from the outlet of the Strait, presented the most eligible, on that frontier.   At this point on the Strait, and one mile east on the ridge road, the land is more elevated, gravelly and dry.   To this place the sick and wounded, about two hundred, were removed from Fort Niagara, the middle of June. By the first of August the patients were increased in number to between six and seven hundred, and were comfortably accommodated in two spacious barns, and hospital tents. Here bunks and bed-sacks filled with straw were furnished each individual. The wounds immediately assumed a more healthy appearance, produced in part, by a change from an insalubrious to a more healthy position. A liberal supply of milk contributed not a little to this salutary effect.

Typhous fever and diarrhœa pervaded the army after their retrograde march from Stony Creek. Numbers who had been admitted into this hospital improved also in their health by change of position and milk regimen, with which they were liberally supplied. This bland diet, well suited to the condition of the sick and convalescents, and proved more beneficial than medicine, to check the diarrhœas, which prevailed from the time the troops arrived on the frontiers.

Many of the soldiers, when embarked at Sackett's Harbour, had but a short time previously recovered from the epidemic of the preceding winter. During their passage to Little York, they were night and day unavoidably exposed to the weather, and so much crowded on board the transports, that little opportunity was had for repose. After the attack upon Little York, and when the army had re-embarked, the troops were exposed a number of days on the decks of the vessels to a violent storm; during which period they were constantly soaked with rain. Under these circumstances, diarrhœas supervened most universally among the men. After landing at Niagara, the men, in many instances, were attacked with typhous fever; which became more frequent after the capture of Fort George. Subsequent to the retrograde march of the army from Stony Creek, a combination of typhous fever and diarrhœa was very general.

It may not be improper to notice, that the greater part of the army were recruits, and, previous to the assault on Fort George, had either marched or been transported the distance or our hundred miles, by rapid movements, exposed to the weather and its varying changes, during March and April, which months, in the

northern district, were experienced severely cold and wet. The
brigade of Generals CHANDLER and PIKE encountered, while on
their route from Lake Champlain to Sackett's Harbour, a violent
storm of snow, during the month of March, in the wilds which
border the river St. Lawrence. Other detachments, after a
march of two hundred miles, were transported up Lake Ontario
in batteaus, in April and May. The vernal months of this year
were wet and cold. During the greater part of these routes, the
men were destitute of covers to shelter them from the inclemency of the climate.

An army on expeditious movements have little or no opportunity given to pitch their tents, and time too short suitably to
prepare their rations. Their meals are generally cold; their
lodgings hard, wet, and comfortless.

Such long unremitted exposures to cold and excessive fatigues,
with a diet, which, under existent circumstances, could not
prove nutritious, exhausted the vital principle, and diseases supervened in the following order: first, diarrhœas; next, typhous fever; and then typhous fever and diarrhœa combined.

The productions of animal putrefaction and excrementitious
materials were also sources of these diseases. Armies always
accumulate these noxious principles about their encampment in a
few days, when attention is not called to their daily removal.
The bread was believed to be another source of these complaints.
It was bad and unfit for nutriment in several respects. In some
instances the flour furnished had commenced a fermentative
process, which rendered the bread sour; in others, had progressed so far to a state of putrefaction, that its nutritive property
was destroyed. At one period, the flour issued was believed to
be adulterated with plaister of Paris, (gypsum) ground fine. So
large a proportion of this last article was mixed with the flour,
that it was detected in the bread by the eye. This adulteration
was also known by its specific weight.

Excepting a few hot days in the first week of June, the remainder of that month and July following, were cold and unpleasant for the season. The month of August was extremely
hot and oppressive, as were the first weeks in September. The

last of this month, the weather became very pleasant, and the troops generally more healthy; while those, who had been prostrated and wasted by disease, convalesced in a rapid manner. At the flying hospital encampment, Lewistown, the sick particularly improved in their health; the convalescents experienced no relapses; nor were they seized with any new form of disease. The convalescents were put on light duty at that place; and out of some hundreds of these, not more than three were returned to the hospital during the campaign. This is full evidence of the healthy position of this cantonment. The means employed to preserve it in a state of cleanliness were conducive to ameliorate the bad condition of the men who were admitted into the hospital; yet these means could not have added salubrity to its natural situation, being seventy feet above the surface of the lake waters.

Fort George and Newark, from their position, might be supposed healthy also. The site of these places is elevated 50 feet above the surface of the lake. The forests in their vicinity had been cut and cleared away for cultivation. The country to a great extent is level, without a hill until we arrive at Queenstown height. Wherefore, from the land-side of the position, a free circulation of air might be expected. The daily breezes from the wide expanse of the lake, were cool and refreshing, during the hot season. The encampment of the army appeared clean. Newark previous to the war, was thought healthful, as it was a most delightful village. Notwithstanding all these favourable appearances, the army did not enjoy so much health, as had been anticipated from its situation. The village of Newark, interposed between the lake and encamping ground, was an obstruction to the breezes from that quarter. The east bank of the Niagara strait was bounded by an immense forest, which extended up the strait to the south; in which quarter, was also a ridge of land, one hundred feet in height. These severally were obstructions to free currents of air, from the eastern and southern quarters. From these points, the wind blows four fifths of the time, during the summer months.

One of the efficient causes of the sickness at Fort George,

assigned by myself at that time, was the effluvia from the sinks. This evil was reported by myself to General BOYD; on whom devolved the command of the army, after General DEARBORN was ordered to the eastern district. The General repeatedly called the attention of the officers commanding corps, to the important necessity of daily covering the sinks with earth. Nevertheless, the exhalations from them to me, who occasionally visited the post, were very offensive; while no unpleasant odour was noticed, or complained of by those of the army, who were continually exposed to the offensive gasses emanating from these reservoirs of filth.

This fact is one evidence among many, of the force of habits. In this instance, the faculty of smelling was so blunted by the impure exhalations, that it became insensible to their influence; so as the constitution was imperceptibly impaired, and a predisposition to disease induced, before the patient was conscious of the cause.

During the month of August, an uncommon proportion of the army were sick, or unfit for duty. More than one third of the soldiers were on the sick reports. The officers shared with the privates, in the prevailing diseases. Half of the medical staff attached to regiments, were also unable to perform their duty. Of seven surgeon's mates attached to the hospital department, one died, and three had leave of absence, by reason of indisposition; the other three were, for a short period, sick. So general was the sickness, the few remaining surgeons could not do full justice to their patients. At the time when the returns of the sick in the general hospital, counted between six and seven hundred, there were only three surgeons of this department, present for duty. At this period of General BOYD's command, the troops were under excellent discipline, the encampment in good condition, and the men neat in their apparel. The general and regimental hospitals were reported during the summer months, by the inspectors of the army, "in the best possible order."

Doctor LOVELL, hospital surgeon, (late surgeon of the 9th regiment of Infantry,) who was attached to the army at Fort

George, thus observes, " the division of the army stationed at
Fort George, from the beginning of June, to the beginning of
October, 1813, was encamped on the bank of the Niagara, extending from the fort to the village, nearly on the lake shore.
The surrounding country is flat, and the camp was deprived of
the benefit of the lake breezes, from the position of Newark.
During the month of June, it rained almost incessantly ; while
the latter part of July, and the whole of August, were extremely
hot; the whole of September however, was remarkably mild
and pleasant. Thus after having been wet for nearly a month,
the troops were exposed for six or seven weeks to intense heat
during the day, and at night, to a cold and chilly atmosphere,
in consequence of the fog arising from the lake and river. The
enemies' advance being within a short distance of the camp, the
details for duty were large, and skirmishes taking place at the
piquets every morning ; the soldiers were, for a length of time,
stationed at the several works, for several hours before day-light ;
and thus exposed to the effects of a cold damp atmosphere, at
the time the system is most susceptible of morbid impressions.
The diseases consequent to this alternate exposure to a dry, hot,
and cold damp atmosphere, were such as might have been expected ; typhous and intermittent fevers, diarrhœa and dysentery. A detachment of artillery, stationed at the right wing near
the lake, was particularly exposed to the heat of the day, and
dampness of the night, and suffered much from typhus and intermittents. I do not recollect a single instance, in which typhus came on with a sudden and complete paroxism. It attacked in a slow and insidious manner, which almost invariably
denotes an obstinate and long continued fever ; and in which
we are seldom to expect a crisis. The symptoms were those,
denominated typhus gravior; although severe, they were generally regular. In some cases however, delirium came on very
early, and was much more severe than the other symptoms. It
was of that species, attended with an obvious increase of arterial
action in the brain ; and relieved by the application of cold, or
blisters to the part effected. The disease began to subside about
the fourteenth day, and gradually disappeared during the third

week ; but in some cases, no symptoms of recovery were to be noticed, until the end of the third week."

" The treatment adopted was, with a few variations, that recommended by Fordyce, in his dissertations of fever, and the success was complete ; not one case of death occurring of this complaint, in the corps to which I was attached."

" The cases of intermittents were numerous, and generally of the tertian type ; not however very obstinate. The remedies employed were emetics, opium, bark, and Fowler's solution. Opium, and particularly bark, had not a very good effect. I was particularly unsuccessful with the latter ; whereas, the mineral solution universally succeeded, both in those cases, where other medicines had failed, and those where it was used alone. I shall have occasion to observe the contrary effects of the medicines, during the campaign on this frontier, in 1814. That this was not owing to the quality of the medicine, would appear evident from their having been procured from different places, and not shewing any defect of power in other complaints."

" These diseases, however, though severe, bore but a small proportion to the usual pestilences of our army, diarrhœa, and dysentery. During two years and a half, I was on the frontiers, at every post from Buffalo to Burlington, Vermont, these complaints almost invariably absorbed all others. They were the only ones which could be called our camp diseases. All others arose from obvious or local causes, and were as common to the citizen as the soldier."

" By dysentery, is not meant that idiopathic form of disease described in books, as an almost invariably attendant on a camp ; for during the whole war, I saw idiopathic dysentery but once ; and then it was confined to the militia under General Porter, in the latter part of 1814. The complaint above referred to, consisted simply of dysenteric symptoms, consequent upon the violence or long continuance of simple diarrhœa. The two complaints would sometimes alternate very early ; but the symptoms of dysentery were easily removed at this period, by the simplest means. After the diarrhœa had continued several weeks or months, the mucous coat of the rectum became inflamed;

o be

rec-

l the

' this

ly of

edies

ition.

was

neral

other

e. I

medi-

t this

' evi-

i, and

small

i, and

itiers,

com-

re the

others

to the

isease

:amp;

once;

ORTER,

red to,

on the

e two

symp-

by the

everal

amed,

in consequence of perpetual irritation; and finally, ulceration took place, as appeared on dissection. Though the rectum was the part principally affected, in many cases, the whole intestinal canal bore marks of inflammation; being covered with large spots of a dark or livid appearance; and sometimes, spots of effused lymph were found in the mucus coat of the ileum. Cases of this nature were probably often relieved by the application of blisters, or poultices to the abdomen, as will be presently mentioned. The inflammatory appearances after death, however, were not so remarkable as might have been expected from the symptoms during life."

" In its incipient stage, diarrhœa was easily cured by evacuations, followed by opiates and astringents; but after having continued some time, it was accompanied with severe febrile symptoms; a contracted wiry pulse; tongue perfectly dry, and covered with a dark brown or black fur; or of a dark colour, and as if glazed; skin extremely dry and scaly. The emaciation equal or surpassed what occurs in any other disease. The dysenteric symptoms being kept up by the continual irritation of the diarrhœa, could only be relieved by anodyne and emolient injections, and mucilaginous food. All attempts to check the diarrhœa by opiates and astringents were immediately followed by an increase of febrile affection. They (the above medicines) had but a temporary effect on the diarrhœa, and if persisted in, speedily destroyed the patient. Antacids, and particularly lime water, often had a very good but temporary effect. The only medicine, in fact, that I found generally to have beneficial effects, was ipecacuanha. When the state of the stomach, tongue and skin indicated it, a gentle emetic of ipecacuanha had a most beneficial effect, and often laid the foundation for a cure. At other times, doses of from two to three grains often repeated, so as to produce catharsis, gave speedy and permanent relief; and very many were restored to health by small doses, for a length of time combined with opium, or in the form of DOVER's powder."

" The only cathartic I found beneficial, at this period, was Ol. Ricini, which generally produced an alteration of the symptoms for several days. The application of a large blister to the

10

abdomen would often have the same effect. But it was difficult to determine *à priori*, whether it would produce this effect
or not; for the relief was not in proportion to the dysenteric
symptoms. It appeared from some dissections, that this result
took place, in those cases, where the small intestines were principally inflamed; upon such patients, mild and mucilaginous
food was found beneficial. Very great relief was also obtained
by the application of a poultice of the inner bark of the slippery
elm, to the whole abdomen. After obtaining a truce with the
complaint by one of these means, the cure was effected by small
doses of ipecacuanha, or of DOVERS' powder, continued for a
long time, repeating the remedy first used, as occasion required.
This was the only treatment that appeared to be generally attended with any success. It should be added, however, that
many who had so far recovered, as to be reported fit for light
duty, would be taken with so violent a relapse, as to sink in one
night; while others would die suddenly, without any adequate
cause discoverable, either before or after death.

"During the whole of October, and part of November, most of
the troops were exposed to excessive fatigue, and almost incessant rains, in open boats on the lake. On their arrival at the
French mills, about the 14th of November, the weather became
intensely cold, and remained so during the winter months."

Typhous fever, dysentery, diarrhœa, and these variously combined were the prevailing diseases, during the months of May,
June, July, and August. Intermittent and synochal fevers appeared in the months of September and October. But dysentery and diarrhœa were the most general diseases through the
summer months, and they continued into autumn. The last
form of these diseases was the most obstinate. These complaints of the bowels were not confined to the tented field;
neither were typhous, synochal, and intermittent fevers. They
did not appear, however, with all those severe and aggravated
symptoms among citizens, as in the army. Hence an inference
was drawn, that as the citizens were subjected to the above
forms of disease; their causes were, but in part, connected with
the life and habits of a soldier; or the casualties to which he

was unavoidably exposed. These diseases were consequently
considered endemic, on the Niagara frontier, and excited by
additional causes, than those which depended on local situation,
were most severe among the troops. The bowel complaints,
among the inhabitants, were supposed by them, to have been
produced by the water on that frontier. It was the sentiment
of the first settlers, that the water possesses a purgative quality.
This opinion was current also in the army. The citizens stated, that the new settlers were always attacked with these disorders of the bowels, the first summer after their arrival; and that
but few escaped them. Lime-stone, or calcareous rock, a sub-
stratum of the earth in the vicinity of Ontario, which the waters
hold in a state of solution, was conjectured by some, a cause of
these complaints of the bowels. A more probable cause of these
endemic diseases is, in my opinion, the production of vegetable
putrefaction; with which the springs, rivulets, large rivers, and
the waters of Ontario, are impregnated during the summer and
autumnal months. The clearing the lands of their forests, and
cultivation of the soil, by producing earlier evaporations of waters from their surface, before the heat of the summer is so high
in degree, as to produce a putrefactive process upon vegetable
substances, in a state of decay, will obviate these complaints of
the bowels, and likewise those autumnal fevers, to which the
inhabitants are subjected.

The intermittents and synochal forms of disease, which supervened during the months of September and October, were
more immediately under the control of remedies, than typhus,
diarrhœa, and dysentery. The first forms of disease appeared
among several officers, who were permitted to leave the encampment at Fort George, soon after they were indisposed. Whereas, the privates were generally attended by their own surgeons,
in the regimental hospitals, and were seldom removed to the
flying hospital, until their diseases had progressed to the last
stage.

These synochal fevers were accompanied with pain in the
head, increased heat, fullness and hardness of the pulse; all of
which indicated an excess of excitement, which demanded

bleeding, and an antiphlogistic regimen. In most cases, which fell under my observation, blood-letting to the quantity of sixteen ounces, a cathartic of calomel and jalap, removed the excess of excitement, and placed the patient in a condition, in which antimonials in small doses, removed the remains of diseased action. About the same period, a case called my attention, which had been of some duration, perhaps twelve or fourteen days. What the symptoms were, at the first onset of the disease, I did not learn. This patient was extremely debilitated, when he was removed to the flying hospital encampment. At this period, the pulse was contracted, quick and hard; the skin dry, and cool in the mornings, but hot in the evenings. These symptoms were attended with delirium. Some inflammation on the eyes indicated an excess of excitement on the brain, as did the other symptoms, especially delirium. A blister was applied upon the neck; one grain of calomel night and morning, and one fourth of a grain of tartrite of antimony, every four hours, were prescribed. The delirium continued with watchfulness; the above medicines were directed the second and third day. The disease remained *in statu quo.* The bark and wine were proposed by a surgeon of the army. The experiment was acceded to by myself, but not with a high degree of confidence. As had been anticipated; the before mentioned febrile symptoms were all aggravated; while the remissions were shortened, and the fever assumed a more continued form. A cathartic was then administered, the antimonials in small doses were again resorted to, and were continued. The paroxisms of fever, under this last process, daily lessened, and gradually disappeared, with an abatement of delirium, and a return of appetite.

This is one case among many, which might be recorded, where the bark and wine have been injudiciously administered, within my own observation. The practice of administering bark, during remissions of fever, is in conformity to that of CULLEN. Long experience has convinced me, that the practice of introducing bark and wine, as soon as there is a remission of fever, will not generally succeed in the autumnal mixed fevers, as they appear in the eastern and northern states. After there is

a complete resolution of fever, these remedies are proper, sometimes indispensable to give tone to the stomach, and excite the
organs subservient to digestion into action.

*Summary of the causes which were believed to be active in the pro-
duction of the various diseases on the Niagara, during the campaign of 1813.*

1st. PREDISPONENT.

The debilitating effects of the epidemic of the preceding
winter. From these the soldiers had not fully recovered, before
they were subjected to severe duty, during inclement weather
in the month of March, when on their routes from the interior to
the frontiers, and exposures on the lake in open transports, as
well as in the field.

2d. HURTFUL AGENTS.

These acted as both predisponent and exciting causes, and
generally might have been obviated.

1. *Bad bread.* It was notorious that the bread on the Niagara
was made of damaged flour ; such as was either not nutritious, or
absolutely deleterious. It was also believed, that the flour contained in some instances an earthy substance, and that this ad-
ulterating substance was plaster of Paris (gypsum.)

2. *Bad water*, impregnated with the production of vegetable
putrefaction, more or less active in producing the endemic diseases of the country.

3. *The effluvia from the sinks*, materials of animal production,
with which the circumambient air was replete. This evil might
have been remedied by a rigid police, and more thorough covering of the sinks, or by a change of position, a distance of one or
two hundred yards.

3d. EXCITEMENTS.

As more immediate causes,

1. *Heat and cold*, alternating with each other, and inducing in
the system unequal excitement. Both these powers were more
active in producing their deleterious effects, when combined

with moisture, in the form of rains, fogs, and dews. The effects of heat and cold might have been in some degree obviated, by woolen garments.

2. *Fatigues of body, and severe hardships*, comprising the whole routine of duty, both by day and night. These were unavoidable.

3. *Inebriation.* The effects of ardent spirits were both pre-disponent, and immediate. These, when received into the stomach in undue quantities, induced on the brain engorgement; or when they were repeatedly drank to an excess short of absolute intoxication, general debility. These last agents were more active in the production of violent diseases, than many of the other deleterious powers combined.

The several causes above enumerated, will suggest, at first view, the forms of disease which occur to those exposed to their influences, or subjected to their agency.

It is to be observed, few *recent* causes of either diarrhœa, dysentery or typhous fever fell under our observation in hospital practice. As we are giving sketches of diseases as they appeared to us, it must not be expected, that these will be detailed from their commencement, through all their several stages, in a systematic order. The practical physician must not look for new theories, nor will he be instructed by many practical observations, which are not to be met with in books found in the library of every medical man.

The object here intended is to exhibit what was done in certain states of disease, and under certain circumstances; not what should have been directed to the patient, under different states and circumstances. It must be remembered, the means of affording relief to the distressed in an army are few, compared with those which present themselves in domestic practice.

The patients, generally ordered to our hospitals, were such as had been unsuccessfully treated by the regimental surgeons in camp, where the accommodations were less eligible than in the hospitals, with all their defects. Flying hospitals attached to an army, from their instability, cannot be expected to be in the highest possible order. It is the work of months and persevering labour, as well as unremitted attention, to render two hundred patients very comfortable in a permanent hospital. But when the number is increased to five hundred or one thousand patients, under one establishment, (and such has been the sickness in the army, as thus to gorge the hospitals) the duty which devolved on the surgeons was severe beyond calculation. It may be a question, whether it is better policy to detain the sick with their regiment, until they are reduced to the last extremity by disease, or order them to the hospital at an earlier period.

Those patients only were ordered to the general hospital, who had been long unsuccessfully treated by the regimental surgeons in camp. Consequently the cases admitted were either chronic, or in the last stages of their disease, many of which were most obstinate, or irremediable. These patients had already pass d thro' the usual routine of emetics and cathartics, and were found in bad condition, with their skin scaly, dry, and cold; pulse quick and weak; total loss of appetite; stomachs nauseated with every species of nutriment, and extremely debilitated; such were the states of those who were afflicted with diarrhœas, and dysenteric symptoms. The indications were to excite the stomach to action, by grateful stimulants; wine, diluted spirits, spices. To restrain profuse evacuations, by opium, or by medicine possessing more permanent restrictive powers. With this last intention Moseley's vitriolic mixture was prescribed; not, however, with all the benefit wished for, or expected. For the same purpose astringents of many kinds were tried in vain. Having been informed by some regimental surgeons, that they had experienced success in the removal of these diseases by acetite of lead, experiments were made in hospital practice also with this medicince, but not succeeding immediately with it, we desisted from its use as an internal remedy. Of strong prejudices early acquired we could not divest ourselves; and later experience has convinced us, this drug has been frequently administered for these complaints of the bowels with too little caution.

In most obstinate chronic diarrhœa, the following preparation was administered with more success than any other astringent remedy. To two quarts of strong decoction of white oak bark,

was added one ounce of alum in powder, and one quart of brandy.   A table spoonful of this mixture was administered once in
three or four hours ; one grain of opium occasionally, most generally at night.   This astringent stimulus was inadmissible
where fever existed.   It was resorted to where the patient was
reduced, and the evacuations from the bowels profuse.   The
above formula was introduced into hospital practice by Doctor
WHITRIDGE, hospital surgeon's mate on the Niagara.

Persuaded as I was, that these obstinate diarrhœas required
a long course of diaphoretic medicine to remove them ; recourse
was had to Dover's powders.   In this preparation we possess
the restrictive powers of opium, and the diaphoretic property of
ipecacuanha combined.   This medicine, when the patient was
confined to his bed between blankets, was productive of happy
effects.   To those who were able to walk, it was prescribed
without great precaution.   Patients labouring under chronic diarrhœa took this medicine, when unavoidably exposed to transitions of weather, without any increased inconvenience.   In most
obstinate cases its beneficial effects were slow, but permanent ;
although the obstinacy of the disease was very discouraging, yet
by perseverance, it was in most cases overcome.   In cases where
nausea indicated an emetic, ipecacuanhas were preferred to any
other, and where cathartics were demanded to obviate tenesmal irritation, manna and cream. tart. combined in solution, or
ol ricini, were the most suitable.   To remove pain, the consequence of chronic inflammation on the mucous coats of the intestines, blisters sometimes acted as a counter stimulus, and gave relief.   'n all cases the patients were put on a soft nutritious diet.
No article prescribed proved so beneficial as milk and its preparations.   It was most grateful to the patients ; it was an article
they could take, when other kinds of food were rejected.   By
milk alone, it was my persuasion, that many lives were saved,
which, without it, would have been lost.   I have been highly
gratified, as well as astonished, to see with what avidity milk
was devoured by those enfeebled by diseases, who had not been
accustomed to it when in health.   These patients were daily indulged, also, with wine or diluted spirits, in moderate quantities.

CAMPAIGN OF 1813. 77

During the month of May a number of patients were admitted into the hospital, from those regiments who had been previously employed on the expedition to Little York. It has been already observed, the troops, previous to their embarkation at Sackett's Harbour, had been long exposed to fatiguing marches, during the severe cold and wet month of March. On their passage up the lake on board the transports, they were not covered from the weather: after the reduction of that post in Upper Canada, they were soaked with rains for several days on board the fleet. Many of these, soon after debarkation on the Niagara, were taken down with typhous fever. Their first indispositions were scarcely attended to by themselves. At first there was dyspepsia, heaviness in the head, accompanied with dizziness, without any evident regular paroxisms of fever. These symptoms daily increased, until the patient complained of weakness, without being able to assign any particular cause. The above symptoms progressing were attended also with lassitude, mental depression, and soreness throughout the muscles of the body. Then followed watchfulness, or interrupted sleep, reveries, false imaginations, confusion of thought, a dull pain in the head and down the dorsal muscles, intervals of mental derangement, torpor and low delirium. The above symptoms progressed so slow from day to day, the change was scarcely perceptible.

During the progress of the above symptoms, a small increase of heat was noticed with but little alteration in the pulse, except it was somewhat accelerated.

When the first symptoms of dyspepsia and heaviness were attended to, an emetic of tartrite of antimony, or ipecacuanha, interrupted the chain of diseased actions, and if followed by a cathartic, obviated the succeeding symptoms, and arrested their course. When a soft nutriment, as soups, and wine in moderate quantity, effected a restoration.

It was too frequently the case, that the surgeons had not an opportunity to effect the above favorable termination of the first indisposition. Either the patient neglected to apply, as soon as the first complaint commenced, or his continued exposure to those causes which induced a predisposition, obviated those salutary

11

effects of emetics and cathartics which might have been expected, had he been placed under circumstances more favorable to
health.

When the patient was found laboring under the whole, or many
of the above unfavorable symptoms, the disease, although insidious at first, no longer left us in doubt as to its nature. Its features were more strongly delineated by a dry skin, with an increase of heat; dry tongue with a brown incrustation; pains in
the head and back; and soreness in the muscles; watchings in
the first stages; stupor and delirium in the last.

Emetics and cathartics were indicated to remove irritation
from the first passages, after which the following prescription
was administered with benefit: R. Cal. gr. 10. Opium, gr. 5.
Tartrite antim. gr. 1. M. fiant Pillulæ, 10. of which the patient took one every fourth hour, and intermediately the Vinum
antimon. in nauseating doses to procure a diaphoresis. But
when this disease was accompanied with diarrhœa, a dose of 5
to 10 grains of Dover's powder was substituted for the medicine
last mentioned. When the typhous symptoms of disease were
accompanied with tenesmal diarrhœa, indicating irritation and
inflammation on some portion of the intestinal canal; a cathartic of jalap and calomel, or rhubarb and cal. or castor oil were
found necessary; after which opium and mucilaginous injections.
After a resolution of fever, known by a moist tongue, moist and
soft skin, natural sleep, a return of some appetite, the following
were administered: R. Spt. Nit. dulcis oz. 1. Aqua. ammon.
oz. 2. A tea spoonful of the above mixture was administered
every two hours. Or spirit of lavend comp. or tinct. cort. comp.
or a decoction of snake root or bark. Wine, during this state,
became an important remedy.

During the course of the fever, a blister on the neck or head,
or on various parts successively, was sometimes found necessary
to counteract local pains, and equalise excitement.

The above remedies were more certainly efficacious, when
the patient was placed in a situation wherein cold and moisture
did not operate upon the body, so as to counteract a gentle diaphoresis. The nutriment was adapted to the state of the stom-

ach. There was a period of this disease, previous to its complete resolution, and where the powers of life seem to be on the point of yielding to the insidious effects of its hurtful agents, that wine alone became the most appropriate remedy. This state was better known than can be described, even by the discriminating physician.

During the summer months, the typhoid symptoms of fever were so intimately combined with the dysenteric and diarrhœa, it was not easy to discriminate between the two forms of disease. These complaints were considered varieties of one and the same disease, depending on the same general causes for their existence, and required but a little variation in their treatment. There were but a few instances of diarrhœa, unaccompanied with more or less febrile action, in some one of its stages; as there were no instances of typhus, in which diarrhœa or dysenteric symptoms did not form a part of the disease. The general remedies were the same; some regard being had to the prevalent forms of the disease. Those patients, who had been reduced by disease, or the various means employed previous to their admission into the hospital, required, in most cases, opium, wine, soft nutriment, comfortable lodgings, cleanliness from dirt and vermin. Some few were afflicted with the last. A patient was admitted, whose clothes were not only dirty in the extreme, but had become habitations for armies of lice; his hair was also filled with this tribe of insects. He was cleansed by the removal of his dirty linnen, and the hair from his head. The patient was not exposed, as the day was warm, and no water was employed on his body. He survived only twelve hours, the abstraction of this stimulus from the skin. So necessary had this unnatural stimulus become to support life, in his enfeebled condition, that he sunk and died almost immediately upon its removal.

ABUSE OF CALOMEL.

Submuriate of mercury, (calomel) was in general use among the army and hospital surgeons. The well-known fact that fever, under some of its forms, will yield to its operation when administered in full doses for a cathartic, and that beneficial effects have been noticed, when given in small doses as an alterative; led to its incautious employment in field practice. When calomel was administered in camp with no more precaution than a very inactive medicine might have been; if it did not produce immediately its salutary effect, it induced a dangerous state of debility on the stomach and bowels. Hence it was, that calomel proved frequently injurious in disorders of the bowels, as also typhous fever on the Niagara, during the summer and autumn of 1813, while the men were exposed in tents to the diurnal transitions of weather.

Some of the surgeons of the army did not reflect, that calomel should not be administered to their patients when exposed to cold and moisture, even if in a dry habitation it might have been the most suitable medicine in similar states of disease. Upon a body exposed to the weather, calomel loses its salutary powers, and exhibits its deleterious effects.

It was most evident, calomel, under the above circumstances, co-operated with the existent causes, to render the disorders of the bowels, and diseases combined with them, more formidable.

Calomel should never be administered, unless the patient is so situated, that the skin may be preserved in its natural warmth. If this was not attended to during its administration, either the bowels or the glands of the mouth suffered. To one of these parts it frequently directed its whole stimulating powers, and induced on one or the other high degrees of inflammation, which terminated in mortification of the intestines, or destruction of not only the muscles, but the bones of the face.

Four cases, under these formidable effects of mercurial ptyalism, were admitted into the general hospital at Lewistown;

three of whom died with their jaws and faces dreadfully muti-
lated. The fourth recovered with the loss of the inferior maxilla on one side, and the teeth on the other. He lived a most
wretched life, deformed in his features, (when I last saw the patient) incapable of taking food, except through a small aperture
in place of his mouth. The above interesting case is described
at large, by Doctor Whitridge, one of my assistants in the hospital at Lewistown, in the following manner :

Greenbush, 25th May, 1814.

" Sir,—Mercury has very justly been styled the " Sampson
of the Materia Medica." It has also (by a physician of my acquaintance) been emphatically called his " sheet anchor." It is
a medicine of such gigantic strength, which may, according to
the application of it, either build up or pull down the " pillars of
the constitution."

" In the hands of the judicious physician, it is an article of in-
estimable value, and one of the greatest blessings to the human
race, not only as a prophalactic, but an agent by which he erad-
icates disease, and restores health. On the contrary, in the
hands of the ignorant or the empyric, it may, and sometimes does
prove an agent by which he not only augments the maladies of
human flesh, but produces new diseases, subverts the laws of nature, breaks down the human constitution, and often proves the
source of incalculable mischief.

" An able writer, in speaking of mercury, observes, that it is an
' article of materia medica, possessing such activity in some conditions of the living system, as may be capable of producing great
and salutary changes. But in effecting these, certain premises
and indications are to be attended to, to justify the exhibition ;
and the physician, who does not give himself the trouble to consider these circumstances, may perform the part of an execu-
tioner.'

" I have seen no less than four cases, where death was produced outright by the improper administration of mercury ; besides innumerable instances, in which the constitution was either partially or wholly destroyed : coughs, rheumatisms and other

disorders, many of which-were incurable, produced by the improper exhibition of this most potent article.

"You must, sir, as well as myself, in the course of your or my practice, have seen much injury done in this way, by the indiscriminate, and improper administration of mercury, in its various forms to soldiers, in northern latitudes; placed in bad quarters, or in camp, or on marshes, exposed to a cold and damp atmosphere, to night air, storms and vapour, whose bed is the earth, and, perhaps, whose only covering is the canopy of heaven!

"After what has been said by Wilson, Trotter, Warren, and others on the use and abuse of mercury, is it not surprising, that we should, every day, have so many instances presented to us, of the flagrant abuse of this important remedy?

"I have selected the following case, (though not a fatal one) chiefly because it affords a striking illustration of the baneful effects of the improper use of mercury, and also, because it involves an important surgical operation. I shall describe the case in as brief a manner as possible.

"Thomas Broughton, of the 6th regiment of U. S. infantry, a sprightly lad of about seventeen years of age, fell into my hands upon the Niagara frontier, (Lewistown hospital,) in July last, with a disease at that time wholly mercurial. I could not, with certainty or precision, ascertain the nature of the disease, which occasioned the exhibition of the mineral; but believe it was a febrile complaint.

"When he was first placed under my charge, he was extremely weak and emaciated, had a slight cough, attended with a profuse diarrhœa, cheerful, and in good spirits, feared nothing—which, by the by, is characteristic of most soldiers, but was remarkably the case in this instance. Mortification had taken place in the buccinator muscle of his right cheek, and under his jaw, and had been progressing several days. The hole in his cheek, occasioned by the sloughing, (when I first saw him,) was about three quarters of an inch in diameter, perfectly round, and had the appearance of being cut out with a knife, or some sharp instrument. That under his jaw, about the size of a goose quill.

"I placed him under the charge of a faithful nurse, whose sole care was to attend this one patient. I directed his mouth (which was very offensive) to be kept perfectly clean, by injecting into his mouth, and through each of these orifices, warm water, diluted brandy, &c. by means of a small syringe. I ordered at first gr. xxv, and afterwards gt. c. L. Fowl. min. solut. to be mixed with a little water, and his mouth syringed with it: I directed a repetition of this quantity five or six times a day, taking care that it was not swallowed. In the interim to be washed every half hour with tinc. cinc. offic.

"Bark (cinc. off.) and wine or brandy was given him internally, in large quantities :—the tinc. opii. was also administered largely, not only to check the diarrhœa, but as a general stimulant (upon the principles of Pott,[*]) to arrest the progress of the mortification. Under this treatment, sphcelation continued to progress, until the orifice in the cheek had attained to about the size of half a crown, and that under his tongue to the size of half a pistarene.

"In a few days, however, his system became braced, his diarrhœa abated, his appetite improved, and his general health amended; so that the progress of the mortification was arrested.

"Shortly after, granulations were thrown out from the edges of each of the orifices, and their sides gradually approximated. Notwithstanding the caries of the bone continued to progress slowly, the teeth were loose, and as they became troublesome were taken out, one after another, until all the teeth upon the right side of the jaw were removed, the incisivi first, and afterwards the molares.

"Much advantage seemed to be derived from the local applications, as well as the general remedies, particularly the arsenis as potassæ.

"This system was rigidly pursued several months, great attention paid to him, and particular care taken to keep his mouth clean, and to prevent as much as possible the fœtor arising from the carious jaw. The diseased bone at length became loose, and gradually separated at the symphysis. With a pair of for-

* Vide Pott's Works.

ceps, I frequently raised it a little from its natural situation, and by impressing lateral motion upon it, could move it a little from side to side, but was at that time unable to extract it. The alveolar processes of the incisores and cuspiditi irritated and cut his tongue considerably, in consequence of which I removed them. The two orifices though much contracted did not close.

" He remained in this situation until after the capture of fort Niagara, and burning of the villages upon that frontier by the British army; when I took him (in January, 1814) together with all the sick and wounded upon that station, and brought them to Greenbush; after which I did not see Broughton for several weeks; during which time the diseased bone had become more firm, and shewed very little disposition to separate. Indeed, I considered the removal of the bone altogether impracticable by any other means than that of an operation.

" Two unsuccessful attempts were made by a surgeon (chief of the medical staff at this post) to pull it out of his mouth with a pair of forceps, when at the same time his mouth could not be opened to exceed half an inch. And at another time to saw off the end of it. He affirmed, that the operation I proposed could not be performed; and if it were, the wound occasioned by it could not be healed.

" As the diseased portion of the bone nauseated the patient, and was very offensive to those around him, not finding any advantage from further delay, I stated to him what would be necessary in order to complete the cure, and proposed to lay open his cheek, and extract it surgically; to which the patient readily assented.

" Accordingly the necessary preparations were made, and the patient placed in an horizontal position, upon a table of convenient height, and the operation performed. With a probe pointed bistoury, I commenced my incision at the angle of the mouth, divided the orbicularis oris, and the muscles of the cheek to the orifice in the buccinator, and continued the incision through this, into the substance of the masseter muscle. The facial artery, by this incision, was divided. The hemorrhagy was such as to render ligatures necessary before I could proceed with the

and
rom
: al-
cut
ved
ose.
fort
the
ther
ught
: for
i be-
:rate.
prac-

chief
with
:ot be
:w off
could
by it

:tient,
:y ad-
e nec-
: open
readi-

nd the
onven-
point-
mouth,
: to the
hrough
cial ar-
as such
vith the

operation. I made a ligature upon each of the mouths of the divided artery, and then proceeded to separate the bone from its lateral connections, and to dissect it up from the subjacent muscles, to which it was still firmly attached; after which, with a zigzag motion, together with a little extension upon the bone, I was enabled to separate it from the sound portion of the maxilla inferior about half way between the angle of the jaw, and the condyloid process.

"The parts were then brought together, their edges kept in contact by means of the interrupted suture, at the angle of the mouth, and by strips of adhesive plaster through the remainder of the incision. Perhaps the twisted suture would have been better, but this I was unable to employ for want of hare-lip pins. The dressings were then applied, and the patient taken to his quarters, placed in bed upon his left side, and kept in that situation to prevent the saliva from insinuating itself between the lips of the wound. The wound healed by the first intention through the principal part of its course. The fistulous openings both soon closed, and the patient gradually recovered without much disfiguration. The chasm has been filled up by ossific matter, thrown out by the secerning arteries; ossification seems already to have commenced, and it is probable a new bone will eventually supply the place of the old one by the process of osteogeny. He now eats and converses very well, which before were performed with difficulty. His general health is good, and the contour of his face is daily improving, so that there is a prospect of his yet becoming quite a handsome man."

(Signed)   J. B. WHITRIDGE,
Assistant Hospital Surgeon.

To James Mann, *Hospital Surgeon,*
U. S. Army, at Burlington, Vermont.

I have so frequently witnessed the injurious effects of mercurials, particularly calomel, when administered to soldiers in the field, it is my decided opinion, it never should be employed to men under such circumstances, except in combination with some active cathartic. To soldiers under typhous fever, or of an in-

12

flammatory type, it was equally injurious when daily repeated. Instead of remedying those diseases of the bowels, which prevailed in our armies on the frontiers, when exhibited to men exposed to all the casualties of a camp, those complaints deteriorated by its frequent repetition. Syphilitic diseases were but seldom permanently cured by it, during campaigns. This was made most evident to the surgeons of hospitals, by the numbers admitted with these complaints, which had been of some months duration, after the army retired into winter quarters.

The following Syphilitic cases were recorded by Doctor March *of the Hospital department, and are here inserted to shew the injurious effects of mercurial practice in tents.*

CASE FIRST.

" Richard Mahhar, private of the 16th regiment, was admitted into general hospital, at Greenbush, October 13, 1812, with the venereal disease. He had administered him by a regimental surgeon, five or six doses of calomel; also had used an injection of a solution of the acetite of lead. October 15th—His mouth had become very sore, having also a profuse ptyalism; a dose of salts was prescribed. 17th—The mouth extremely sore; gums and face much swollen; the saliva profuse and mixed with blood; effluvia consequent upon salivation, very disagreeable. A solution of alum was used as a gargle. 18th—Mouth still extremely sore; blood and saliva flowing continually. The discharge was not less than a pint, or a pint and half in twenty-four hours. Bark and wine were directed. 19th—Mouth and face as yesterday. Bark and wine continued. A decoction of white oak bark in which alum was dissolved, was prescribed for a wash and gargle for the mouth. 20th—Bleeding had somewhat abated. Medicines as yesterday. 21st—Symptoms continued the same, and the same medicines repeated, with the addition of a dose of sulphate of soda for a cathartic. From the 22d to the 24th, the last medicines were continued, excepting the cathartic; two teeth fell out of his jaw, followed by a discharge of pus mixed with blood and saliva. 27th—Sulphate of soda for a cathartic. 28th—Hemorrhage considerably abat-

ed; bark and wine continued. 30th—Much better; bark and
wine as before. 31st—Cathartic of sulphate of soda. November 1st—Convalesced fast. The cathartics seemed of great
benefit; the succeeding days took bark and wine. 4th—Took
a dose of sulphate of soda. From this time recovery was rapid,
and the ptyalism had almost ceased; and by the 17th of November he was entirely recovered from the venereal affection,
and also from the distressing effects of mercury. This case il-
lustrates the beneficial effects of cathartics in checking the excitement on the salivary glands; also, the alarming effects of
mercury under exposed circumstances. This patient scarcely
escaped death. For several days appeared in a moribund
state."

CASE SECOND.

" James Cady, private, regiment light artillery, admitted into
the general hospital at Greenbush, October 4, 1812, with lues
venerealis. The prepuce and glans penis were much swollen
and inflamed, with several chancres. This patient had been
treated, while in his tent, by calomel; in consequence of exposures and irregularities, the complaint increased. He was put
on calomel, gr. 2. night and morning, sometimes it was combined with opium to prevent its operation on the intestines, and to
allay the pain of the local irritation. A solution of acetite of
lead was applied to the inflamed parts. October 5th and 6th,
the calomel was continued and the chancres dressed with cerate
armed precip. rub.—swelling had little subsided. 7th—Calomel
continued; the gums began to be slightly affected; swelling
continued to subside. 8th—Ptyalism had commenced; calomel
omitted; chancres assumed more favorable appearance; continued the mercurial dressings. 9th to 12th—Swelling of prepuce
increased in consequence of irregularities, and exposures to
cold; mercurial frictions on the thighs; pill of opium at night.
20th—The prepuce in a suppurating state; an emollient poultice; ptyalism continued; the above method was pursued, varying the treatment according to symptoms, several weeks, when
the patient was discharged cured. In this case it was most evident that cold had a strong tendency to increase every alarm-

IMAGE EVALUATION
TEST TARGET (MT-3)

6"

Photographic
Sciences
Corporation

23 WEST MAIN STREET
WEBSTER, N.Y. 14580
(716) 872-4503

ing symptom of disease, at the same time the mercurial action on the glands of the mouth was aggravated."

In similar cases of this disease, the nitro-muriate of gold has since been employed with the best effect, without the unpleasant salivation produced by mercurials.

A discriminating line between those cases where calomel is admissible, and those where it may prove injurious, even under the most favourable circumstances, is not always correctly drawn. Calomel, in full doses for a cathartic, is a powerful and safe remedy in sthenic diathesis. But its administration in small doses, with a view of removing the primary strong diseased action of this diathesis, by inducing a new mercurial action, previous to its reduction by depleting the blood vessels, and evacuating the contents of the intestines, will frequently defeat the intention.

I have witnessed a febrile disease of the sthenic diathesis to increase during the continued exhibition of calomel in small doses, until the mouth was very much inflamed; so that it was not easy to determine whether the existent state of the disease was the effect of its original cause, or the consequence of mercurial excitement.

It has been also observed, in asthenic fevers attended with great debility, with torpor of the stomach and bowels, and profuse diarrhœa—that calomel increased the dangerous state.

<hr/>

ABUSE OF TARTRITE OF ANTIMONY.

Pringle, in his " diseases of the army," noticed the injurious effects of antimonials, or their inefficiency to cure the diseases incident to soldiers, when exposed in camp. It is with regret that I feel myself bound to record the bad consequences of the administration also of tartrite of antimony, in one of the hospital wards ,at Lewistown. A young surgeon, upon taking charge of this ward of about 60, observed to me that these bowel complaints would readily yield to emetic tartar, in small doses. He was cautioned not to employ this medicine. It was observed, these diseases were not recent affections; and having been of some duration, evacuants had been carried to their full extent, previous to their admittance into the hospital; and furthermore, antimonials were, but in few instances, admissible in field practice, while men were exposed to the transitions of weather in tents. These precautions were disregarded. The following weekly report, out of 500 patients, gave 10 deaths; 9 of whom were out of the above ward of 60.—The succeeding week 8 deaths were reported; 6 of whom out of the same ward. At this time I was confined to my tent, and unable directly to correct the abuse by prescribing to the sick. The other two gentlemen, Surgeons Whitridge and Vanhovenburgh, had more in their wards than they were able to attend and do them strict justice.

Having been informed that I was dissatisfied with so disproportionate ill success, as was exemplified by reports; this young surgeon wished to be informed the practice pursued by myself. Too feeble to enter into a minute detail of practice most suitable in these diseases of the bowels, he was referred to Doctors Whitridge and Vanhovenburgh, whose practice had been accompanied with more success.

From the 1st of July to the 30th of December, the number of sick admitted into the general hospital at Lewistown, were between 950 and 1000. During this period, 59 deaths were reported—nearly half of whom died in a small ward of 60 patients in the course of about three weeks; most of these by an imprudent and injudicious administration of tartrite of antimony.

It has been observed that intermittents were among the forms of disease on the Niagara, during this campaign. A company of volunteers stationed at Schlosser, one mile from the great cataract, during the summer months, were nearly all attacked with intermittent fevers of the tertian type. There are, in this vicinity, extensive swamps and stagnant waters. Twenty-five privates of this company were admitted at one time into the general hospital, sick with this disease; who, previous to their admittance, had been destitute of medical aid. A few cases among the number were found, which, during the hot stage of the fever, exhibited great increase of heat and arterial excitement. These were bled, apparently, with benefit. Emetics and cathartics were prescribed for the whole; the first, with intention of counteracting the cold stage of the fever, were administered at its accession; the last, with a view of removing irritation from the intestines, and reducing sthenic diathesis; and both, having for our object a more equalised excitement. After these evacuations had been carried to an extent which was judged sufficient, bark, snakeroot, aromatics, and wine were directed, in moderate and larger quantities during the intermission of fever; not, however, with all the benefit which was expected. The last medicines, in a few instances, arrested the paroxisms a short period only; while, in general, they had no effect. Not one experienced a permanent cure by the above means.

After being thus disappointed with remedies in most common use, recourse was had to Fowler's mineral solution, a remedy held in high estimation for the cure of intermittent fevers. This experiment made by us at this time confirmed the great reputation which this arsenical preparation had acquired, in the hands of other physicans. This potent medicine acted almost like a charm. It did not fail in one instance, to remove the paroxisms of fever within five or six days, some of whom had taken the bark a fortnight, or more, without permanent effect. In a few cases two or three doses of from five to ten drops of the mineral solution effectually removed the paroxisms. The convalescents from this fever were benefitted by the bark and wine, inasmuch as the stomach and digestive powers were improved by their use.

After the retrograde march of the army from Stony Creek, no expedition against the enemy was undertaken, except the disastrous movement of a detachment to the Beaver dams; at which place, 600 men under the command of Colonel Borstler, after a feeble resistance, surrendered to an inferior force.

While waiting the arrival of the fleet from Sackett's harbour, under the command of Commodore Chauncy, to co-operate with the army; and the drying of the roads, which had been impassable for waggons, most necessary for the transportation of provisions, in a contemplated expedition against the enemy at Burlington heights, in the event of any failure of assistance from the fleet; General Dearborn was employed the month of June and part of July, in making preparations for the expedition, by organizing and disciplining the troops, a considerable part of whom had been recruited the preceding winter. In the mean time the encampment was secured against surprise. Fort George was reduced in its dimensions, and its lines of defence strengthened by a deep ditch and palisades. These preparations were in forwardness to recommence operations against the enemy, which were momently and anxiously anticipated by the officers of the army, when General Dearborn was removed from this command.*

From this period, 14th July, until the first week in September, when General Wilkinson assumed the command, the army at Fort George consumed the most eligible season of this summer and autumn, for effective service; cooped within the narrow limits of a few acres of land, by a force of the enemy not exceeding one half its strength. And under constant apprehension of an attack, placed itself wholly in a state of defence. This apparent pusillanimity, or want of energy on the part of the army, emboldened the enemy to insult it, by repeated attacks upon its advanced piquets, night after night, during the above period; and on the 24th of August, a general attack was made on the lines by Sir George Prevost, and was repulsed with loss.

This petit guerre kept the army in constant alarm, and sub-

---

* The removal of Major General Dearborn from this command, was exceedingly regretted by the officers of the army. Whatever might have been the object of this procedure, subsequent events have demonstrated that its policy was very injudicious. General Dearborn, at the time of his removal, had recovered his health; and preparations were in forwardness to recommence active operations against the enemy; which had been delayed in consequence of the badness of the roads, almost impassable for waggons, until the month of July, waiting the arrival of the fleet to cooperate with him. The fullest evidence which can be given, that the General possessed the entire confidence of the army, is the affectionate address to him, signed by General Boyd and every field officer present, when he took his leave

jected the troops to vexatious fatigues, unremitted duty, and multiplied exposures, which prevented them from taking their necessary repose.

Under the above mortifying circumstances, the army, in consequence of its stationary position, suffered from diseases, aggravated by filth accumulated in its vicinity.

From this last period, arrangements were ordered for some important movement. These were actively and unremittedly executed. Boats, in particular, were wanting for the transportation of at least four thousand men. Those attached to the army were repairing, while others from various parts were collecting.

The object of the expedition was kept a profound secret. It called forth variant opinions, and excited lively anticipations, that the reputation and honor, which had been lost by inglorious inactivity, would be retrieved by some bold and decisive stroke upon the enemy. These animating sensations were highly exalted by the annunciation of the capture of the enemy's flotilla on lake Erie, by Commodore Perry; and the surrender of the British forces in the vicinity of Malden, to General Harrison. These sanguine expectations were almost realised when those glorious events were succeeded by reports that General Harrison had already embarked on board transports a part of his division, to form a junction with that of General Wilkinson. With this united force, it was expected the army would recommence offensive operations, against which the enemy could have made but a feeble resistance.

These high wrought anticipations were only visionary suggestions of the soldier, ardent in the cause of his country, and emulous of fame and glory. These, which seemed to have been already within the grasp of the army, were thrown at a distance, by the orders of the commander in chief, to embark the troops, including the convalescents, and move down lake Ontario, to Grenadier Island; this place being assigned a general rendezvous for the army.

"Obedience to orders is the first and last duty of a soldier." It was, nevertheless, deeply regretted by the officers, that the army, respectable as it was, should retire in the presence of the enemy, much inferiour in force.   And after having gained, with some loss, and a high degree of honor, one of his most important posts, and held possession of it five months, should abandon the conquest, without accomplishing the primary object of the campaign; by either destroying, or capturing that division of the enemy which composed his right wing, in Upper Canada.

When an enemy exhibits great military talents, we are disposed to allow him all the credit due him, in a martial point of view, even when by artful deceptions and judicious management, with a force inferior, he was enabled to apparently check the offensive operations of our army, and compel it to place itself in a position entirely defensive.

This inactivity while the army was under the command of General BOYD, upon whom it devolved when General DEARBORN retired, excited at the time severe public animadversions. General BOYD had in possession the means of his own justification; he owed it to the high station he held in the army, as well as the nation, to have brought to public view at an earlier period those documents from higher authority, which governed him in the measures he adopted, while he commanded at Niagara. The orders which he received from the department of war, if more publicly known, would exonerate him from that censure, with which he is now loaded in the opinion of the public, who, on national concerns, are too much disposed to pronounce judgment, before they hear the cause.   (See Note F.)

General WILKINSON, at the time he issued his orders to move down Lake Ontario, directed the sick and convalescents, too feeble to accompany the army, should be sent to Lewistown, under my charge, with an order to " furnish them with winter quarters out of the reach of the enemy," in a situation which I might esteem most eligible.

The last weeks of October were most uncomfortable for the sick in tents.   The weather had become cold, rainy and boisterous.   Winter, with its dreary attendants, progressed in November with rapid movement. The convalescents, from typhous and diarrhœa, in consequence of the sudden transitions of weath-

13

er, had renewed attacks of disease under the form of pneumonia; coughs had become general among them. These changes determined me, after spending some days to select a secure position, and prepare quarters for the approaching winter, to break up the encampment at Lewistown. We had at this time about three hundred and fifty in the hospital, including the sick, convalescents and invalids. The last were subjects for discharge, in consequence of wounds and other disabilities. After selecting one hundred who had so far recovered from wounds and bodily infirmities, as to be able to perform a journey of three hundred miles to Greenbush, the remainder were ordered to Eleven Mile Creek, called Williamsville.

These arrangements were communicated to Colonel (now General) SCOTT, who had been left in command at Fort George, and met with his full approbation. To the assistant quarter master General of the post, he gave his order to furnish the necessary means of transportation. The invalids destined for Greenbush were committed to the charge of Lieutenant ARCHER, regimental pay master, and Doctor HUGO. The remainder of the sick and convalescents, two hundred and fifty in number, some of whom very debilitated, were transported to Schlosser, a distance of eight miles, in waggons; thence to Black Rock, in boats; from the last place in waggons to Williamsville. This was a tedious journey of forty miles for sick men, many of whom were destitute of cloathing, suitable for the approaching inclement season. Previous to this movement, the roads, bad at best, had been rendered almost impassable by heavy rains. During the journey the weather was cold and wet. The evening on which the sick arrived at Black Rock, a storm of rain commenced, with a violent wind from the west, which raised the waters of the strait at the outlet of Lake Erie, eight feet in two hours; which swept the baggage belonging to the men, and a quantity of hospital stores, that had been deposited during the night at the landing, down the river. This loss was severely felt by many, who, previous to this unfortunate casualty, had exceedingly suffered for want of clothing. It left them without a change of garments of any description. The hospital department by this sudden flood of water, besides many articles very necessary, lost between 150 and 200 blankets, a more serious deprivation than every thing besides, under existent circumstances, as it was impossible to replace them.

In addition to the above disasters, six of the most enfeebled died during the removal, who, although too weak to encounter the cold and fatigues attendant, importunately objected to being left at Lewistown, exposed, as they must have been, to the depredations of the savages attached to the British army. These depredations were strongly apprehended, after the army retired from this frontier. That these apprehensions were not without foundation, subsequent events have fully and shamefully demonstrated. Four weeks previous to those fatal and painful disasters, which succeeded the removal of the army from the Niagara, they had been predicted. At that time, upon learning that the few troops who had been left at Fort George, mostly militia, were evacuating the post, it was observed, that Fort Niagara would fall into the hands of the enemy, and the country in the vicinity would be invaded and plundered.

At Williamsville, the barracks which the preceding winter had been occupied by General SMYTHE's division, were put into a comfortable state of repair, and improved during this winter as hospitals. These quarters were very extensive, and were, by much labor, rendered commodious for the number who composed this detachment of sick and convalescents. The wards were made warm; this was more important, as the men were destitute of clothing. The wards were not crowded, consequently were less liable to become infectious. Six patients only were placed in a room; wherefore it required but little labor and attention to preserve them in a state of cleanliness. This part of duty the soldiers were, at all times, obliged punctually to execute. Those regulations which had respect to cleanliness were always scrupulously enforced within the hospitals under my direction.

The sick in their new habitations recovered their health and strength in a wonderful manner. Here it was made most evident, that the health of the body was intimately connected with an equable and uniform warmth of the circumambient atmosphere. Animal life cannot be supported but a short time during the seasons of severe cold, unless the temperature of the body is preserved in an equable state, by both natural and artificial means. The first are suitable nutriment taken into the stomach, and fresh air : the last are gentle exercise, warm clothing, and comfortable habitations. Even during the hot season, life may be destroyed by a sudden evaporation of heat from the surface of the body. In the hottest day of our summers, a healthy man may be placed in a situation where he may be literally chilled to death in a very short period of time.

At Williamsville, before three weeks had expired, fifty of the convalescents were reported fit for duty, and were ordered to Fort Niagara. The barbarous deaths of most of these men, with the rest of that ill-fated garrison, we have to lament, while emotions of just indignation irresistibly obtrude themselves, when reflecting upon the manner. Surprised, and taken without resistance, most of the garrison were deliberately murdered by the bayonet, after surrender.

Having disposed of the sick in quarters for the winter, in conformity to the orders received from General WILKINSON, and finding their number daily decreasing ; my services at Williamsville were believed to be no longer absolutely necessary. It became my duty, as it was my inclination, to pursue the army of General WILKINSON by land to Sackett's Harbor, where information might be obtained to what point from Grenadier's Island it had directed its course. It was my persuasion, that at the last place, or more probably at Kingston, in Canada, it would be overtaken. Which position being considered the key of the upper province, would, in possession of the army, have been of high importance to its future operations. With these impressions, it was my expectation, that this important post, previous to the severe frosts of winter, would fall into the hands of our army.

Permission was received from General HARRISON, who had but just arrived from Detroit, and on whom the command of the post devolved, to leave the Niagara frontier, and join the division of General WILKINSON. The charge of the hospital at

Williamsville was resigned to Doctor WHITRIDGE, who, for assiduous attention to duty, was exceeded by no physician of the
army. The services of this gentleman cannot be too highly ap-
preciated. To him not only the nation is indebted, but my
grateful acknowledgments are due ; and this opportunity is improved, more fully to express them. A full share of the high
reputation, which the hospital at Lewistown supported during
the campaign ; as announced in the flattering reports of the Inspector General to the Commander in Chief of the army, is attributed to his fidelity and good judgment.

NIAGARA FRONTIER.

FORT NIAGARA is situated on the east side of the strait or river of the same name, at its outlet into Lake Ontario. It is a
commanding position as a military post. This fortress was
built by the French about 1725, was surrendered 1759 to the
arms of Great Britain, under the command of Sir William Johnson, and by the line of demarkation settled at the treaty of peace,
1783, fell within the bounds of the United States ; but was not
given up until 1796. The river or strait, 35 miles in length
forms the water communication between lakes Ontario and Erie,
of unequal width, from half to six miles ; in the upper part between the falls and Erie are several islands, the largest being
13 miles long, and six broad, equal in dimensions to a large township. Seven miles above the mouth of the river is the head of
navigation, where the village of Lewistown is laid out into house-
lots ; eight miles south is the celebrated cataract. The banks
from the lake to Lewistown are as perpendicular as they can be,
composed as they are of clay and loom, from fifty to seventy
feet above the surface of the water, and are different from all I
have seen. They have more the appearance of art than nature.
From Lewistown to the falls the sides of the banks are perpen-

dicular 160 feet in height, supported from their foundations to their tops by strata of calcareous rocks, as regularly fixed as if they were mason work. Through the whole extent of the river to the falls, the banks do not slope, as is usual; from whose summit there is no passage to the water's edge, except where artificial roads have been constructed.

The distance from the falls to Black rock, a village of ten or fifteen houses, the river banks are from four to twelve feet high. At some points, marshes, which terminate in low swamps, border the river; over which the river road, during wet seasons, is miry and almost impassable for waggons. Buffalo, two miles above Black Rock, previous to the war was a considerable village, rapidly increasing in population and trade, beautifully situated on a creek of the same name. At the time it was burnt by the British army in December, 1813, it comprised between one and two hundred houses. The whole of the thinly scattered settlements on the Niagara were at the same time pillaged and burnt. Directly opposite Fort Niagara, on the Canada side, the beautiful village of Newark presents itself to view. The whole country on the Canada side is under a good state of cultivation, and pleasant. From Newark, after passing a number of fine farms and settlements, we arrive at Queenstown, opposite Lewistown. This is a charming little village. An adjoining eminence, known by the name of Queenstown Heights, commands a most extensive prospect. From this place the eye comprehends, at one scope, the whole country to the borders of Lake Ontario north distant eight miles, variegated with woods and cultivated lands, and to the village of St. Davids west four miles, which prospect overlooks the vast forests beyond. At the same time a full view of the Niagara meandering to the lake, the waters of Ontario, as well as the remote high lands of Little York, distant forty miles. All these combined render this a most delightful situation. The sceneries from this elevated ridge will enlarge and extend; and for many years will become more and more beautifully picturesque, as improvements progress. Queenstown Heights will long be remembered in the annals of history, where the first important battle, after the declaration of war, was fought

on the Canada side, between a small body of United States'
troops and New-York volunteers, under the command of General Van Ranselaer, and the British under the command of General Brock ; in which ill-conducted, unfortunate action, unpro-
pitious to the arms of the United States, five hundred men were
either killed or taken prisoners of war; and in which the British General lost his life.

Lewistown is a handsome site for a town, the name of which
it only bears, comprising, before this frontier was devasted, a few
log houses.   Situated as it is, at the head of navigation of Lake
Ontario, it will become a place of importance, as a deposit for
goods transported to and from the shores of the lakes west, as
well as the country east.   The exuberant productions of this
fertile country will here concentrate.   The portage from the
navigable waters of Ontario to Erie, is eight miles.

From Lewistown, as we proceed south up the Niagara, an eminence is abruptly ascended one hundred feet, or more, above the
tract which borders Ontario, and more than one hundred and
fifty feet above its waters.   The traveller, when climbing this
precipice, feels that from its summit he would find a descent
somewhat proportionate to the ascent.   He is both disappointed
and astonished to learn, that the precipice ascended is but the
edge, or abutment of a vast and extensive plain, or table of land,
which contains within its enormous excavation, the waters of
Erie, three hundred miles in length, and one hundred miles in
breadth, which disembogue themselves from Erie, through the
strait or river above described, to Lake Ontario.

This abutment extends east a great distance, and with some
broken inequalities, gradually loses itself in lands descending in
gentle swells from the south.   To possess a correct idea of the
general face of the country which comprehends the waters of
Ontario and Erie, it will be understood they are severally contained in two vast basins, supported in two extensive plains, or
more strictly speaking, gently undulate .ands.   One of which,
with an elevation of one hundred and fifty feet, seems as if lap-
ped on the lower, while the waters of the upper are restrained
by lands on the north the distance of Lewistown from Lake

Erie, bounded by the above described precipice or abutment. This abutment, for its greater security, is strengthened by layers of rocks from its foundation *stratum super stratum*, coated with earth, which, through a long series of ages, has been washed by rains from the summit. This abutment, after being divided by Niagara river, at Lewistown is, on the Canada side of the river from Queenstown, extended as far as the heights of Burlington, at the west extremity of Ontario.

The cataract, eight miles south of Lewistown, is one of the wonders of this continent. To give a just description of this amazing fall of water, exhibiting a sheet 600 yards in width, divided by Goat's island, rolling from a perpendicular precipice to a vast and awful chasm 150 feet deep, might appear a vain attempt after the very correct descriptions which have been already published. The picture of this sublime natural exhibition, had been painted in a language so picturesque, its reality to my view, was less majestic, than what had been formed on the imagination. Observations similar, have been expressed by others after visiting this cataract.

The rapids, on the American side above the falls, are in extent half a mile. Where, in broken sheets, the waters seem in full career, white with foams, down a huge bed of broken rocks, in a descent of 50 or 60 feet, bounding over crags and steeps, with a movement accelerated as they approach the brink of the precipice. Above these rapids the river is two miles wide, where the waters pressed by broader torrents, seem, by their impetuous race down a declined plane, to be accelerated to unite with the preceding contending floods, in one tumultuous stunning roar. The waters, on the Canada side, in their course, perform, with increased celerity, their race to meet the awful conflicting scene.

The accumulated body of water on the Canada side is so forcibly pressed forward by floods behind, and quickened by its movement on a descending plane, and accelerated by its own voluminous weight, as it approaches the cataract, that it shoots over the precipice, forming, at the distance of 40 or 50 feet from its perpendicular, a curved white sheet. On the United States' side, the water falls in a thinner perpendicular sheet. The grand falls are divided by Goat island. The sheet on the American side forms an angle of 120 degrees with that on the Canada at Goat island.

The uninterrupted conflicting current of this broad cataract immediately below the falls, exhibits a scene, although less majestic, still more awful. From this thundering precipitated torrent, in wild commotion, rises a foam to half the height of the precipice; where, intermixed with air, the lighter sprays are suspended in clouds and become the sport of the winds. These clouds are seen thirty miles. The vast sheet of water, precipitated by its weight to the bottom of the gulph, seems lost for a short time; then swelling from beneath the superincumbent waters, bursts upon the surface in spouts, forming figures of various and changing shapes, which move in every direction, and in hurried disorder and giddy whirls dance upon the wave; while the great body of the flood, emerging at some distance below the falls, pursues its rapid course. Sixty rods below the falls, the river is passed in a small boat with safety.

With wonder we view a mountain's summit; and the sublime precipice, from its base, affords delight. But, when we cast our eyes down on deep sounding caverns, or on yawning broad chasms below, all is apprehension. Our heads turn giddy; we tremble in every joint; we seize on every bush, and cling to every tree, as we approach the brink; and still feel we may be precipitated in a moment to the dreadful gulph. Such is the force of association of ideas, that the body irresistibly becomes the sport of its influence.

Two miles above the falls the Chippawa empties its waters. A signal victory was gained over the British army at this place, 5th of July, 1814, by a detachment of General Brown's division, led by the intrepid General Scott. Four miles north of Chippawa, on the heights of Bridgewater, the 25th of July following, was fought a second battle, in which Generals Brown, Scott, Rifley, Porter and Miller were conspicuously engaged; and in which there was exhibited a most brilliant display of undaunted courage and cool bravery by the whole army.

14

After Generals Brown and Scott were wounded, the command devolved on General Ripley, who with six hundred and fifty of his own brigade and volunteers under the command of General Porter, charged the British line, three times their number, and repulsed it at every point. In this action, General Miller, with the 21st regiment, distinguished himself in a particular manner, by a charge with the bayonet, upon a battery of nine pieces of artillery, which fell into his hands. The killed and wounded of both armies were great for the numbers engaged. Fort Erie, situated opposite Buffaloe, will ever be remembered in history, for the gallant defence made by General Ripley, during five weeks; as well as a subsequent repulse the enemy met with, when he assailed the works defended in a most gallant manner by troops under the command of Generals Gaines and Ripley; also on account of the successful sortie made by orders of General Brown upon the enemy's batteries, which compelled him to raise the siege.

The country which borders the Ontario east of Niagara, from eight to twelve miles from its shores is flat, intersected by ravines, at distances of two, four, and six miles; formed by waters which, in times of rains and freshets, run from the high lands south. These ravines communicate with the lake by creeks, which originally were land-marks of distances from the Niagara down the lake shore; at this day are known by the name of two miles, four miles creeks, according to their respective distances. The same mode of estimating distances from Niagara west has obtained on the Canada side. The flat lands above mentioned are wet into mid summer, except where openings into the forests have been made for cultivation. These improvements are neither frequent nor extensive. Not over four or five years had settlements been made on this frontier previous to the war. This tract is known by the name of Holland purchase.

The whole of this territory, comprising a diversity of soil, has the reputation of being the most fertile in the northern states; perhaps not inferior to any in America, productive in all kinds of grains, and every species of fruit which grow in New-England. The meadows particularly are luxriant. The crops of wheat on every soil are abundant, amply remunerating the husbandman for his labor. The forests are composed of large and lofty beach, maple, and the aspiring elm, interspersed with groves of majestic oaks.

The lands in the vicinity of Fort Niagara, and on the borders of the strait to Lewistown, were very wet until the middle of July, in 1813, in consequence of repeated rains, when the weather became dry and hot. The waters on the surface of the ground soon evaporated ; the roads, which had been bad, soon became passable. Transitions from cold to excessive heat were so sudden during the month of August, that to me it was almost insupportable ; more oppressive than had ever been experienced by myself in the atlantic states.

While contemplating the above wonderful works of nature, the relative positions of lakes Ontario and Erie; the elevation of the last 300 feet above the former, with only 35 miles of intervening distance; we are irresistibly carried back to remote antiquity ;—a period when the wonderful cataract of Niagara was advanced eight miles lower on the strait or river. If any dates were obtained, how far it has retroceded in a given number of years, a tolerably correct calculation might be made at what period of antiquity the waters rolled over the abutment at Lewistown; the number of years, also, before the falls will recede to the northern extremity of Erie, the present outlet of that lake ; provided the river the whole distance glides over a bed of rocks to the cataract, as it must have done from its present position to Lewistown.

Such are the evidences of this statement, the spectator must yield to it his assent; while the philosopher, upon examining the complicated sceneries on the Niagara, will advance in his conjectures one step beyond, convinced by still stronger marks of changes having taken place from more remote antiquity to that period previous to a communication between Erie and Ontario ; when the northern abutment of Erie was entire and its waters disembogued themselves south through a different channel, which held intercourse with the Mississippi. He will be also forcibly impressed by evidence demonstrative, that the waters of Ontario have retired from eight to twelve miles from its most ancient banks; leaving a tract of alluvial land of the first quality once submerged, now covered with forests of superb growth and capable of the highest cultivation. Upon the most ancient bank of lake Ontario, which is improved as a road, petrifactions of various species of water shells have been dug eight feet below its surface. Specimens of which were presented me by colonel BARTON an inhabitant of Lewistown. These without other evidence force a belief, that the waters of Ontario were anciently seventy feet perpendicular above their present level. The lands which border Erie exhibit appearances of having been once overflowed with water. Rocks and stones interspersed through the country have marks of having been worn smooth by water and sand; in some of which are found imbedded petrifactions of shells. These are demonstrations that the above lakes were, at some former period, vastly more extensive than at the present.

It may be thought a bold conjecture, too improbable for belief, to say the river Niagara is of modern date, compared with the most ancient state of the lakes; previous to a water communication between them, when the waters of Erie with the lakes west emptied themselves through a channel south.

To seek for causes of an obstruction of the ancient outlet of these waters, previous to the existent Niagara, and account for its present channel, we may not go back but a few years to find one; similar to that, but more powerful, which lately overturned from their bases extensive banks on the Mississippi into its channel. That a similar concussion has either tumbled into the ancient channel of the outlet of the waters of the upper lakes, or raised its bed so as to obstruct their course is probable. To corroborate the hypothesis, it is stated that even now there is a water communication between the waters of the upper lakes to the waters which empty into the Mississippi, which admits of boat navigation; through which the baggage of a detachment from a post on the lakes, was transported to the Mississippi in batteaus; that the route was through a champain country, without an intervening hill. The last statement was given me by the commanding officer of the detachment.

A sudden accumulation of the waters not only of Erie, but the upper lakes would have been a consequence of an obstruction of its most ancient outlet. The increasing flood would continually encroach upon the bordering lands, until the old outlet was opened, or a new one formed at some point; that point was, where the banks of the vast basin of Erie were the lowest. Such being the state of the waters, at this ancient period, the current of the overwhelming flood of Erie irresistibly forced its passage to Ontario; by which event the channel of Niagara was opened. Lake Ontario, extending then to its ancient bounds, experienced an increase of its waters from Erie through its recently formed outlet. What were the consequences of the rise of waters in Ontario, with all which has been adduced, are conjectural; nevertheless, the present appearances warrant every supposition which has been advanced.

To account for the recession of the waters of Ontario, from its ancient banks, an additional flood was necessary to accomplish so great a work—an enlargement of its own outlet the St. Lawrence. It was not only the accumulated waters of Erie, but those of Huron and Superior with their tributary streams which aided. The channel of St. Lawrence deepened and enlarged by these overwhelming floods, as soon as those of the upper lakes had subsided to, or probably below their most natural level; the waters of Ontario sunk below their ancient bounds, as the St. Lawrence was necessarily enlarged and deepened.

In consequence of the increased depth of the St. Lawrence, lake Champlain, communicating with it by the Sorel, experienced a similar recession of its waters from its ancient banks. There is presumptive evidence that all the high plains on its borders, extending to the mountainous parts, were, at a very remote period of time, submerged. (See Note G.)

Some point on the Niagara frontier will, one day, become the grand emporium of this north-western territory. If we may be allowed to form an opinion from the existent astonishing improvements, that period is not very remote. The fertility of the soil not excelled by any i ne United States, intersected by rivers capable of boat navigation, bordering on inland waters not

inferior in extent to seas, navigable for vessels of the largest bur-
thens, and possessing the advantages of a navigable communication, excepting the short distance of seven miles, with the Atlantic ocean, will, within a few years, be capable of affording to
the nation resources which may rival, and even surpass those of
the Atlantic states of the same extent of navigable waters.

This is not a mere speculative suggestion, nor a wild anticipation of an extravagant imagination. The sentiment admits
of actual demonstration. This tract, embracing an extent from
Utica, near the source of the Mohawk, to Buffalo, the east extremity of Lake Erie, thence to Detroit, a length of five hundred
miles, and a width of 150 to 200, twenty years previous to the
late war, was a wilderness unfrequented by civilized man. But
at the present period many parts of it are in the highest state of
cultivation. New towns and villages, which in point of population equal, and of ornamental appearance, surpass the ancient
villages in the Atlantic states, are interspersed amidst the vast
forests of this district.

Should we cast our eyes stil further west, and look only a few
years into futurity, we shall see, by anticipation, settlements no
less important on the waters of the Michigan, and even to the
western extremity of Superior; when a commerce will necessarily require vessels whose aggregate of tonnage will not be less
than that on the whole Atlantic shores.

What is there to prevent, if luxury and thirst of opulence
keep pace with improvements? The soil of this district, being
much superior, is capable of supporting, on a territory of equal
magnitude, a population vastly more numerous than that in the
Atlantic states can. The productions of the earth, with the
same labor, are three and four fold.

A free navigation of these waters to the ocean would, even at
this period, be of infinite importance to the United States, while
the consequences of the natural advantages which this territory
possesses will increase with the population of the country.

To possess a correct opinion of the value of this country, which
the command of these western lakes and rivers, communicating
with the Atlantic, would give; the parts of the whole district in

relation to each other, and the extent of an inland navigation intimately connected with a foreign, must be viewed. The politician cannot be convinced with any representation short of ocular demonstration. While in his closet, with even a correct map of the country before him, he can acquire but an imperfect idea of the immense wealth it will in a few years afford. It is anticipated, that one of the greatest sources of the national revenue may be the commerce of the north-western district; but which, while Canada is possessed by the British government, may not pay the expenses of collection. Under existent circumstances, at peace with Great Britain, innumerable avenues will be open for smuggling, which may be carried on to such an extent between Canada and the north-western territory, as not only to diminish the public resources, but render them subservient to the British government.

The inhabitants of the northern and western parts of New-York are mostly emigrants from the New-England states. The fertility of the soil of this district invites enterprising adventurers to those regions; where the laborer is amply remunerated for his toils, while changing the face of the earth, and converting the wilderness into pleasant cultivated fields.

It is that class of people generally, who are endowed with good educations, that first adventure into this territory. They possess not only high degrees of resolution and industry, but a knowledge, which, by inductions drawn from causes and their effects, leads them to foresee the future importance of this territory.

The traveller, on his journey through this district, is astonished to find so large a proportion of its inhabitants well educated. There are at this period more men possessing literary information to be found in these new settlements, in proportion to their population, than in the old towns and villages of New-England. These emigrants from the old states bring with them habits of industry necessarily acquired in a country where a man, to enjoy the blessings of life, must be indefatigable in the employment in which he is engaged.

The marks of a strong attachment to the religion of their ancestors are exhibited by beautiful edifices dedicated to the LORD. In every village are seen buildings for public worship, highly ornamental. Having experienced themselves the benefits of an early education, they know how to appreciate its value; and are therefore not inattentive to furnish the means of literary acquirements for the rising generations. In every village are found schools where the first rudiments of letters are taught by classic scholars. In many, also, are seen seminaries of learning and academies, in which the higher and more important branches of literature may be acquired.

What are the motives which induce the inhabitants of the old towns to quit the places of their nativity, and leave connexions and friends, to commence new settlements in a wilderness? has frequently been asked. The acquisition of a more comfortable subsistence, and accumulation of wealth. These, the main springs of action in social life, inspire a man with courage and fortitude to embark in vast enterprises—to endure fatigues—to submit to privations—and encounter dangers.

Great undertakings are meritorious, when they promote the interests of the public, and enlarge the sphere of private happiness. It is then they deservedly receive universal applause.

The "wilderness" cannot "blossom like a rose," without the aid of man; who must encounter difficulties, and undergo infinite toils. With cheerfulness and patience these are endured by the first settlers of a country; from whose soil its resources are not evolved, except by indefatigable industry and persevering labour. By these means it is, the hardy husbandman of the forrests accumulates riches in these fertile regions, from the productions of his farms; the mechanic, from his ingenuity and unremitted attention to his occupation, increases his wealth; and the merchant, by his accurate and economical calculations, enlarges his fortunes.

The northern and western frontiers of New-York, like all new countries emerging from a wilderness state, are more unhealthy than the old settled towns in the same latitudes in the New-England states. A country in a state of nature, previous to openings for cultivation, is less subject to diseases than the same district after improvements are commenced by the agriculturist. Hunters and surveyors of woodlands, exposed during many months to all the vicissitudes of weather, with little or no shelters from cold storms, seldom suffer from diseases. The aborigines experience fewer diseases, than the inhabitants of new settled countries.

Upon opening a farm in the midst of a wilderness, the putrefaction of vegetable substances is promoted in higher degrees by the increased rays of the sun upon the surface of the recently exposed earth, during the hot seasons of the year. The deleterious gasses emanating by the process of putrefactive decomposition are suspended over the cultivated spot in greater or less proportions, as currents of air are impeded by surrounding forests. Under these circumstances, heat and moisture are not evaporated in proportion to their extrication from the earth; while the inhabitants are enveloped in a warm vapour bath charged with offensive gasses, eliminated from substances in a state of decay, by which they are predisposed to diseases, and suffer from them more or less, as artificial causes co-operate to excite the diseased actions. Severe labor under a hot sun; a neglect of cleanliness in log houses—habitations of the first settlers; a coarse diet, ill adapted to easy digestion and nourishment, as meats fryed in fat, instead of being boiled, or prepared in the form of soups; and ardent spirits of the worst quality—new rum and whiskey, are among the co-operating causes productive of diseases in new settlements.

In proportion as cultivation of the earth is extended by opening the forests and draining the lands, so will climate be improved, and its endemic diseases disappear. The heavy fogs of lakes and large rivers, which are impeded and suspended over their borders by woodlands until a late hour of the day, abstract from the body its vital heat, and subject the inhabitants to intermittent fevers, and other autumnal diseases, as dysentery and diarrhœa. They, however, are less frequent at those points, on the lake shores, where cultivation has made some progress, and have disappeared where the lands are extensively improved. These

15

autumnal diseases, which are now considered endemic in new settlements on the frontiers, will vanish as the forests are subdued, and the marshes and swamps drained ; while the husbandman will be remunerated by a two-fold reward—higher degrees of health, as well as accumulation of wealth.

The transitions of weather on the northern and western frontiers are less frequent, and not so sudden and great, as on the Atlantic shores. With the same extensive improvement, their inhabitants will not be scourged by diseases more, than those of the eastern states ; the first settlers of which, (if historians and the most aged of the inhabitants are to be credited) were subjected to the same diseases, which are now endemic on the north-western territories. Intermittent fevers, one hundred years ago, were common in the lower towns of Massachusetts, where a single case has not been known to have originated within the past fifty years. The few autumnal fevers, which are sporadic, generally, may be traced to well known exciting causes, independent of atmospheric influences arising from local positions.

The diseases of winter, in the northern and western districts of New-York, are mostly pneumonia of every grade from a slight cough to high inflammation. The most severe form of this disease prevailed, during the war, among the inhabitants, as well as soldiers of the army, and was no less fatal to the first, than the last. These complaints of the breast are seldom seen among that class of citizens the most temperate, especially its severest forms ; but among those who indulge in a free use of whiskey and rum.

The means employed to obviate the deleterious effects of cold become the exciting causes of dieases. Long exposures to inclement weather exhaust the excitement, and waste the vital principle. To remove unpleasant sensations, a gill of whiskey is resorted to. The stomach may be charged with three or four of these potations, with the best intentions to fortify the body against disease. A cough, increase of heat, pain, and perhaps high degrees of inflammation may be the consequence. The whole of this indisposition may have been obviated by tepid drinks, or a soft diet.

Although local positions influence the states of health, and predispose to diseases; yet causes which may be denominated artificial excite the greatest number which exist. A laborious man, replete with health, seldom believes the observance of rules and regulations of temperance is necessary. While he is free from pain, he v'ws disease at a distance—with a bottle of whiskey in his hand, he bids defiance to death and its terrors. Instances like this are frequent; with which every physician is conversant. The following anecdote is not a fictitious picture, but a painting from the life.

I was once called to visit a child whose father was absent when taken sick. Before my prescription was made, he returned; when petulantly asking his wife why a physician was called, said, he consulted no physician, and took no drug; that his *bottle* was his only *physician*, and *rum* his only *medicine*. Rum to him was all in all, as it cured every disease. My reply to this devotee of Bacchus was, that rum to *him* was a *good god*. Not many days had passed, when this man, being attacked with a violent pain in his side, the effect of severe labor, and liberal potations of spirits, under the rays of a hot sun, sent for me in haste. My astonishment was expressed he should call the aid of a physician, having his IDOL at hand; affecting to be unwilling to prescribe, when I had so potent a DEITY as a competitor; from whose assistance he had heretofore experienced so much benefit. The man was tantalized until confession was extorted, he had tried his favorite medicine without good effect, and in vain. This was too evident to have been mistaken. An acknowledgment of the fact only was required. As soon as he was convinced of his folly, the requisite means to mitigate distress were administered.

Intermittent fevers, dysentery, diarrhœa and jaundice may be considered the endemic diseases of this frontier. Jaundice, however, is most generally a secondary disease, subsequent to intermittents and diarrhœas, frequently accompanied with an enlargement of the liver. Rheumatism and rheumatalgia are also common: they attack, during the cold seasons of the year, those who indulge in the use of ardent spirits. This is sufficient evidence, that these liquors, taken to excess, do not obviate diseases, but are highly injurious. As spring opens, by the genial influences of the sun, the last diseases disappear. This fact demonstrates, that the excitement of spirits is more deleterious to animal life during the cold, than the hot seasons.

The several types of fever appear under more aggravated forms on the north-western frontiers, than in the New-England states, under the same latitudes. The greater humidity of the atmosphere, in the vicinity of the lakes, combined with the hurtful agents heretofore enumerated, is assigned as a cause.

———

THE last week of November, I departed from the Niagara frontier, to follow the division of General Wilkinson. After leaving Williamsville, thirty miles east, we arrive at Batavia, a new well built village, surrounded with farms extensively opened, comprising a soil of the best quality. The village contains 40 houses, a handsome court house, jail and a county arsenal. It is a place of considerable business. Over a tract of territory of 20 miles square within the limits of the town, according to the census of 1810, there are 3645 inhabitants. The head branches of Tonnewonta river rise in this town, which running west empties itself into the Niagara, ten miles north of Black Rock. On this river is a town of the Seneca Indians. This village is situated 256 miles west from Albany. Ten miles east lies Le Roy village, comprising 30 houses in the town of Caledonia, which has a population, by the census of 1810, of 2353 inhabitants. This village is 246 mile from Albany; the Genesee river is its eastern boundary, where commences that stupendous work of nature, which extending to Lewistown, distant 70 miles, forms the great barrier or abutment, which confines the waters of Erie in its own basin, excepting a breach which has been made through it by Niagara river. This ridge, throughout its whole distance, overlooks the alluvial lands which border Ontario, and when the forests are cut down for cultivation, will command more beautiful uninterrupted sceneries than can be found perhaps in the known world. The county of Genesee between forty and fifty miles square, 14 years ago a wilderness, contains a population, by the census of 1810, of 12,644 inhabitants, and a taxable property of three millions of dollars. Genesee river is distant 226 miles west from Albany. From Caledonia, after passing new settlements and some inconsiderable villages, we arrive at Bloomfield, a populous well settled town, in which are highly improved farms. The soil is of the first quality, productive of every species of grain, grass and fruit trees. Their dairies furnish large supplies of butter and cheese for market. Domestic manufactories of cloth are carried on to considerable extent, in which are employed between two and three hundred looms; in 1810, by the census, the town contained 4425 inhabitants. During the war the inhabitants of this town and its vicinity found in the army an excellent market for the surplus productions of their farms. On the Niagara their cheese sold for 50 cents per pound, butter 40, cyder 8 dollars per barrel, potatoes from 2 to 4 dollars per bushel, onions from 2 to 4 dollars per bushel, and other articles in the same ratio.

The next place of considerable note is Canandaigua village, situated near the outlet of a lake of the same name, 208 miles west from Albany and 111 from Utica. This village is built on the lake hill, which rises from the shore by a gentle ascent, and commands an extensive view of the lake thirty miles in length, and the handsome improvements on its banks. In 1810, by the census, it contained 137 houses and stores, county buildings, an elegantly built academy, a spacious arsenal, and several superb private seats, in point of elegance and taste inferior to none in the United States. Twenty years previous to the war, the first house was erected here from logs, which were felled to make an opening for the house. Since which it has increased in an astonishing manner. The academy is richly endowed---Messrs. GORHAM and PHELPS are among its most liberal benefactors. Canandaigua is esteemed by travellers the most beautiful inland village in the United States. Progressing east 16 miles from the last place, we arrive at Geneva, 192 miles west from Albany, within the town of Seneca, elegantly situated on the west bank of Seneca lake. It is a place of considerable trade, having 130 houses, 3 places of public worship, and 4 public schools. The soil on the borders of this lake is excellent and under good cultivation. Geneva is about 25 miles south of lake Ontario. The population of this town, by the census in 1810, was 3431. While continuing our route through a country having more extensive improvements and greater population, we arrive at Cayuga lake, which is passed over on a very handsome bridge, one mile in length; at the east end of which we enter the village of the same name. From which position, the country bordering the lake presents a great variety of beautiful sceneries, variegated from low banks gently ascending to bolder swells from 100 to 200 feet in height. The lake discharges its waters at the north end, where it soon meets the waters from Seneca lake, through the river of the same name; thence continuing their winding course disembogue themselves into lake Ontario, distant 25 miles. The lands are rich and fertile. Seneca lake is 38 miles long, and from 1 to 4 miles broad. Cayuga village is in the town of Aurelius, 175 miles west from Albany. This town has a population, by the census in 1810, of 4642 inhabitants. Its inhabitants are cultivators of the soil, and if we may judge from appearances, generally, and particularly the state of cultivation and improvement, all of which have been made the last 20 or 25 years, we must infer that they abound not only in the necessaries and conveniences of life, but in the luxuries, sources of wealth and opulence. After leaving Cayuga village, we pass Camillus, and fine farms under good cultivation, when we arrive at Onondaga hill, to distinguish it from a village two miles east, in the hollow; the first contains 40 houses; here the county courts are held; the last village contains 60 houses, in which is an elegant meeting-house. Three miles south, is the residence of part of a tribe of 200 in number, anciently known by the name of Onondaga Indians. Onondaga is 50 miles west of Utica and 147 miles west of Albany. From this, east, we pass Manlius, 137 miles west of Albany. This town like others already noticed on this route, exhibits riches and increasing affluence. The population consists, by last census, of 3127 inhabitants.

From this to Utica, a distance of forty miles, to a person who had been twelve months conversant with vast forests and new villages interspered in the wilderness; the increasing improvements of the country are peculiarly interesting.   New objects and changing sceneries continually unfold themselves.   Every mile on the route presents older states of cultivation, where increasing elegance is displayed; which, had the journey been reversed, and the traveller immediately from the Atlantic shores, he would have viewed new, as being less improved.   Thus, the mind is vario v and oppositely affected by the same objects. What renders the most remote new settlements, when first beheld, more astonishing is, they are approached through an uncultivated wilderness, dreary to the lonely traveller; and while his mind is shrouded in darkness proportionate to the gloomy shades of the forests, which bend over his head, the cheering light of an open country suddenly bursts upon his eyes; the extensive improvements before him announce a village near, in which he expects to find, knowing its recent date, a few og houses, or more decent comfortable habitations covered with boards.   But this exhilarating light, as of a new world, with mansions of painted wood work and bricks, erected with taste, and in an elegant style of modern architecture, rich and superb, astonishes the beholder.

These enlivening sceneries are more extensively opened as we approach Utica from the west.   The transition is not less pleasing than the Elysian fields were to Æneas, after traversing the dismal regions of Avernus.

Upon my arrival at Utica, information was obtained, that the flotilla conveying the army, instead of crossing the St. Lawrence to Kingston, as had been expected by those unacquainted with the real design of this expedition, had directed its course down the St. Lawrence; having now evidently for its object, the reduction of Montreal.   The disappointment was universally felt and expressed by all not immediately connected with the army.   My own feelings compelled me to concur with the prevailing public opinion, that the campaign of this year, which had early opened with flattering prospects—prospects propitious to our arms, under the command of General DEARBORN, would close with irrepar-

able disasters; productive of disappointment mortifying to national feelings, as well as lasting disgrace to the projectors of the expedition. Little is hazarded, when it is declared, this unfortunate movement of the army was made in direct opposition to the
sentiments and opinions of the major part of the officers of the
army.

The road from Utica direct to Montreal was bad, and the accommodations worse. It was expected, at the last place, or some
other point between Ogdensburgh and Chateaugay, the army
might take a position. Having been advised the enemy had,
in some instances, crossed small parties upon the south bank of
the St. Lawrence, in the rear of our army, during its progress
down, and some hazard apprehended from these marauders, a
more circuitous route, by Albany and Lake Champlain, was pursued. After this unpleasant journey of nearly five hundred
miles, I arrived at Plattsburgh the first week of December;
where an effort was made to place the hospitals, now in extreme
disorder, under some regulations. In the execution of which
duty, many obstacles presented themselves, while the division
of General HAMPTON, still in tents, were occupied in erecting
their barracks. The requisitions upon the Quarter Master General's department were so pressing to furnish materials for barracks, little or nothing adequate to the erection of hospitals, could
be obtained. My most pressing remonstrances, for the neglect
of the hospital department, were not or could not be regarded, so
long as the barracks for the troops were considered the primary
object. The first consideration, with officers of every grade,
should be to provide comfortable accommodations for their sick.
The healthy and robust can better endure exposures to cold and
inclement seasons in tents. Under these comfortless coverings,
many, enfeebled by diseases, who might have been preserved,
in warmer habitations, were daily sinking to the grave. At this
period, the 10th regiment, the only one from south of Delaware
at this post, suffered extremely by the prevailing mortality. The
disease was similar to that of the preceding winter. My stay
here was of too short duration, to form an opinion of the practice

adopted; more especially, as the most of my time was employed to provide more suitable quarters for the sick of this division.

Orders received from General WILKINSON, (who had then taken quarters at Malone, eighteen miles south of French Mills, and fifty miles from Plattsburgh) hastened my departure for that place, where I reported myself the 15th of December.

The General had contemplated to establish hospitals for the sick of his division, in this pleasant village. In pursuance of orders, the Assistant Quarter Master General had appropriated an academy, the arsenal and two private houses, to hospital purposes. Within ten days, these buildings, sufficiently capacious to accommodate 250 men, were made comfortable; in which each patient had a separate bed. The wards were warm, even during the utmost severity of cold. The sick admitted here, except such as were quite exhausted by disease, daily improved in their health, by the change from cold lodgings in tents, to more temperate in houses. The above establishment was placed under my direction. To Captain DWIGHT, A. Q. M. General, who promptly afforded every assistance in his province to bestow, and the circumstances of the country would allow, this establishment was much indebted.

This division of the army witnessed a series of unfortunate movements after the capture of Fort George, until it retired into winter quarters at French Mills. To combat the elements, was attended with more losses than to fight the enemy. The unseasonable expedition of the army, down the St. Lawrence, was not the final evil which it had to encounter.

We shall, here, give a retrospective view of the general health of the army, when it embarked on board the flotilla at Niagara. A large proportion of the soldiers were convalescent, and could but illy endure the fatigues and exposures in open boats, during the passage down Lake Ontario, to Grenadier Island. The weather was cold, accompanied with rain, the whole route. The flotilla was scattered. The boats transporting this army were, wholly, at the mercy of the winds and waves; and were not collected within a fortnight of each other, at the place of rendezvous. While on their tedious passage, attended with great haz-

16

ard and serious disasters, many of the convalescents relapsed into former, or were seized with new diseases. Some of the most
indisposed were transported from Grenadier Island to Sackett's
harbour, and there left in hospitals.

From Grenadier Island, the flotilla, progressing down the St.
Lawrence, met with no serious obstructions from the enemy.
Three hundred boats passed the batteries at Prescott, opposite
Ogdensburgh, under a tremendous fire, with the loss of one man
killed and two wounded. General Wilkinson, from the time he
took command of the army at Fort George, until his embarkation, was sick. At Grenadier Island, he became more indisposed; and during his movement down, was mostly confined to his
bed. It having been ascertained that the enemy with his disposable force was in pursuit of the army; with a view to prevent its rear from being molested, General BOYD was ordered
with detachments from his own, and General COVINGTON's brigades to land and beat them. In pursuance to orders, a landing
was effected with about 1200 men; who, in Williamstown, on
the Canada shore of St. Lawrence, engaged a superior force.
The field of battle was contested three hours. At the commencement of the action, the enemy was beaten; but neither
army in the event gained any important advantage; but, in
which, were displayed by the officers and men generally, the
highest degrees of courage, against superior discipline and force;
and in which the enemy claimed a victory. By their strong
position and superior management they frustrated the object of
this rencounter, when General BOYD was ordered to reembark
the army. The attack was so severely felt by the British, the
retrograde march of this detachment was effected without molest-
ation. In the battle fell, much lamented, General COVINGTON,
a brave and accomplished officer. The loss on either side was
stated to have been five hundred killed and wounded. Those
of the United States' troops badly wounded were left on the
field of battle.

This action closed the hostile operations of the army against
the enemy this campaign. It belongs to officers versed in high
military tacticks, to reconcile the plan of invading an enemy's

country, and entering it at its centre of population, during an inclement season of the year, and when its severity was rapidly progressing, with an army feeble, destitute of clothing and provisions :—in which, when possession was gained, it would have to contend with a far superior force at every point ; and where resources could not be obtained, except by way of Champlain ; nor from that quarter without opening a communication by the strong posts of Isle au Noix and Stone Mill, by force of arms.

Doctor LOVELL further observes, that " during the whole of October, and part of November, most of the troops were subjected to excessive fatigues, and exposed in open boats on the lake, when it rained almost every day. On their arrival at the French Mills, about the 14th of November, the weather became intensely cold, and remained so all the winter. In addition to the great fatigue to which the soldiers had been exposed, especially the division from Fort George, most of them had lost their blankets and extra clothing, on their march, or in the action of 11th November, at Creistler's fields, in Canada. Even the sick had no covering except tents, from the period they debarked at the Mills, until the 1st of January in the severe latitude of 45 degrees. Provisions were scarce, and of a bad quality. Medicine and hospital stores were not to be found, having been lost or destroyed during the passage down the St. Lawrence. Under these circumstances sickness and mortality were very great. A morning report now before me gives 75 sick out of a small corps of 160. The several regiments of the army, in their returns, exhibited a proportional number unfit for duty. Of the 75 referred to, 39 were reported of diarrhœa and dysentery ; 18 of pneumonia; 6 of typhus, and 12 of paralysis of all the extremities. Many of the paralytics, on our arrival at the Mills, were attended with mortification of the toes and feet. In a few of these, the pain was severe; wherein opium not only relieved the pain, but checked the progress of mortification. Stimulants, both internally and externally, were beneficial ; and when these remedies were assisted by a nutritious diet, warm lodging and clothing, a cure was effected. The last complaint, generally, seized those, who, previously had been extremely reduced

by disease ; and under our unavoidably bad situation, frequently in a few days proved fatal."

The statement given by Doctor LOVELL was confirmed by
spital Surgeon Ross, the senior of the medical department,
accompanied the army down the St. Lawrence.

In the vicinity of the French Mills, the country was a wilderness. Huts and hospitals were necessary, to render the army
comfortable. The erection of these was a work of great labour,
and required several weeks to complete. A supply of hospital
stores could not be obtained nearer than Albany, a distance of
250 miles. The want of these necessaries, for the support of the
very wretched and enfeebled soldier, was most severely felt. The
poor subsistence, which the bread of the worst quality afforded,
was almost the only support which could be had for nearly seven
weeks.

These accumulated evils the army encountered with much
patience and heroic fortitude. Now it was the chief surgeon,
who was with the flotilla, found himself loaded with a weight
of censure; of which he should be fairly exonerated, so far as he
was blamed for the loss or waste of medicine and hospital stores
on the St. Lawrence. It was abundantly demonstrated, that
no separate transportation for these stores, although expressly
ordered by the Commander in Chief, had been provided ; but
that they had been improvidently distributed throughout the
boats of the flotilla, and for the security of which no officer had
been, nor could have been made accountable.

The deaths, sickness, and distress at French Mills, excited
general alarm. The great mortality had obvious causes for
its existence. In all such cases, censure will fall on some department. And as each was disposed to exonerate itself, upon which
was blame more probably to have alighted, than the medical—
than upon the surgeons of the army, under whose immediate care
the victims of disease were daily prostrated ? There are to be
found some, who, ignorant of the effects of medicine on the human constitution, are too prone to believe, its exhibition may
be equally efficacious, under every circumstance and condition to which the patient may be subjected. Hence it was in-

correctly inferred, when men were beheld expiring under the prescriptions of the surgeons, the mortality was a consequence of injudicious management, or neglect of duty. Predispositions to disease, the effects of obvious causes, the comfortless conditions of men exposed to cold, wanting the common necessaries of life to support them, in their exhausted states, were seldom taken into consideration. Doctor LOVELL, one of the most able and attentive surgeons of the army, emphatically observed, " It was impossible for the sick to be restored, with nothing to subsist upon except damaged bread."

At the time the division of General WILKINSON was delayed at Grenadier Island; and the flotilla put in motion down the St. Lawrence, General HAMPTON's division penetrated from lake Champlain, on a bad road, some parts of which almost impassable by nature, in the direction of Chateaugay, to the bounds of Canada, where it met with some opposition from the Canadian militia and Indians. After a feeble effort to repel the enemy, and advance into the lower Province; a retrograde march to Plattsburgh, from whence the army had previously moved, was ordered. By this unfortunate, imbecile attempt to invade the lower Province of Canada by General HAMPTON, some loss was experienced, and less honour was acquired. Whether this apparent vacillancy of judgment resulted from insuperable obstacles, unforeseen and not anticipated, or a matured determination not to co-operate with General WILKINSON, has not as yet been developed.

For the disasters which attended the army, and the non-accomplishment of the object of this movement, General WILKINSON has been arraigned before a court martial, composed of officers of a high grade and most respectable standing; and of the host of charges and specifications preferred against him, has been acquitted. Success, however, often makes the celebrated general; while want of success, in the public estimation, ensures his condemnation. The documents exhibited before the court, upon his trial, are a full exposition of all the important circumstances relating to the movement of his division, from Fort George, until the campaign terminated ; and, when made public, will give stability to floating public opinion.

The medical sketches of this campaign will be concluded with the substance of a communication made to an officer of high grade, at the French Mills.

The greatest evils, to which the army has been subjected since the war, are diseases and their consequent mortality.

How are these to be remedied? is a question of the highest moment. As causes and effects are intimately connected, by the removal of the first, the last cease. Long exposures to inclement weather, independent of other causes, are sufficient to produce a catalogue of diseases. But in the event of active operations, these causes are not under our control. The unavoidable casualties to which an army at times may be subjected, during cold seasons, may be partially remedied by additional clothing.

It may not be as generally known as it should be, that, a large proportion of the army were not, when first enlisted, fit for soldiers. At the time of entering the service, many of them were incapable of enduring the fatigues and hardships incident to war, during all seasons of the year. Many of these, habitually intemperate, with constitutions broken down by inebriation and its consequent diseases; whose bloated countenances exhibited false and insidious marks of health, contribute to fill our hospitals. It has already fallen to my lot, since the commencement of the war, to recommend more than two hundred of the above description for discharge; many of whom had not been enlisted three months, and had performed only a few days' march, during the most pleasant season of the year. It has been too much an object with officers on the recruiting service, to fill up their rolls with numbers; without reflecting, that the strength of an army consists in able-bodied men. These infirm men were always a dead weight, requiring a detachment of the more efficient, as nurses, or attendants. A body of five thousand composing our troops, seldom have furnished more than three thousand capable of active duty in the field. Government has the means of remedying the last evil.

The health of men depends much on the officers immediately commanding companies. Their cleanliness has not at all times been promptly attended to. The most suitable manner of preparing their diet has been neglected. An improvement in the dietetic management would be made, should each corps and regiment detail a police officer to inspect daily, the kitchens, and enforce upon the men the importance of preparing their rations in a manner most conducive to their healths. A surgeon may be ordered to accompany the police officer, when employed on this duty of culinary inspection. A surgeon of regiment should not feel his duty ends with his prescriptions for the day; but to obviate disease, as well as to cure, is a part of his province. Less trouble and expense are required to employ prophylactic means, than cure diseases.

The quarters of soldiers are generally too much crowded. To place 16 or 20 men in a room 16 feet square, is very injudicious. Officers are not fully sensible of the evils which arise from close rooms, charged with contaminated air. It is an opinion too prevalent in the army, that, in this cold season, men cannot be made too warm; the closer they are stowed the better, because warmer, has been often alleged; without reflecting, that unoxygenated air is more injurious to health, than absolute cold, in pure air. The evils which originate from crowded rooms, and which accumulate during the long nights of winter, are not remedied by breathing a purer air, during the active employments of the day. The constitutions of men, subjected to these transitions, shew their morbid effects, by coughs and pneumatic fevers; which, when the causes are of long continuance, assume forms the most mortal, rapid in their progress, terminating the fatal scene, sometimes in the short space of 24 hours. Such were the morbid effects of the pneumonia of 1812. Such have been described, at various periods, under its most mortal form, the spotted fever, by many physicians of respectability; particularly by North and Gallup. Here the disease, like a devouring element, quickly dissolves the fabric of the constitution, or, like an explosion of a loaded mine, subverts from their basis the foundations of life in a moment.

An ill-timed distribution of clothing is among the causes of disease. It has been found, the woolen garments allowed the soldiers have not been issued until the warm weather of summer commenced, when winter finds them either naked, or clad in their summer dresses, perishing with cold. It may be added, the allowance of clothing is not sufficient to protect the men on the northern frontiers from the severe frosts of this inclement climate.

It cannot be too frequently repeated, an intemperate use of ardent spirits, is also among the destructive evils attached to our armies. The high excitement produced by ardent spirits is more injurious to life in cold, than hot seasons of the year ; especially if drank when the system is exhausted of its vital heat by cold. This most noxious of all causes of disease, to which our army is exposed, may be obviated by prohibiting sutlers to sell these deleterious liquors in the vicinity of the cantonment.

To elucidate the correctness of the above positions does not require the aid of philosophic demonstration. It is only necessary to present them to the eye of the understanding, and they cannot fail to be comprehended. The above, however, are only a partial representation of the causes of disease and death.

To exonerate the medical staff of the army from censure, is not my design. For a neglect of duty they may sometimes stand chargeable. Not more should be placed to their account, than is just. Is a soldier sick under circumstances already described, and does he die under the hands of his surgeon ? his death is too often imputed, either to his ignorance or inattention, by officers who are no less, perhaps more greatly deserving of blame. It is a disingenuous fact, the surgeons of the army are made mere scape-goats, on whom are heaped a multitude of sins ; which, without a figure of speech, are imputable to causes, over which they have no control.

END OF CAMPAIGN 1813.

CAMPAIGN OF 1814.

~~~~~~~~~~~~~~~~~~

At MALONE Hospital, on the 1st of February, 1814, the number of sick had increased to 450. For an additional number of 200 sent from French Mills, rooms were wanted; which were promptly provided by Captain DWIGHT, A. Q. M. General; who continued to give me his assistance.

In addition to diseases already enumerated the preceding campaign, (among which, diarrhœas were the most prevalent,) was the pneumonia of 1812-13. The disease was accompanied with all the same symptoms under which it appeared the preceding winter; but, its attacks were less frequent. There were two cases where the patient did not survive 12 hours after the first indisposition supervened. There were a few cases of disease which assumed the form of spotted fever—in which the brain seemed to be the seat of disease; a mental derangement having been the first alarming symptom, without any pneumonic affection. The progress of the symptoms was so rapid, that no decisive mode of practice was adopted. All of these died within the first 24 hours. Two of the number, within six hours. A nurse in the hospital, apparently in good health in the morning at 9 o'clock, became deranged; soon after comatose, at 3 P. M. was a corpse. Many of the sick had swelled feet and legs; some of these were accompanied with mortifications; the consequence of long confinement and inactivity in the boats, wet and cold, during the passage of the army down Lake Ontario and the river St. Lawrence.

Six or seven weeks elapsed before the men were made comfortable in their barracks, at the Mills. By this time, provisions had arrived from Plattsburgh and Utica, of a better quality than

17

had previously been issued. Ample supplies of hospital stores were received from Albany, under the charge of Doctor Low, Assistant to the Apothecary General. The men daily improved in their appearance; time was had to clean themselves; while order and discipline assumed the place of apparent confusion and bustle, which, during the building of huts, seemed to exist.

This relaxation from severe toils and labour was but momentary. About the 9th of February, an order was issued to leave this cantonment. One division, under the command of General BROWN, moved up the St. Lawrence to Sackett's Harbour; the other, under the immediate command of the Commander in Chief, directed its march to Plattsburgh.

In consequence of this retrograde movement of the army from French Mills, the hospital, at Malone, at this time, under good regulations was broken up, and the sick were ordered to proceed on routes destined for their respective regiments. Those for Plattsburgh and Burlington were accompanied by myself. It was no inconsiderable task to transport 450 sick men, or more, at this season of the year, through a country almost destitute of inhabitants, a distance of 70 miles. Some of whom were extremely reduced with fevers and diarrhœas. Others were convalescent. The few accommodations on this route were wretched. The inhabitants, although kind, were not under circumstances to furnish means to render the situation of sick men even comfortable. Nothing was omitted within their abilities, to meliorate their miserable condition.

Knowing that so large a detachment of sick and invalids could not be covered at night, if they moved in a body; the sleighs which transported them were successively put in motion, in small divisions. Their line of movement, three days forming, extended the whole distance from Malone. The first division arrived at Plattsburgh, the place of their destination, about the time the last commenced its progress. About 20 very sick, who were left in the hospitals, under the care of a citizen physician, were made prisoners of war by the British; who immediately followed the retrograde march of the army, as far as Malone. Those left in the hospitals were not molested in their persons, but were only obliged to sign their paroles. The greater part of whom, after five and six weeks, joined the hospital at Burlington. During this movement of the sick, six died, while many improved in their healths; notwithstanding it snowed or rained during the whole journey.

Upon the 16th of February, I arrived at Burlington; where about half of this detachment of sick had arrived. There were, then in the hospital here, about 160 of General HAMPTON's division.

After preparations were made for our increasing number, for whose accommodation, in addition to the hospital house, 20 rooms of the common barracks were provided, the wards were inspected, and the men classed and distributed according to their diseases and conditions.

The epidemic of 1812–18 was among the prominent diseases also, in this hospital. Although it was not so generally prevalent as the preceding winter, there were some strongly marked cases, sudden in their onset, with suffocated respiration, contracted pulse, cold extremities, and a heavy dull pain in the chest.

My attention was called to one case, of a few hours duration. After directing heated woolen clothes to his extremities, bleeding was directed; when it was understood, there had been some disagreement between four or five young gentlemen attached to the hospital, respecting the proper method of treatment. All of whom, excepting one, objected to bleeding; having never witnessed its employment under similar states of disease; and consequently were strangers to its beneficial effects. The quantity first taken away was eight ounces. About one hour after the operation, I visited the man, and found him relieved, as to the laborious respiration. In the evening of the same day, difficult respiration had returned with increased heat and fuller pulse; when eight ounces were again taken away. The day following, he was bled eight ounces the third time. After which, he convalesced, and in three days was able to walk his ward, having a returning appetite.

The following days, five or six similar cases were treated in

like manner, under my immediate direction; who also recovered. After these successful exhibitions of bleedings in these
pneumonic diseases, no further opposition was made to the use of
the lancet in hospital practice, in similar forms of disease. I do
not hesitate to say, that more than one hundred were saved by
this operation. We had this disease completely under our control, if seasonable application was made. The auxiliary remedies were a cath. of jalap and calomel; calomel and opium in
small doses; antimonial wine and camphorated tinc. of opium,
as expectorants; and blisters upon the chest. Small emetics,
after bleeding and evacuations by the bowels, were occasionally
employed. The epidemic of this winter, as heretofore, fell upon those with the greatest force, who were either advanced in
years, or intemperate.

Intermittents shewed themselves, in a few instances, during
the months of February and March, 1814. Some of these cases
were admmitted patients, who had been treated by regimental
surgeons in quarters; wherein the disease appeared obstinate—
not yielding to remedies commonly employed. Previous to
their admittance, emetics and cathartics had been administered;
after which, the bark, aromatics, bitters and wine in large quantity without any benefit. Their treatment in the hospital was
commenced with Fowler's mineral solution; not with those good
effects, however, which had been experienced from its employment, on former occasions, at Lewistown, on the Niagara. This
unsuccessful practice, by the most usual means, persuaded me
that these intermittents partook of the type of the prevailing
pneumonia. Sydenham and Rush have observed, that during
epidemics, all complaints assume the nature of the prevailing
disease. Recourse was next had to remedies employed in the
epidemic pneumonia; as bleeding, calomel in small doses, and
antimonials. This practice was more especially adopted, inasmuch as these intermittent fevers were accompanied with some
slight affections of the lungs.

The patients with these intermittents were bled from 12 to 16
ounces during the exacerbation of the febrile stage. Then jalap
gr. x. calomel gr. x. were administered for a cathartic; or sul-

phate of soda ; or ol. ricini. From one to two grains of calomel were administered every six or eight hours, and intermediately a tea-spoonful of antimonial wine. The paroxism seldom returned after bleeding and the operation of a cathartic. Bark and wine were of no use, until the excitement was equalized throughout the system, and became permanent, and the local affection of the lungs entirely removed.

Epilepsy was among the diseases with which we had to contend in the hospital at Burlington ; and over which we made ourselves completely triumphant by the employment of nitrate of silver. By this medicine alone, the morbid action, which constituted the disease, was entirely subdued.

The following cases were taken from the prescription books of the Hospital, and will be here inserted, in the form as therein appeared.

CASE FIRST.

GEORGE WATKINS, 10th regiment, admitted 5th March, 1814. The preceding month, this patient had been daily attacked with fits four or five times. His treatment was not known, when with his regiment.

March 6th. Rs. Calomel gr. x. pro cath.

7th. The fits continuing as heretofore. Venæsectio $\frac{z}{3}$ xvi.

8th. The disease continues. Emplas. epispastic. pro capite.

9th. The fits continue.

10th. Rs. Nitras argent. gr. ½. fiat pill. Sexta quaque hora capiat.

12th. No fit yesterday. Nitras pill. cont. ut. supra.

13th. No fits. Nitras pill. cont. ut supra.

14th. The nitrate pill discontinued, in consequence of a sore mouth, and small discharges of blood with the fœcal evacuations, and gripes.

15th. Rs. Nitras pill. bis in die, cum laud. liquid. gt. xx. capiat æger.

16th, 17th, 18th, 19th. The last medicines were continued. Since which there was no return of fits.

May 1st. Reported for duty.

CASE SECOND.

OLIVER SPENCER, 29th regiment, had been subjected to epilepsy seven months. During which period, he had been treated in the hospital by a routine of evacuants, antispasmodics, tonics and blisters, without any benefit. The following was his treatment.

February 28th. Rs. Calomel gr. x. Rhœi. gr. x. pro cathart.

March 1st. Rs. Laud. liquid $\bar{3}$ i. Sp. Nit. dulcis $\bar{3}$ i. capiant. gutt x. quaque hora.

The above was continued until March 16th; during which period the fits recurred from ten to twenty times in a day.

March 16th. Rs. Nitras argent gr. $\frac{1}{4}$. fiat pill. quaque sexta hora capiat æger.

After the first dose was administered, there was no return of fits.

17th to 20th. The above medicine was continued; after which date, the nitrate was discontinued; and believing the disease to be overcome, medicine was deemed unnecessary.

Three similar cases were also treated in a similar manner with the nitrate pill, and with like good effects. In every instance, the fits did not recur, after the administration of the first dose. The nitrate of silver was made into a pill with crumbs of bread, and solution of gum arabic.

The result of the above cases is evidence the nitras argenti is a valuable medicine in this form of disease. The present communication might be more valuable, if it were possible to state all the circumstances which preceded, or accompanied the first attacks of the complaint.

A history of the causes which induce a predisposition, or those which more immediately excite a morbid action in the system, might, in many instances, direct to the most appropriate remedy.

———

DROPSIES were very frequent in the hospital at Burlington, particularly among those soldiers who belonged to the division from Fort George. It is worthy of observation, that dropsies

frequently occurred, where chronic diarrhœa was suddenly checked. These dropsical swellings appeared under forms of general
anasarca, or ascites, or both combined.

Previous to taking direction of the hospital at Burlington, in
February, 1814, acetite of lead had become a common prescription, in the hospital practice, in cases of chronic diarrhœa. Prejudices against the internal use of acetite of lead, from education,
I had always possessed. To the indiscriminate employment of
this medicine, in the above disease, strong objections were opposed. Soon after taking charge of this hospital there were noticed, when visiting the wards, an astonishing number among six
hundred patients, some of whom young men afflicted with dropsical swellings. The circumstance led me to enquire, the conditions of these patients, when admitted into the hospital. It was
made known, they all had diarrhœas; and as soon as the diarrhœas were stopped, the body and lower extremities became
bloated, œdematous and dropsical. It was also ascertained, that
these diarrhœas had been checked, while under the use of acetite
of lead. There was no hesitation in my mind to believe, these
dropsies were a consequence of the sudden check of discharges
from the bowels, caused by the injudicious administration of this
poisonous drug.

The acetite of lead has been introduced into practice, as a
safe and valuable medicine, in dysentery and diarrhœa, by some
very respectable physicians. It will effect a cure of these diseases without ill consequences, when managed with prudence.
Notwithstanding the high reputation of this medicine, its long administration, in any case, renders it dangerous. The obstinate
diarrhœas in the army often required its long use; hence the injurious consequences which followed.

The formidable dropsical swellings were removed by drastic
purges. The digitalis purpurea was resorted to, as a remedy in
obstinate cases. These complaints were, sometimes, accompanied with an enlargement of the liver, and obstructions in the ductus
communis choledocus; as jaundice associated itself with the other symptoms. When the last states were evident, calomel was
directed, in small doses; also mercurial embrocations, on the re-

gion of that viscus were in some instances employed with success. Some few, however, resisted every mean employed. That these dropsies were the consequence of the sudden check of diarrhœas by acetite of lead, was most evident; for, as soon as the diarrhœas returned by the employment of cathartics, the swellings subsided. It was observed also, there was a strong constipation of the bowels, especially a rigid contraction of the *sphincter ani;* which was not overcome, except by frequent repetition of cathartics. Whenever a diarrhœa was induced by medicine, these dropsical swellings rapidly disappeared.

The deleterious effects of acetite of lead were most evident, in two cases, circumstantially reported by Doctor HENRY HUNT, hospital surgeon in the army. His communication has been, already, published in the Medical Repository, at New York. To one of these I was called, occasionally, in consultation. It is here inserted, in connection with other injurious effects of this potent medicine.

" GENERAL HOSPITAL, *Burlington, Vt. Sept.* 15, 1814.
" The following is a statement which was given me, [writes Doctor Hunt,] by Major BEBEE, one of the sufferers, at my first interview with him, which was several months after the commencement of the disease.

" About the middle of November last, Colonel JOHNSON and myself were attacked with diarrhœa, and consulted at Malone a surgeon, (then belonging to the army,) who gave us a box of astringent pills about the size of large peas (afterwards discovered to be the acetite of lead) with directions to take them *frequently,* until our disease was checked. On an average we took five or six a day. Much relief was procured by them, and by the last of the month we returned to duty at French Mills, apparently cured. We were so much pleased with these pills, that each of us took a large box on our departure, and frequently afterwards had recourse to them, whenever our disease shewed a disposition to return.

" On the 5th of December, Colonel JOHNSON was attacked with a violent pain in his stomach and bowels, attended with a

frequen
aid was
remedie
creased
excrucia
" Aft
death, c
my box
wet we
which v
blistered
with sic
violent
of swee
time. I
and bow
over my
entirely
mouth w
the oper
bowels.
sphincter
pain and
" Abo
rived at
again sal
ders duri
more vio
tremities
" In A
The syn
aid of lar
Docto:
was call
was lyi:
sunk, his

frequent disposition to puke, and a powerful tenesmus. Medical aid was immediately procured, and the most prompt and active remedies were applied without relief. The symptoms daily increased in violence, and he lingered seven days, tortured with excruciating pain, and retained his senses until he died.

" After the death of my friend (not knowing the cause of his death, or the composition of the pills) I frequently resorted to my box. Early in January, being much exposed to cold and wet weather, I was suddenly seized with a pain in my side, which was supposed to be the pleurisy : for this I was bled and blistered with considerable relief. Soon afterwards I was taken with sickness at my stomach, attended with flatulences, and a violent pain in my bowels, with tenesmus. A copious discharge of sweet saliva soon followed this attack, and continued some time. During this month I suffered great pain in my stomach and bowels, likewise in all my joints, and bunches of knots arose over my abdomen. My bowels were costive, and my appetite entirely destroyed. For these I took pills of calomel until my mouth was sore, and a large dose of sulphur was given daily ; the operation of which never failed to increase the pain in my bowels. Injections were used with some palliation ; but the sphincter ani soon became so contracted, that the pipe was with pain and difficulty introduced.

" About the middle of February I left French Mills, and arrived at this place (Burlington) the 20th, in great pain. I was again salivated without relief, and afterwards took Dover's powders during the month of March. My disease continued to grow more violent and alarming, with pain and numbness in my extremities, and an abscess on each of my legs.

" In April I took wine and bark, but had no appetite to eat. The symptoms all continued, and I could not sleep, without the aid of large quantities of opium."

Doctor Hunt, in continuance of his communication, says, " I was called on to visit the Major about the middle of May. He was lying in bed, and looked pale and emaciated, his eyes were sunk, his cheeks hollow, and his countenance dejected.

18

" He told me he was in violent pain, which could not be palliated without taking two or three grains of opium every three or four hours. His bowels were obstinately costive, and he was obliged to take some purgative medicine every day ; the operation of which was severely painful, (the sphincter ani being still much contracted.) Food was loathsome to him, and he had profuse perspirations, for which he was taking wine and bark. A deep seated abscess was formed on one leg, and a superficial ulcer on the other. The gastrocnemii muscles were enlarged and indurated, and his arms partially paralized.

I soon discovered that the wine and bark aggravated his disease, and substituted milder tonics, until I had tried the whole list of metalic and vegetable tonics without any good effect; when I was obliged to abandon them altogether, although his feeble pulse, cold skin, and great debility fully justified the practice.

" I endeavored to restore his appetite, by lessening the quantity of opium, and substituting the tinc. of hops, as much as possible. Sweet oil was given every day, for the constipation of his bowels, large blisters were applied over the abdomen, for the pain ; and his arms were freely blistered for the paralysis. His legs were washed with a decoction of galls twice a day, and lightly dressed, (the irritation being so great, that the slightest touch was painful to him.) His appetite was frequently coaxed by some delicacy, and the sweet oil was frequently alternated by magnesia and rhubarb.

" This treatment was regularly pursued until the last of June ; and although he suffered much pain during that time, he was evidently much better, and his appetite improved. He slept much better at night, and took but little opium; he had no profuse perspirations ; the sphincter ani was more relaxed, and his legs were nearly cured. The pain in his bowels was less frequent, and not so violent. He was cheerful, and talked of soon returning to his duty.

" July 4th. I was sent for in great haste to visit him. When I entered his room, I was astonished at his altered appearance. His countenance was pale and fallen ; he was sitting up in his bed, struggling for breath; his body was covered with cold and

clammy sweats; and he had a most anxious and desponding
look. In a few words he informed me that he was suddenly
seized with a violent pain in his stomach and breast; that he
could not breathe, and must die in a few moments. I immediately gave him large quantities of æther and laudanum; applied
flannel dipped in hot spirits to his stomach and breast, and ordered anodine injections to be frequently and copiously used,
until the pain subsided. This treatment gradually relieved him
during the day; at night a large blister was applied over the
stomach and breast, and the æther and laudanum continued.

" The injections brought away from his bowels large quantities of dark and hardened fæces. They were repeated every
day during this month, with the happiest effect; and it was astonishing what masses of these dark and indurated fæces were
evacuated during this time.

" About the latter end of this month he complained of great
difficulty in voiding his urine, and was always obliged to make
strong efforts for several minutes before he could accomplish his
wishes; when the urine would suddenly start in a full and copious stream.

" August—In the commencement of this month, his thorax
and abdomen were entirely relieved from all uneasiness, and he
was again flattering himself, that his disease was subdued; when
he was suddenly seized with a violent pain in his left hand and
arm, attended with an emphysematous swelling. This continued until the middle of the month, without the least abatement,
when a similar affection commenced in the right knee; and in
proportion to the increase of pain and swelling in this part, those
of the hand and arm diminished. He was tortured with the most
agonizing pain the rest of the month, which nothing but large
quantities of opium could lull for a moment. Repeated blisters
and other applications were used without any relief.

" September 1st. Is much emaciated and exhausted by want
of sleep. His left foot and knee are also affected with great pain
and swelling.

" 6th. The pain and swelling have pervaded all his extremities. Opium can no longer lull his pain, and nothing but death
now seems to offer him any hope of relief.

" 8th. His extremities are completely paralized.

" 10th. Is affected with erysipelas, and is gradually sinking into a state of insensibility. In this state he lingered until the 13th, when he expired without a struggle.

" HENRY HUNT,

" *Hospital Surgeon U. S. Army.*

" P. S. In addition to the above cases, I have seen several others produced by the same cause, since I have been on this frontier. Chronic diarrhœa is a common complaint on the borders of Lake Champlain, and the sugar of lead was, at one time, a fashionable remedy among the surgeons of the army. It was often given to the men, while in the tented field, and exposed to all the varieties of this fickle climate. Without being cautioned, and, ignorant of its baneful effects, no doubt some of them used it improperly.

" No one appreciates more highly than I do, this valuable article of the materia medica; but great *caution* ought to be observed in its administration, without which much is to be feared, that it will oftener prove a *bane*, than an antidote to man; especially, as some physicians express *doubts* of its deleterious effects."   H. H. &c.

" April 20th, 1315."

The above effects of acetite of lead, at Burlington hospital, brought to mind two cases of colica pictonum, which occurred at Lewistown, on the Niagara, the preceding summer, when diarrhœa was the prevailing epidemic, and sugar of lead was by some employed as a remedy. One of these expired on the .d day after the attack. The other, by the use of cathartics; calomel in large doses; olium ricini; injections frequently repeated, and warm baths, recovered. Having no suspicion at the time, that these attacks might have been occasioned by the previous employment of medicine, no enquiries were made, what their states had been previous to their seizure. It was, however, conjectured at the time by myself, that these complaints might have been produced by adulterated wine, which was sold at the stores and by sutlers of the army; as it is well known, that wine-sellers frequently sweeten their low and sour wines, by acetite of lead.

The case of Major BEEBE requires a more full exposition. When he first arrived at Burlington, in February, he was attended by myself. At that time he was not extremely reduced. A journey of ninety miles, added to the stimulants with which he had indulged himself, to resist the inclemency of the weather during the route, had induced a high degree of arterial action, and considerable increase of heat. There was a small abscess on one leg, and a large intumescence on the other, in an incipient state. To reduce the sthenic diathesis, which evidently existed, blood-letting and a cathartic were prescribed. The relief procured by these was small and temporary. After administering some small doses of antimonials, it was agreed, in consultation with two physicians of the army, to put him upon small doses of calomel, until his mouth became sore. This was again advised, as he had found some benefit by this process, when first employed at Constable, near French Mills. His greatest painful suffering seemed to arise from the forming abscess; upon which emolient poultices were appllied several days. These had little or no effect to bring it to a state of maturation; when a blister over the swelling was directed with no better success; after which was applied a stimulating plaster of the gums. The pain increased with the enlargement of the swelling, until a deep seated fluctuation was distinctly perceived under the gastrocnemius muscle. It is to be noticed, that even now the superincumbent teguments were not inflamed, the skin not in the least discoloured. An opening was made into the encysted matter, which was sanious instead of being purulent, as was expected. No relief was procured by this operation, but the swelling continued extremely painful. The sore was dressed with a simple pledgit of cerate.

After the calomel was employed to an extent which had been proposed, and no relief procured by all the means employed, he was advised to warm baths, to remove general wandering pains. These not giving relief proportionate to the trouble of employing

them, were strenuously objected to by the patient, being apprehensive he was weakened by them.

He was then put on a course of Dover's powders. While under their influence the patient seemed to be in a better condition, than I had seen him. There was sufficient ipecacuanha
in this preparation to counteract the restrictive powers of the
opium, which was necessary to procure a respite from pain; also some sleep. By this medicine the necessity of cathartics
was obviated; at the same time the powders induced a gentle
diaphoresis upon the skin, universally, which previous to their
administration had been dry and hard.

Although I could with propriety pronounce him in a favourable condition, having more appetite, and less pain; yet he was
very impatient under his circumstances. His friends advised
him to invite a physician to consult upon his case.

Upon an interview my plan was opposed. The bark, wine,
spirits, and opium were proposed in large quantities. To these
I objected, under existing circumstances. My principal objections arose from the constipated state of the bowels and rigidity
of the sphincter ani. The patient had his choice. He preferred the stimulating process, as being more congenial to his own
sentiments, that they were necessary to give strength, as they
were more agreeable to his propensities. In consequence of
some indecorous language of the consulting physician who was a
citizen, I refused to visit the Major again, in the character of a
physician. However, the last stimulating prescriber was eventually dismissed with a load of imprecations from his patient, after he had taken bark, wine, spirits and opium, until he was
disgusted with the sight of them, and with no melioration of his
condition. These medicines had the effect to place his stomach
and bowels in an irremediable state, in which Doctor HUNT found
them, when he made his first visit.

If we may be allowed to theorise in what manner the acetite
of lead may act to induce dropsies, when administered to patients extremely reduced by chronic diarrhœa, we shall observe,
that the increased evacuations from the internal, diminished
those upon the external surface of the body. During the course

of the diarrhœa, the skin was remarkably dry. Unless perspiration was restored, as diarrhœa was checked, there was an accumulation of lymph in the large and small cavities of the body; whence hydro-thorax, ascites, and anasarca. Perhaps there is not in the materia medica, a more powerful and permanent astringent, than sugar of lead. May not this potent medicine be equally efficacious as an astringent, and less deleterious, in combination with some article whose known effect is to determine the material of perspiration to the skin? such as ipecacuanha. The tepid bath may be an appropriate remedy, while the patient is under the effects of the acetite of lead. The above is suggested to those who are persuaded, that sugar of lead is not, in any case, an unsafe internal medicine. Opium has been advised to obviate the colic pains, which sugar of lead, frequently induces, when continued a long time. Doctor FISHER, President of the Massachusetts Medical Society, in a communication published with their papers, has related several cases of colica pictonum, in which opium in large quantities was administered, not only with safety until pain was overcome, but with happy effects. He obviated the restrictive powers of opium on the intestines, by some cathartic medicine. In hemorrhagic diseases, as menorrhagia, and hemo-phthysis, the acetite of lead is now resorted to as a safe remedy: here a few doses generally will cure the disease, without any subsequent bad effects; but since experiencing that sulphate of copper is equally efficacious in these diseases, and in my estimation a safer remedy, it is substituted in my practice in all those hemorrhagic diseases, where, formerly, the acetite of lead was employed.

RHEUMATALGIA was a frequent disease in the hospital at Burlington, in the winters of 1813—14. The patients dated the origin of this complaint from some period of the movement of the army from Niagara to French Mills. It has already been noticed, that the weather was rainy, boisterous and cold. The men were frequently employed up to their arms in water, to secure their boats and baggage from being lost in the surging surf when they approached the shore of the lake.

Calomel and opium, or Dover's powder, under different states of their diseases, were found beneficial. Under the most chronic forms, the following was directed.

> R. Tinc. guaic. ℥ i.
> Laud. liquid. ℥ i.
> Vinum antimon. ℥ i.
> Aqua Amonia. ℥ ii.　m.

Of the above mixture, a teaspoonful was administered every four or six hours.

In some instances, swelling of the joints accompanied this complaint. The camphorated volatile liniment was used by way of embrocation, and blisters. These diseases terminated, in some instances, in confirmed white swellings, which were remedied most generally, by long continued applications of blisters on the part affected, as recommended by Doctor DEXTER, in his communication published with the papers of the Massachusetts Medical Society, and at the same time, one grain of calomel, combined with half grain of opium, was given night and morning.

The steams rising from the wash-tubs in the hospital proved salutary to such as were able to exercise their bodies over them. The rheumatic patients were put to the duty of washing an hour or two daily, which proved more permanently beneficial, than temporary immersions in tepid water ; and when care was taken that subsequently they did not expose themselves to cold, steam baths proved a convenient remedy. Some were cured by this employment. The spirituous vapour bath of Doctor Jennings was experienced an improved method of communicating warmth to the body, and of equalizing the excitement throughout the system ; thereby relieving the fixed, as well as wandering pains, which constitute the above forms of disease. His method of practice was not introduced into the hospital until the close of the war.

Syphilitic complaints we also numbered among our diseases. Many of these had been of long duration, from three to fifteen months, and were accompanied with all the various symptoms of confirmed lues. Some of these patients had been in the hospital several months previous to my taking the charge of it, with obstinate chancres and ulcers, accompanied with pains in different parts of the body, and exceedingly emaciated. These men had already gone through with repeated courses of mercurials, under every form, without any abatement of the disease; to which had been added, tonics, bark, sarsaparilla, guaicum, &c. with little or no benefit.

After the above reports had been circumstantially made by the surgeons who last prescribed for these patients, I believed it useless to employ mercurials, or common medicines any further. The reputation, which the nirtro-muriate of gold had acquired in most obstinate cases of this disease in the city of New-York, followed by favourable reports of its use from Doctor Low of Albany, determined me to give this last medicine a trial upon our hospital patients. They all were placed under the care of hospital surgeon's mate WALKER, from whom I had the satisfaction to learn, within a fortnight, the greater part were either entirely cured, or in a happy way of recovery. In a short time after they were all reported well.

At the close of the year 1814, a patient placed himself under my care, who had performed his duty the whole campaign under this disease; and while in the use of mercurials, had exposed himself to all the varying changes of weather. At the time I was called to advise in his case, there was upon the glans penis an obstinate ulcer, which had destroyed half of it; while the chancre continued to progress. The patient was directed to take a pill composed of bread and $\frac{1}{8}$th grain of the nitro-muriate of gold, night and morning. The ulcer, in a few days, assumed a healthy appearance, and healed in three weeks.

The winter following a second patient, who had exposed himself, during the preceding campaign, while taking medicine for the cure of a syphilitic disorder, asked my advice, on account of an ulcer in his groin, of four months duration; when he was ordered the nitro-muriate of gold; which, in seven days, chang-

10

ed its appearance for the better; and, in the course of fourteen days, completely effected a cure.

Phthisis pulmonalis, in a few instances, followed the winter epidemic, denominated pneumonia. It generally had a fatal termination. Life was, in some instances, prolonged by a soft nutritious regimen, wine, and diluted brandy. Hope of recovery was always entertained by the patient to the last expiring moment. Such was, as has ever been described, this insidious and flattering disease.

At the commencement of the war, most unfavourable representati'.s were publicly made, of every department of the army. The medical, in connexion with others, was exhibited in reproachful language. The bad management of hospitals was a subject of severe animadversion. The physicians and surgeons of the army were either ignorant of their professions, or inattentive to their duty. The distresses of the sick were portrayed in gloomy colours. The number of deaths in consequence of disease, although the mortality was great, was vastly exaggerated.

Such were the statements given to the public, by characters oppor'd to the war; the object of which was, to defeat the measures of the government, by discouraging the recruiting of the army.

Man, under all situations, is subject to disease and its concomitant evils. That the soldier in the field is more exposed to disasters, than the citizen at his ease, is believed and acknowledged by all. Candour would have made allowances for the extraordinary mortality, which has visited the army, and not have implicated the officers of the medical department, nor the improvidence of government, as being instrumental to these scenes of distress.

It should be remembered, that in addition to unavoidable exposures of the army, during long rapid marches, and water-transportations, as well as the other duties of the camp and field, as being causes of sickness and deaths; a considerable proportion of the soldiers, when enlisted, were either too old or infirm to endure those fatigues. Many of them became fit subjects for hospitals, as soon as they commenced their military ser vices. This last circumstance was an evil more especially of the first campaign, when a healthy young man would not engage in the army, where dangers in many shapes assail him, for a less compensation than he could receive in domestic employment, safe from harm, and no way exposed to severe hardships. Wherefore many men were mustered as soldiers, who, in consequence of bad habits, and infirm constitutions, could find no other employment.

When the numerous decrepid men, of whom our army has been composed, are taken into consideration, the number of deaths were fewer than might have been expected, by those acquainted with these facts; and we are, notwithstanding all the inconveniences to which the sick were subjected in the camp and field, persuaded, even during the extreme mortality of the winter 1812—13, the number of deaths in the army did not exceed, proportionably, the number among citizens in any district where the epidemic prevailed; but much less than in some.

Had these mortal visitations been confined to the army, those who have reasoned themselves into a belief, that the war was unjust, might with some propriety have proclaimed, that divine providence in wrath executed judgment, and inflicted retributive justice upon the aggressors. It was not only absurd, but impious, to assign for events subject to divine control, the feeble agency of man. Such is the pestilence which walks in darkness, and exhibits its progress only by its direful effects.

Independent of diseases produced by pestilential states of atmosphere, there were periods when the condition of the soldier was wretched. On the field of battle, tortured by the anguish of his wounds—during inclement seasons, exposed to frosts and raging storms—while preparing quarters for winter, in wild and frigid regions—the hardships of a soldier are severe. Such were his sufferings; such were his painful toils and labours on extraordinary occasions. Such were the sacrifices he made for the *public good.* His country demanded them of him. Similar were the sacrifices made during the revolutionary war. Then the offerings on the altars of Liberty were honorably noticed. Then the memory of the self-devoted hero was cherished, while his hard fate was lamented. At that momentous period, when the nation was contending for her Liberties and Independence, the sufferings of her armies were severer than in the last war, equally struggling with a powerful enemy for her rights. During the adventurous times of the first, the sensibilities and passions of the people were not excited to counteract the just measures of the government, to oppose the violent aggressions of a savage and infuriated enemy.

The exaggerated accounts of deaths on the northern frontiers, and in the hospital at Burlington, with which some of the weekly papers were pregnant during periods of the war, have never been contradicted. I have to regret that few of the official reports of the general hospitals are to be found. Copies of those made at Malone, near the French Mills, and at Burlington, for the months of January, February, March and April, of 1814, are all which are at this time in my possession. Into these hospitals, the largest proportion of the sick of the army were admitted, after the close of the unfortunate campaign of 1813. While the army were in cantonments at French Mills, the sick, as soon as hospitals were established, were ordered to Malone. After the army, under the immediate command of General WILKINSON, and the division of General HAMPTON, retrograded from the lines of Canada, the sick were generally sent to Burlington hospital, except those attached to the division of General BROWN, who were ordered from the Mills to Sackett's Harbour.

An abstract of the hospital report of the sick at Malone, from 1st Jan. to 9th Feb. 1814,	Admitted.	Deaths.
	380	20
Report at Burlington for January,	180	7
Do. for February,	671	17
Do. for March,	931	29
Do. for April,	630	22

There remained in the hospital at Burlington upon the 30th April, 161 patients, not 50 of whom required medical aid.

From the first of May to the last of July, 1814, the numbers on the sick reports weekly diminished. For the month of June or July, (which I do not now recollect,) not one death was reported, at Chazy and Champlain, when the strength of the army exceeded 6000 men. It was not until the middle of August, that our old visitors, dysentery and diarrhœa made their appearance among the troops.

When the army under the command of General IZARD retrograded from Champlain to Plattsburgh, the last week in August, and continued its route to Sackett's Harbour, the sick of that division were left at Plattsburgh, under my direction, with only one assistant capable of duty. Upon the 1st of September, the returns of the sick, including the regimental and hospitals reports, were 921.

The British army followed General IZARD's retrograde march. Upon the 6th of September, Plattsburgh was invested with an army of between 14 and 15,000 men; when the sick unable to perform garrison duty were ordered to be transported to Crab Island, about two miles from the fortifications; as they could not be covered within the lines of defence. At this time the general hospital reports alone counted 720 men.

General M'COMB, learning that General Prevost, Commander in Chief of the British forces, was in full march over the line, had no doubt this powerful army, with the co-operation of the fleet, was destined to take possession of the post at Plattsburgh; which, at that time, was the depot of the munitions of war, for an army of ten thousand men, and which no time was had to remove, after General IZARD marched to the west.

The day previous to the investment of the post, General M'COMB ordered a detachment of 300 men under the command of Major WOOLS, to cross the Sarenac, and advance upon the enemy, who were met at Beeckman's town, distant eight miles. Major WOOLS fell back, skirmishing, until he arrived at the lower bridge over the Sarenac, where its passage was disputed from ten o'clock in the morning until evening. Here Lieutenant RUNT received a mortal wound while employed in taking up the planks of the bridge; which he survived two days; the only officer of the army killed during the investment.

Between the 6th and 10th, feints were made by the British to cross the river at the several fording places; in consequence repeated skirmishings took place between the light troops.

On the 10th, the enemy fell back from the river, and firing ceased between the advanced piquets of the hostile armies preparatory to the ensuing attack.

On the 11th, the British fleet under the command of Commodore DOWNIE, bore down upon Commodore MACDONOUGH. At the same time the enemy, with a division of 2000 men, evinced his determination to cross the river, five miles south of the fortifications. He gained the southern bank without much opposition. The enemy, having advanced its column about one mile from the river, was met by the volunteers from Vermont, under General STRONG, and the drafted militia of the northern counties of New York, under the command of General MOERES. The enemy retreated with considerable loss in killed, wounded, and prisoners; and recrossed the river with precipitation.

During this gallant resistance made by the volunteers and militia, a heavy fire was opened from seven batteries upon the fortifications, some of which within the distance of 400 yards. These movements and operations on land were simultaneous with the attack of the British Commodore, upon the fleet under the command of Commodore MACDONOUGH.

These combined assaults exhibited one vast military effort of the British general to gain the ascendency of the waters, and the borders of Lake Champlain.

The fire, which was unceasingly vomited from the mouths of two hundred pieces of cannon, was terrible. The whole exhibition on water and land, in addition to the uninterrupted cracks of musketry, in the forests south of the fortifications, to a spectator in full view of the fleets and batteries, was awfully grand.

The army of General M'COMB seemed regardless of the cannonade against themselves; but were interested spectators of the conflict on the lake, looking forward to the event with extreme anxiety, well-knowing, that the security of this important post much depended on the success of the fleet.   Two full hours victory was held in suspense ; when an huzza on board the ship Saratoga announced its victory over its antagonist the British Commodore's ship, the Confiance.   The brilliancy of this action was never surpassed, especially as the event was of the highest importance to the nation.

It belongs to the historian to do ample justice to the commanders of the land and navy forces; who directed, under Providence, the destinies of that day.   These transactions are here noticed, as being connected with the general movements of the several divisions of the army on the frontiers.

This memorable action gave full employment to the surgeons of the army and navy.   The wounded of both fleets, as well as the army, were ordered to Crab Island encampment, under my immediate charge.   Within four days more than thirty amputations were performed on the United States' troops and seamen, and the British prisoners of war.   A variety of gun-shot wounds came under my observation ; some of which will be recorded, as being important to the young surgeon.

It is worthy of remark, that the convalescents of the army, after this glorious victory, recovered their healths in a rapid manner.   This was most evident among a number, who had been ordered into the fortifications, at the time the post was invested.   These men suffered no inconvenience from exposures day and night without tents, although it rained part of the time. Similar occurrences have been noticed, as effects of exhilirating excitements on the mind, produced by important victories over an enemy.

It has been before noticed, that diseases of the bowels first appeared in this campaign about the middle of August.   The troops previously had not been subjected to hard duty, until the earth was dry.   The preceding campaign the troops were attacked with the same complaints in the month of May, the men having been put on most severe duty, as early as March.   Having an opportunity this campaign, to see men sick with these diseases, during the first stage of indisposition ; it was learnt, they supervened, without a loss of appetite on their first attack, and when immediately attended to were readily removed. Soldiers generally did not report themselves sick, while they were able to take their common rations, which often were devoured with impaired appetites. The consequences were total indigestion, loss of appetite, and gradual increase of their bowel complaints. To these sypmtoms were added increase of heat and dry skin. Where these derangements of the functions were not obviated, fever deteriorated, and assumed a typhoid form. These fevers became typhous, also, where attempts were made to check the diarrhœa by early administration of astringents and stimulants; more especially ardent spirits and opium, previous to evacuating the stomach and bowels by emetics and cathartics. When highly excited by ardent spirits, these complaints were accompanied with accelerated action of the arteries, and assumed a synochal form of fever, wherein bleeding was indicated.

The diseases of this campaign, as has been noticed, did not supervene, until the greatest heat of summer had commenced. We know from experience that transitions, from one temperature to another when sudden, induce unequal excitement in the system. This effect was most evident, when the body was enveloped in a moist atmosphere. Subjected to rains and cold fogs, the pores of the body become impervious to the matter of perspiration, caused by loss of heat upon the surface, then by a collapse or spasm of the minute vessels of the skin. The glands, subservient to the secretion of the perspirable matter, cease to perform their offices. The other secretory organs, by association, are also deranged. The liver partakes of this general affection, and neglects to execute its appropriate functions, made most evident by the appearance of the fœcal evacuations, which, in simple diarrhœa, were generally white or clay coloured; the dejections accompanied with griping pains and tenesmus, were dark, sanious, slimy, and streaked with blood. These several appearances depend on degrees of derangement within the intestines, and morbid secretions of inflamed vessels; not on states of the bile. For want of digestion, every article of food taken into the stomach was converted into an irritating material, which induced inflammation on the villous coats of the bowels, which were vellicated, more or less proportionate to the degree of the deleterious power. Dejections of a natural colour were favourable appearances, inasmuch as they demonstrated that the liver still continued to perform its secretory offices. When these dejections were accompanied with large secretions of bile, from its superabundance less danger was apprehended, than when there was no evidence of bile in the evacuations; the bile it is believed may prove salutary by washing from the intestinal canal offending materials. After a similar manner, a flood of tears wash irritating materials from the eyes. These salutary effects of bile, a cathartic furnished by nature, have long since been noticed by physicians, inasmuch as bilious diarrhœas, frequently accompany the resolution of acute diseases.

That these diseases of the intestines were accompanied with inflammation of their internal coats, was inferred from pain, tenesmus, mucous evacuations, heat and soreness at the inferior portion of the rectum; and, especially from dissections of some who were victims to these diseases.

During the wet season, which, this campaign, commenced the last of August, and continued into September, it was not possible to treat these diseases with success, while the sick were in tents. These complaints, under such exposures, frequently run on a length of time, and become habitual; and under a chronic form, were obstinate, and resisted all remedies; while the patients were exposed to rains, and the night fogs of the lakes. The most efficient remedy, employed under my observation, for these habitual diarrhœas of the bowels, was Dover's powders repeated every four, six, or eight hours, as the symptoms demanded. It was now, as heretofore experienced, a safe and frequently an efficient medicine, productive of no new disease. Whereas, when these diseases were suddenly checked by astringents, and especially by acetite of lead, dropsical swellings supervened. Chronic diarrhœas were cured with the greatest safety by such medicine as promoted perspiration, combined with those which were pacific, and took off irritation. To this intention, Dover's powder was admirably adapted. To possess the full effects of

20

this powder, or any appropriate medicine, the patient should be placed in a dry situation, kept warm, and fed with a soft farinaceous diet. Perhaps nothing, as nutriment, was preferable to milk and its soft preparations. When the patients were reduced by excessive evacuations, stimulants were highly important to support the powers of life, such as wine and diluted spirits. To these were added anodynes at night; and in some cases frequently repeated through the day.

I have always experienced, that even after a return of appetite, animal nutriment, prepared in the softest manner, was not well adapted to restore the convalescents from this disease to health. The last observation is not confined to army practice.

GENERAL CURATIVE INDICATIONS.

1st.—To remove the irritating causes of inflammation from the
    bowels;
    A. by evacuations.
    a. emetics;
    b. cathartics.
    B. By restoring to the skin its secretory offices, by
    a. avoiding cold and wet;
    b. tepid baths;
    c. medicine, which determine to the surface; or promote
      perspiration; Dover's powder.
2d.—To counteract irritation, the cause of griping pains; by
    medicines, which are more efficient after suitable evacuations;
    A. by sedatives, as
    a. opium;
    b. tinc. of hops;
    c. mucilages.
3d.—To give tone to the stomach, and promote its digestive
    powers:
    A. by Astringents; always to be employed with caution;
    a. bark; seldom the most suitable;
    b. vegetable bitters;
    c. aromatics;

B. by stimulants, as

a. ardent spirits ;

b. vinous liquors ;

C. by nutriment, as

a. farinacea, and their preparations ;

b. milk, and its several preparations more beneficial, than most kinds of nutriment ;

c. animal nutriment ; prohibited until the diseased organs are restored to their healthy actions.

It has been observed, that typhous fever sometimes accompanied these complaints of the bowels. This form of disease required some additional treatment. The following were its most conspicuous symptoms. Hot and dry skin ; pulse not fuller than in health, but accelerated ; eyes suffused with blood ; tongue brown and dry. These symptoms were accompanied with pain in the head, and throughout the dorsal muscles, and the extremities. The patient when moved, complained of soreness throughout the body. Delirium or coma, sometimes accompanied the febrile state, and shewed that the brain partook of the general derangement.

After evacuating the stomach and bowels, by emetics and cathartics, the following formula was adopted in hospital practice with much success.

R. Calomel gr. x.

Opium gr. v.

Tart. Ant. gr. ii.

Misce, fiant pul. x. capiat. una, quaque secunda vel tertia hora.

By the employment of the above medicine, the skin became soft ; the tongue moist ; and pain in the head, back, and extremities abated. When delirium supervened, blisters upon the neck and head were necessary ; as were sinapisms to the soles of the feet. In some cases, ipecacuanha was substituted for the tartrite of antimony, in the above formula ; especially when the antimony irritated, or ran off by the bowels.

After a resolution of fever, known by a gentle diaphoresis, a moist tongue, and a removal of delirium ; or where a coldness supervened, stimulants were introduced. A mixture of spt. nit.

dul. five parts, and aqua ammonia one part, was here employed; also opt. lavend. comp. and a decoction of serpent. virgin. (aristolochia serpentaria) likewise, tinc. cort. comp. and wine. As soon as the stomach was capable of receiving the bark, (cinchon.) in powder, it became an important remedy. But when the bark in substance offended, its infusion or compound tincture was substituted; and in cases where the bark did not agree with the stomach, colombo root was employed with advantage. Anodynes could not be dispensed with in the last stages; and in states of irritability induced composure and sleep, which seemed to refresh the patient.

The following report of the state of diseases at Burlington, Vermont, in the autumn, 1814, was made by Hospital Surgeon's mate, PURCELL.

"IN consequence of the precipitate removal of the sick to Crab Island, in conformity to the orders of General Mc'COMB of the 5th of September, the day previous to the investment of Plattsburgh by the British army; no straw was procured for their accommodation. The sick were consequently lodged under tents upon wet ground, during two or three days of wet weather, when straw was furnished from Grand Island in lake Champlain.

"Many of the troops were labouring, at this time, under fevers of different forms; and diarrhœas. The bad state of the sick, with their wretched accommodations, made it an object of high importance to remove them to a situation more comfortable. As the larger transports on the lake were employed in transporting warlike stores, no means were provided to convey the sick to Burlington Hospital, a distance of 25 miles, across the lake. Apprehensive that the sick would fall into the hands of the enemy, exposed as they were; and which must have been the case, had he gained the ascendency on the lake; it was suggested to transport as many as were able to be moved in op-

an batteaus to Burlington. The weather had been boisterous,
and passage unsafe in small boats; but providentially, the winds
subsided, and the waters became smooth; so that they arrived
on the opposite shore without any unpleasant accident in small
detachments; the last, on the day of the memorable action, between the fleets.

"The patients, at Burlington, found comfortable accommodations; their number, at this time, amounted to 815; 50 of whom
were wounded. The evils arising from crowded wards were
soon perceived; but could not, under existing circumstances, be
remedied. Every precaution was employed to keep the rooms
clean and ventilated; but the sick were slow in their recovery;
while the diseases of some became worse.

"Typhus, dysentery, and diarrhœa, in most cases, were so
combined, it was with difficulty determined, which was the pre-
dominant disease.

"The men had been so reduced by long sickness, repeated
removals, and exposures for eight or ten days, that evacuations
could not be employed.

"In cases where dysentery was the prevalent symptom, the
patient had more or less fever. Frequent inclination to stool,
tenesmus, gripes, soreness at the sphincter ani were the common
symptoms. The discharges were a mixture of blood and mucus. But as the disease progressed, the symptoms were more
aggravated. The fever assumed a typhoid type, with total loss
of appetite, great thirst, parched brown tongue, sordes on the
teeth, increased heat of the skin—and in the last stage, sores on
the nates, hips, and os sacrum, so deep as to expose, in some cases, the bones.

"In the milder forms of the disease, a cathartic and emetic
were beneficial; and followed with a soft nutritious diet, the patient soon recovered. This happy termination of the disease
was not very frequent.

"In the severer forms, a repetition of a cathartic was found
necessary. After which were administered tartrite of antimony
and nitre, in small doses, frequently repeated. This medicine,
with tepid drinks, while the patient was confined to his bed be-

tween blankets, frequently brought on a free perspiration; by which, the patient found himself relieved from all the attendant symptoms of disease. But, where no ease was procured by the above means, an anodyne, the following night, was proper and advantageous, and seemed to effect all which had been wished for by the preceding medicine. Ipecacuanha, so much recommended by authors in this disease, was seldom of any use unless it was combined with opium in the form of Dover's powder.

" Where the sick were extremely reduced, and no apparent relief was obtained by active medicine, and efforts of some duration to evacuate, accompanied with tenesmus and violent gripes, were fruitless; injections composed of arrow root, water, and laudanum, were found very beneficial, agreeably to the following formula:—To half a pint of water were added a tablespoonful of arrow root and sixty drops of laudanum. The foregoing enema was thrown up the rectum three or four times a day. It removed the tenesmus and gripes, and communicated to the bowels a soothing sensation, by overcoming the spasms, a consequence of extreme irritability of the intestines, more particularly the rectum.

" When dysentery was accompanied with typhous fever, accompanied with great heat, no prescription seemed to fulfil our curative intention, of equalising the excitement, so well as the following:—

" R. Sal. nit. ℥ i.

Tart. Antim. gr. iii.

Gum Opium, gr. vi.

Calomel, gr. viii.

Misce, divide in chart x; capiat. una, quaque tertia hora.

" This, with soft nutritious drinks, was, in most cases, followed by salutary effects; a reduction of heat, soft skin, and moist tongue and mouth.

" The common saline mixture was also administered. As soon as the fever subsided, and the stools became less frequent, and of a more natural appearance, tonics combined with refrigerants were resorted to.

" Of
or four

" If,
only at
was eff
were v

" As
natural
icine;
was dir
necessa

" T
highly
in this
ly dem
quently
cider, t
injuriou
gar dilu
proved

" Ar
ited; a
augmen

" It
safety i
ed seve
induced
remove

" W
dysente
At the
and sm
taste in

" R. Sulphas martis ℥ ss.
   Spt. nit. dulcis ℥ ss.
   Carbon. potassæ ℥ ss.
   Aqua commun. ℔ ss.   fiat solutio.

" Of the above, a table-spoonful was administered every three or four hours.

" If, in this combination of disease, the febrile symptoms were only attended to, and the state of the bowels neglected, little was effected to remove the general complaints ; and unless they were very mild, the disease in a majority of cases proved mortal.

" As soon as fever subsided, and the evacuations became more natural, an infusion of colombo root became an appropriate medicine ; and if the patient was reduced, wine or diluted brandy was directed. An anodyne pill at night, even in this state, was necessary.

" The utmost caution, as to the dietetic management, was highly necessary. Nature was not always correct in her calls, in this disturbed condition of the bowels ; the patients frequently demanded articles which proved very injurious. It was frequently the case that the sick would obtain from their attendants cider, beer, &c. These weak fermenting drinks always proved injurious. If the patients wished for acidulated beverage, vinegar diluted with water was grateful ; it allayed thirst, and never proved detrimental.

" Ardent spirits, in the first stages of the disease, were prohibited ; and when given by the over officious nurse, invariably augmented all the symptoms of disease.

" It was but seldom the bark [cinchona] could be used with safety in the disease, more especially in powder ; as it occasioned severer pains in the bowels, and where they had become calm, induced an irregularity which was obstinate, and with difficulty removed.

" When typhous fever made its appearance, unconnected with dysenteric symptoms, there was more or less simple diarrhœa. At the first attack, the patient complained of pain in the head and small of the back, nausea at the stomach, drowsiness, bitter taste in the mouth, the tongue covered with a white fur on its forepart, and a dark brown colour towards its base. The patient did not often complain of rigors passing over himself. If, however, rigors occurred, more or less inflammation of some of the viscera generally accompanied the disease; and as it progressed, became more violent, with small frequent pulse, disordered head, cold extremities, sordes on the teeth, delirium, stupor, subsultus tendinum, and involuntary discharges of both fæces and urine. With these last symptoms the fatal scene was closed.

" The treatment in the first stage of typhus was commenced by an emetic of fifteen grains of ipecacuanha, with two grains of tartrite of antimony. This not only operated as an emetic, but as a cathartic. If the latter did not follow, and the strength of the patient permitted, the employment of a cathartic, neutral salts, or olium ricini was administered. These remedies commonly relieved, in some measure, the pain in the head, and the patient appeared better. After which were prescribed sal nitri and tart. antim. in small and repeated doses ; and if the head continued to be affected, a blister on the nape of the neck. If the extremities were cold, and a præternatural heat of the chest and head existed, warm flannels were applied to the former, and cold vinegar and water were sponged over the latter parts. A diaphoretic, composed of one drachm of carbonate of potash, half a pint of vinegar, with the same quantity of water, was directed, of which a table spoonful was given every two hours. But no medicine seemed to answer as well as the prescription in dysentery, when fever was combined with it ; viz. nitras potassæ ʒ i. tart. antim. gr. iii. gum opium gr. vi. submuriate of mercury gr. viii ; these were combined and divided into ten powders, of which one was given every three hours.

" The above prescriptions, pursued two or three days, changed the appearance of the tongue from a dry brown colour to a moist, and of a more natural appearance.

" Some were admitted into the hospital so much reduced under the above described form of the disease, that the above practice could not be pursued. In these low cases the emetic and cathartic were inadmissible ; the patients were supported with weak toddy, making use of the last mentioned prescriptions:

In the latter stages of typhus, the patients were supported by a soft nutritive diet; in some cases blisters were applied to the wrist, and sinapisms to the feet. The patients were ordered a liberal use of diluted spirits, with a decoction of the serpentaria.

"In some cases, the patients were disturbed with frightful dreams; in which opium did not succeed to procure sleep, but in which embrocations of volatile spirits upon the head had the desirable effect. Where diarrhœa continued after abatement of fever, Dover's powders were administered in small and repeated doses, and where it was not checked by the last medicine, more powerful astringents were employed, as gum kino, rhubarb and opium.

"In many cases the parotid glands became enlarged and suppurated; where these occurred the patients uniformly recovered.

"In those cases where pain in the chest was an accompanying symptom of disease, attended with cough, a blister over the pained part, and camphorated tinc. of opium, with antimonial wine, given every four or five hours, removed the local affection.

"Success generally followed the above course of practice. But it required the utmost caution to prevent relapses, among a large body of men habitually irregular. Exposures to cold, an intemperate use of liquors, and a hard indigestible diet, with which the convalescents would indulge themselves, frequently brought on relapses which often proved fatal.

"Diarrhœa was the third form of disease that called our attention at Burlington hospital. Even where the men had no fever, diarrhœa supervened in almost every case of disease in the hospital, or previous to their admittance. One fourth of the sick labored under simple diarrhœa, and many under its most obstinate chronic state. Some had previously been so much reduced, no medicine seemed to have any permanent effect upon them; the most potent astringents, sudorifics, and opiates were administered in vain. These unceasing evacuations continued to reduce the patients until death closed the scene. In one case, the efforts were so strong as to cause an umbilical rupture while on his stool; in two instances, inguinal hernias became scrotal, by

21

efforts to evacuate the contents of the bowels. Those predisposed to hemorrhoidal affections had a confirmed state of this disease induced by a constant irritation. The chronic form was accompanied with a loss of appetite, and great debility. As diarrhœas commenced while men were exposed in the field to their causes, a long time; an habitual disease was induced which continued after the primary causes were removed.

" In the more recent cases, a mild cathartic was administered; after which, small and repeated doses of Dover's powder, every few hours; also, tepid drinks and soft nutriment. The body was kept warm by flannel shirts. Diluted brandy was directed as a warm stimulus to the stomach and bowels. In cases where the disease had been of long continuance, excepting opium, diluted brandy was the chief medicine depended upon as a stimulus; the patient also was confined in bed between blankets. In cases where there was a loss of appetite or nausea, a blister applied on the epigastric region, seldom failed to remove the sickness, and eventually of restoring some appetite. To check profuse evacuations, the most powerful astringents were employed, viz. gum kino and alum in combination; to these were added stimulants, as ardent spirits; opium; laudanum and aqua ammonia in equal parts; a tea-spoonful of this mixture was frequently administered, as the case required.

" The following bitter stimulus, after evacuations ceased, was found beneficial.

" R. Rad. gentian. $\frac{2}{3}$ ss.
Cort. Aurant. $\frac{2}{3}$ ss.
Serp. Virgin. ℥ iii.
Canella alba ℥ i.   contus.

" After these had been infused in one quart of brandy a number of days, a table-spoonful was administered three or four times in a day.

" Chalk julap was frequently employed without any benefit. An injection of the infusion of galls had often a good effect, when every other remedy disappointed us; and in the latter stages of disease, when the patient's strength was much reduced, we have employed it combined with laudanum, with great advantage.

"We found it necessary to confine the patients labouring under diarrhœa, to warm drinks, soft diet, and in bed. The preparations of the farinacea and milk were only allowed them. While mentioning milk, we, from experience, found that no article of diet was superiour, not only in this, but other diseases to which soldiers were subjected. The sick soldier accepted of this, in which a little oat-meal was boiled a few minutes, when he refused every other kind of nutriment offered. This alone constituted the nourishment of these sick patients several days; and we are persuaded was, in many instances, conducive to their restoration to health.

"In some instances, great thirst attended this disease, when no quantities of mild drinks seemed to abate the intolerant sensation; nothing contributed to give immediate relief, so soon as spirits and water; but if spirits were largely diluted, this beverage did not have the desired effect." This was the *sitis frigida* of Darwin.

"In curing this disease, or checking the evacuations when they had become chronic, great caution was necessary. Dropsical swellings, anasarca, ascites, supervened on those, where the discharges were suddenly and permanently checked by astringents. This was more particularly the case, where the patient was advanced in years. Whenever these occurred, drastic purges, by producing a recurrence of the former disease, reduced the swellings; after which, it was found most necessary to check diarrhœa in a gradual manner, by small doses of rhubarb; and at the same time, the following tonic preparation:—

"R. Sulph. martis ℥ ss.
Carb. pottas. ℥ i.
Tinc. calom. ℔ i.
Tinc. laud. gt. lxxx.   misce.

"A table spoonful of the above composition was given four times in a day; and occasionally, diluted brandy. When the legs and thighs were much enlarged, as soon as they began to subside, were rubbed with equal parts of spirits and water; when a spiral bandage was neatly applied upon the limb, beginning at the toes and extending it to the groin. This application was in all cases found highly beneficial."

A Report of Hospital Surgeon LOVELL, *of the state of diseases among the troops on the Niagara frontier, during the campaign of* 1814, *is as follows :—*

" THE troops engaged in this brilliant campaign on the Niagara, began to collect there about the beginning of April, under the command of General SCOTT. They were encamped on an eminence north of Buffalo village, having a thick wood in front, which extended to the bank of the river, the ground being in part swampy and wet. On the left of the encampment was a large marsh, extending from the high ground to the margin of the lake. The winds from the lake, at this season, were remarkably cold and chilling; resembling, in sensation, exactly the east winds which prevail on the Atlantic during the spring; and had an astonishing effect upon vegetation. The trees around the encampment having the appearance of winter, while those five or six miles from the lake shore, were covered with verdure. Notwithstanding this, the troops were remarkably healthy; only one or two deaths occurring before they crossed the Niagara, on the 3d of July—even the demon diarrhœa appeared to have been exorcised by the mystical power of strict discipline and rigid police.

" In June a number of new recruits joined the army; and several were collected from the various hospitals; the latter principally composed of the miserable refuse of society, who never had energy enough to demonstrate that they lived, and scarcely enough to prove that they existed. With these last detachments, arrived our old acquaintances, which however were easily checked; and much seldomer returned, than in any former campaign. This was undoubtedly to be attributed to the improvement in police.

" During June, the weather became very warm, and a thick fog arose from the marsh and woods at sunset, and remained for some time after sunrise. During this month, intermittent fever, acute rheumatism, and typhous fever were the prevailing complaints. The intermittents were very irregular and obstinate. Arsenic, which was the sovereign remedy the last year, on this frontier, had now very little effect; while the bark, which then

s-
ic

a-
er
in
it,
in
a
of
·k-
he
nd
nd
)se
re.
ily
on
een
po-

ev-
nci-
ver
:ely
ich-
sily
am-
ove-

hick
l for
:ver,
com-
nate.

this
then

failed, was now generally successful. Some obstinate cases, in which every thin lse had failed, were cured by the sulphate of copper. Three patients, who had tried most of the remedies with which we were supplied, without effect, cured themselves at once, by taking a pint of brandy undiluted, in which was mixed a large quantity of ground black pepper, on the accession of the cold stage. This was not followed by inebriation nor any appearance of undue excitement. It led me to use opium in much larger quantities than I had been accustomed. It was begun with four or five grains at a dose, and increased until some stimulating effects were produced, or the disease cured. The success of this prescription was very great during the whole season. In fine, of the remedies used this season, emetics had but little effect, even at first; and the mineral solution scarcely any—bark succeeded in the majority of cases; and opium very seldom failed. A few obstinate cases were checked for several periods, by the application of tourniquets to one leg and one arm; the disease however recurred; the tourniquets then had no effect; but remedies, which had before failed, now succeeded, after the interruption thus produced in the morbid associations.

" Rheumatism, during the whole war, generally put on a remitting form; this was particularly obvious whenever intermittent fever prevailed, and more especially this season. Bleeding was but seldom necessary; after a brisk cathartic, bark was given in the quantity of from 4 to 8 drachms during the remission, and a large dose of opium on the accession of the fever; and always in sufficient quantity to relieve the pain. This treatment was very generally successful. I was induced to try it, in many cases, where the remissions were very slight, and generally effected a cure. In these, however, bleeding or purging were premised, which produced more perfect remissions. In short, I considered the bark and opium the remedies for rheumatism, particularly when intermittents prevailed, and for the most part succeeded.

" Many of the cases of typhus, about the end of May, were remarkably severe. The most prominent symptoms were great

prostration of strength, and delirium; of the species not attended with symptoms of great arterial action in the head, local applications as usual having no effect upon it. Symptoms of recovery were not observed in these cases, until the end of the
third week. The treatment adopted was strictly that of Fordyce, and recovery took place in every instance.

" On the first of August, a general hospital was established at
Williamsville, eleven miles east from Buffalo. The number of
sick, during the remainder of the season, at this place, varied
from 3 to 400 ; the number of wounded being somewhat greater.

" The troops suffered much during the siege of Fort Erie ;
and soon after it was raised, the rainy season commenced.
Dysentery and diarrhœa were the principal diseases. I became fully convinced after a fair trial of every medicine to be
obtained at this place, of the decided advantage of ipecacuanha
in various forms and doses, to any other remedy. The remarkable effects of this medicine, which Fordyce considers as acting
specifically in typhus fever, led to the conclusion, that the febrile
symtoms attending the latter stages of diarrhœa were in fact a
true typhus, supervening upon the former complaint. Hasty in
his treatise on dysentery, he speaks of several complaints, which
are often combined with typhus fever ; and are then generally
contagious ; and I had observed that the nurses of the wards,
where diarrhœa prevailed, were often attacked with typhus, accompanied with diarrhœa, or a great tendency to it. Decided
benefit had often been observed from small doses of ipecacuanha,
with mucilaginous drinks, in an irritable state of the stomach
and bowels, which appeared to be owing to a degree of inflammation extending through the mucus coats ; and not attended with
febrile symptoms ; and it is probable that the good effects of the
remedy, in the cases now referred to, were in some measure to be
attributed to this mode of operation. Intermittent fevers and
rheumatism prevailed during the whole season, and varied but
little from the cases in May and June. The cases of typhus a-
mong the regular troops were generally mild.

" About the end of September, a large detachment of militia
crossed the Niagara, under General P. B. Porter. Diarrhœa,

typhu
ance
these
had be
compl
the ble
tion of
was ve
ecacua
irritabi
The de
some e
would
often h
peared
elm-bar
tenesm
ed by w
ipecac.
latter s
Typhus
seldom
fever ;
the atte
mong th
his hea
to remo
practice
without
patient.
stances,
cept re
was prin
as appea
ment.
covery ;
ed spot

typhus and idiopathic dysentery very soon made their appearance among them; the two latter were extremely severe. As these patients were not sent to the general hospital, until they had been sick for some time, I saw only the latter stages of these complaints. The dysentery was at this period very obstinate; the bloody discharges and tenesmus incessant, and the prostration of strength as usual most dangerous. In this state, relief was very generally obtained from injections of a decoction of ipecacuanha, sometimes combined with laudanum; at others, the irritability was first reduced by an injection of laudanum alone. The decoction was often rejected immediately; it had however some effect even then, so that by repeating it several times, it would finally remain, and give relief. Blisters to the abdomen often had a very good effect; but no application to the part appeared generally to prove so beneficial, as a poultice of slippery-elm-bark to the whole abdomen, often repeated. It relieved the tenesmus, and produced a gentle diaphoresis, which was promoted by warm mucilaginous drinks, a mixture of tinc. opii. and tinc. ipecac. This was the only treatment found beneficial in the latter stages of this complaint, and it very generally succeeded. Typhus, among the militia, was very severe. Patients were seldom sent to the general hospital, until the third week of the fever; and the treatment had been as different, as the whims of the attending surgeons. The most usual practice, however, among them, was to blister the patient almost from the crown of his head to the soles of his feet; so that the chief difficulty was to remove the irritative fever induced by this *empirical, slovenly* practice. In some, calomel had been employed, but generally without any obvious effect, except increasing the danger of the patient. At this stage of the complaint, and under these circumstances, no general method of treatment could be adopted, except remedying the mischief which had been done. The cure was principally attempted by removing every cause of irritation, as appeared most urgent, and trusting to nursing and nourishment. Under this plan many appeared to be in a fair way of recovery; but in the course of the 4th week, a small circumscribed spot of inflammation shewed itself in the face, generally, near

the angle of the mouth. In a few days, the whole side of the
face swelled; this tumour was hard and pale, resembling the
colour of a white swelling of the joints. It was not in the seat
of the parotid gland, but anterior to the branch of the lower jaw,
and was attended with a most profuse and fetid salivation, apparently from irritation communicated along the salivary duct,
as the liver and gall-bladder are excited by the chyme. In a
few days more, the red spot began to assume a livid appearance,
and symptoms of incipient mortification. In a short time, the
mouth was literally extended from ear to ear, exposing the back-
most grinders on both sides. All the remedies usually employed in this species of disease, were employed without visible benefit. The only article which appeared to produce any good effect was charcoal, which, however, seemed only to prolong the
sufferings of the patients. Three attacked with this affection
had severally so far recovered, as to have a good appetite, and
sit up a great part of the day. Their strength and appetite held
out surprisingly after mortification had taken place. I have
since seen two instances among citizens; one in Boston, on a
young boy. He had so far recovered as to sit up, he took nourishment with a good appetite, and every symptom of fever had
disappeared; when about the middle of the fourth week, the
swelling, salivation and mortification took place, and shortly
sunk. It should be added, that in the majority of these cases,
not a particle of mercury had been used in any form."

*The following cases of a similar disease as the last noticed by
Doctor* LOVELL, *were reported by Doctor* PURCELL, *with his
observations, at Burlington Hospital, in the Autumn of* 1814.

CASE FIRST.

"THOMAS BURNS, a soldier, 16th infantry, was admitted into
the hospital 7th September, with an enlargement of the parotid,
and submaxillary glands, and soreness of the tonsils, accompanied with a large flow of saliva. The tumefaction extended from
the glands down the neck. The tumefied parts were so great
and tender, that the mouth could not be opened sufficiently wide,
to admit of the inspection of the fauces. No food could be

received except in a liquid form. Diseases, at this time, were disposed to run into typhus. This circumstance, and especially as no fevers accompanied the complaint, determined us to dispense with evacuations; and, viewing it as a local disease, not dependent, and unconnected with a general affection, to depend on the employment of local applications.

" The tumid parts were embrocated with volatile liniment every four or five hours; after which a flannel bandage was applied over the jaws. By this management, the swellings in a few days were reduced, while the profuse salivation and soreness of the fauces continued. At first it was believed, that the complaint was produced by mercury; but having been assured by the patient, he had not taken any medicine a long time previous to his admittance into the hospital, and this assurance having been unaccompanied with that peculiar smell of his breath, which denotes mercurial excitement in the system, convinced us that our first conjecture was incorrect.

" A gargle of borax dissolved in water was directed, and the liniment continued. These applications were employed ten or fifteen days, but with very little benefit. By this time the soreness in the glands and tumefaction were so much reduced, as to admit the opening of the mouth, so as to inspect the fauces. The first appearance which attracted the attention was a large ulcer, commencing half an inch from the lip, on the left side of the tongue, and extending half way to its base. Upon pressing the tongue down with a spatula, ulcers appeared on each side of the cheek, and over the anterior surface of the tonsils, the dentes molares were incrusted with a hard substance of some thickness. The breath was intolerably fetid. The surface of these ulcers appeared white, and adhered to the sound parts as if they had been a component part, but now an inorganic substance, which was with difficulty removed.

" At this time the patient was directed to the use of a gargle composed of sulphate of zinc, vinegar, and water, and to continue the volatile liniment. Having continued the above applications twelve days, and no benefit having been experienced, a gargle of alum and kino was substituted. No better effects

22

were experienced from the last medicine. A solution of murias
hydrargyri, one grain to an ounce of water, was next prescribed
as a gargle to be used several times in a day. After continuing
the last medicine three weeks, without any benefit, recourse was
had to Fowler's mineral solution, five drops of which were directed in half a gill of water, three times in twenty-four hours.
There was an apparent change for the better in the ulcer, on the
second day. The inorganic substance had detached itself; the
condition of the ulcers appeared healthy and the breath less fetid. By the continued employment of the last prescription, the
sores in a few days were healed.

"It should be observed, that the pa.ient laboured under no
other disease at the time he was admitted into the hospital, but
was muscular and strong: his complaints had been of three
months duration, previous to the use of the arsenic preparation.
It was employed only six days until every vestige of the disease
disappeared."

CASE SECOND.

The following symptoms of a second case were given by one
of the surgeons, who attended in the early stage of the disease.
"The patient was seized with pain a little above the inferior
portion of the nose which extended to the adjacent parts. It
was light at first, but in eight or ten hours became very severe.
In its incipient stage, an efflorescence appeared, which gradually
assumed a deeper colour, and was accompanied with a little tumefaction, which enlarged until the parts became disorganized.
This process was rapidly performed in three days.

"The ulcer was formed when I first saw the case; (says Doctor PURCELL) then an ichorous corroding matter issued from the
sore, which destroyed the surrounding teguments, and the ossa
naris became carious in a few days. The disorganized muscles
assumed a black and flabby appearance; the edges of the ulcer
were indented, and the circumjacent parts slightly swelled. The
disease progressed until it reached the eye, when that organ became much enlarged, so that the ball protruded from its socket.
The pain, at this stage of the disease, was insupportable.

" The appetite was not impaired until the eye was affected. A delirium then supervened, the patient became raving when the appetite failed, and death soon closed the scene.

" Two other soldiers were attacked after a similar manner. Upon both, the disease commenced and progressed with all the dreadful appearances, as described in the first case, and terminated fatally in a few days.

" The several stages of the disease followed each other in rapid succession. The practice however cannot be particularly detailed. The general remedies, in the first stage, prescribed, were to counteract inflammation; after the ulcers were formed, a carrot poultice was applied; all without any benefit."

CASE THIRD.

" A soldier was attacked soon after the above fatal cases, with symptoms so similar, that an unfavourable termination was prognosticated. It was suggested to the attending surgeon, to administer the Fowler's solution. The plan was adopted, as in the first recited case. To our great satisfaction every unpleasant symptom disappeared, and the man was reported for duty within one week.

" Quere, did the arsenic, in the above cases, act as a stimulus and tonic? The three last patients had been reduced by previous diseases. This circumstance induces a belief, that as the swelling was not truly phlegmonous, these were diseases of debility; and that, in the fortunate cases, the cures were effected by the stimulant and tonic powers of arsenic."

DISSECTIONS.

" Upon dissection, the diseased parts through their whole extent, were found completely disorganized. The nasal bones, and molar teeth on the side affected, were either carious or entirely destroyed; the periosteum of the adjoining bones was removed, even where the superincumbent teguments appeared sound; between which, and the bone, of a dark colour, was lodged a dark ichorous matter."

LAKE CHAMPLAIN, AND RIVER ST. LAWRENCE, FRONTIERS.

BURLINGTON is situated on the east side of Lake Champlain, distant from White Hall 70 miles north; the first village lies 164 miles north from Albany.

From a wilderness, this most beautiful village has, in twentyfive years, become a place of considerable importance. From the lake shore it rises by an easy and regular ascent one mile, to the summit of the lake-hill. Upon the extreme height of land bordering the lake, is erected a handsome college edifice, which overlooks the village below, regularly built on streets which intersect each other at right angles. From this eminence the prospect is extensive and picturesque, possessing an extensive view of the lake, in which, are in sight some small islands. This prospect is terminated by the mountains, which range on the west border of the lake, from south to north, the whole extent of the visible horizon. On the east, the view is interrupted by forests, but which will be more extensive as the country improves. Beyond the intervening woodlands, rise aspiring ridges of mountains, which divide the state of Vermont from south to north its whole extent, known by the name of Green Mountains, from which the state derives its name. From the bases of the mountains to the lake, which is the west boundary of Vermont, the distance is twenty miles. This tract is under good cultivation; the soil rich, and very productive in grass, every species of grain, and fruits. The whole of this district is in an improving state. From the southern extremity to Canada line, are seen farms in a good state of cultivation, and at distances of six and ten miles from each other, pleasant villages; interspersed with seats built in the modern style of architecture, which indicates that the possessors are wealthy and affluent.

The Military Hospital at Burlington is situated on the high bank of the lake shore, elevated 60 feet above its waters; the soil of which is gravel, which immediately drinks up the water as soon as it falls in rain; so that during the wet seasons of the year the ground in the vicinity of the hospital is free from mud and even moisture. The situation of this position is healthy; much preferable to any which I saw on either the northern or western frontiers.

PLATTSBURGH is situated on a bay the west side of Champlain Lake, 80 miles north of its southern extremity. It is 63 miles south of Montreal. The village, handsomely laid out, forms a crescent on the high lake bank. The country in its vicinity is level, but rises gradually to the west, some distance; then abruptly to lofty mountains. The village is intersected by the Saranac, which empties into the bay from the S. W. Its course is, for two or three miles, nearly parallel with the lake shore, from half to one mile distant from it. On the tongue of land comprised between the lake and river, are the United States' fortifications, extending from the lake bank to the river; so situated that they reciprocally defend each other's flanks. This post is three fourths of a mile above the lower bridge over the Saranac, near its outlet, and one mile and half below the upper bridge. The forests are cut to the distance of one mile south; beyond which to Peru, distant nine miles, few settlements are seen on the lake shore; on the Saranac none short of Union village, distant six miles. General PIKE's cantonment, during the winters 1812–13, was about half the distance between the fortifications and the last village. The woods had been cut at this place; on this account this point was selected by the British army to cross the river. After it had gained the eastern bank, and entered the adjacent forest, it was attacked by the New-York militia, under General MOOERS, who retired to Union village, where they were joined by the Vermont volunteers under the command of General STRONG, when the action became warm.

The British retired and recrossed the Saranac at the same point they first forded the river.

The left of the British army rested on Plattsburgh bay, one mile north of the Saranac; its right wing extending to a point on the Saranac near the upper bridge, one and half mile above the fortifications. Between these two extreme points, the distance is three miles. Advanced of their line, the British, between the 6th and 11th, erected seven batteries.

The village of Plattsburgh, comprising 70 houses, is pleasantly situated on the high bank of the lake. It is a place of considerable trade; mostly in lumber, which is rafted over the lake, and down the Sorel and St. Lawrence to Quebec. The courts for the county are held here. The county-house with a number of private dwellings were burnt at the time the post was invested by Sir GEORGE PREVOST.

The soil of this district is good for grazing, but inferior to that west of Utica. After leaving the settlements of Plattsburgh, the route to Malone, distant 52 miles, is dreary, through forests of hard and soft woods intermixed, with a log hut once in four, six and eight miles, until we arrive at Chateaugay four corners, where is a small village of eight or ten houses. From this we pass a forest and few settlements, at a distance of twelve miles, when suddenly opens the pleasant village of Malone. From this to French Mills is a distance of 16 miles; near the point where the 45th degree of north latitude intersects the river St. Lawrence, being the line of demarkation between the United States and Canada. Up this river to Sackett's Harbour, 160 miles, are thinly scattered villages. The most of the road is through a wilderness. The villages are pleasant, particularly Ogdensburgh, ninety miles from Malone, and 70 N. E. from Sackett's Harbour. The brigades of Generals CHANDLER and PIKE endured a severe storm of snow on this route in the month of March, 1813; where they found snow three feet deep on an average, until they arrived in the vicinity of Lake Ontario. The snow never falls the same depth on the borders of the large lakes, and twelve miles back, as it does beyond this distance.

All the mountainous parts of New-England and state of New-York, during winter, are pregnant with storms of snow, when

at the same time on the Atlantic shores, it generally rains.
On the borders of the great lakes, I was always disappointed in
my prognostications of weather from the appearance of the sky.
Even the first settlers acknowledged their ignorance, being unable
to predict in the morning what the weather would be, or in the
evening what the morning would bring forth.   At Lewistown
on the Niagara, storms of rain and snow were experienced, with
winds from every quarter of the compass.   On the Atlantic,
storms of any duration are from the E. and N. E.

On the 29th May, 1813, the enemy seized the opportunity
when Sackett's Harbour was left almost defenceless, under the
command of Major General BROWN, with 300 United States'
troops and a small body of militia, to attack the post with all his
force from Kingston; but after he made good his landing, and
advanced as far as the barracks near the harbour, was repulsed
with considerable loss.   In this action fell Colonel BACKUS of
the army, and Colonel MILLS of the New-York volunteers.
This first action in which General BROWN was engaged, and
which terminated with much honor to the small detachment of
regulars commanded by Major ASPINWALL, after the death of
his superior officers, was honourably noticed by Government;
particularly by the appointment of General BROWN, then of the
Militia, to the rank of Brigadier General in the United States'
army.

At Oswego, in 1814, 60 miles south west of the harbour, Colonel MITCHEL defended himself against a body vastly superior,
in which action the enemy suffered great loss.   In a subsequent
action at Sandy Creek, 200 of the enemy were made prisoners
by an inferior body of riflemen under Major APPLEN.

The route from Plattsburgh to Lake George, south a distance
of one hundred miles, the greatest part of the way, is through a
wild, mountainous, rocky district, whose sceneries are continually varying as we progress, all of which are truly majestic. Between mountains towering to the sky, are small vales, in some of
which, very remote from each other, are situated pleasant villages.
Essex, is one of these beautiful spots, surrounded by mountains,
which, by their vicinity, exclude every other distant object,

except their aspiring summits. These sublime sceneries are too circumscribed to please more than a few days. They gratify the eye no longer than the first surprising impressions remain on the mind. This village is situated thirty miles S. of Plattsburgh. South of Essex, at 45 miles distance from Plattsburgh, we arrive at Pleasant Valley. The valley, planted between two ranges of lofty mountains, very regular, running nearly parrallel with each other eight miles, is a good tract of land from one to one and half miles wide, with settlements through its extent, on which cultivation has made considerable progress. After leaving Pleasant Valley, we plunge into forests, with nothing to attract the attention of the traveller, except the continuation of mountains on every side, which appear to be thrown together in wild confusion; all lofty, and rugged with rocks. Their relative heights may be known by the appearance of their summits. Those of humble elevation are covered with full-grown timber, the more lofty and sublime are covered with wood of dwarfish growth, while the most towering, with bald heads, are capped with the clouds. Through a narrow serpentine road, constantly winding between the precipitous heights, which at some points project their stupendous perpendicular sides faced with rocks—from whose tops the traveller is constantly threatened with overhanging detached fragments—after a route of twenty miles or more, without the sight of a house, except two or three log huts, he arrives at the town of Schroon, so called after a lake of the same name in its vicinity. Here once more the sceneries change: the lofty mountains gradually retire to a respectful distance; between which and Lake Champlain are gently und lated lands, on which are exhibited the works of industry, rural felicity, and domestic enjoyments.

In this vicinity is situated Crown Point, an ancient fortress in ruins, erected on a projection of a rock, north of Ticonderoga, 123 miles from Albany. Lake George lies west of Champlain nearly parallel with the south extremity of that lake, and empties itself between twenty and thirty miles north of its south extremity. These lakes are separated by a ridge of precipitous mountains rising abruptly from their banks. At the south ex tremlty of Lake George, are seen the remains of ancient Fort George; one mile north of which is the charming village of Caldwell in full view, planted on the bank of the lake, having a small tract of plain land on its western quarter, bounded the distance of three fourths of a mile by a range of mountains aspiring and majestic. The sceneries around the village within the view of the eye (the lake being not more than two miles broad) are inexpressibly fine and pleasing. Here one might suppose the muses might delight to take their habitations—here the poet might in verse give scope to his descriptive powers, and sing of rural pleasures and romantic enjoyments; to whose notes the sylvans and woodland nymphs might join in artless mazy dance. Here, where nature is at once displayed in all her rural charms, variegated with mountains, forests, cooling fountains and crystal floods, the painter also might advantageously employ his pencil. This beautiful retreat from the busy scenes of life, and noisy bustle of towns is a resort, during the pleasant months of summer, for parties of pleasure. For whose accommodation an elegant hotel is built, which is furnished with all the delicious viands of the country. The rural repast is supplied from the forests, the lake, and the cultivated fields. The senses are regaled, the philosophic mind feasted by the pleasing and astonishing works of nature, while the body is refreshed from her bountiful stores.

Lake Champlain, which washes the borders of this mountainous and rocky district, will be long remembered on the pages of the historian, as having been a theatre of wars and ruthful waste of human life, both by hard fought battles and disease.

Ticonderoga, now in a state of ruin, at an early period of the country, was considered of high importance as commanding the pass direct from Canada to the settlements on the Hudson and in New-England. The French built Ticonderoga, when they possessed Canada; from whom it was taken by General AMHERST, in the year 1759. At the commencement of the American revolution, this post was taken from the British by Colonel ALLEN in 1775, and abandoned in 1777. At that period the

23

bordering country was a wilderness. The importance of these posts will never be forgotten.

It was the declared intention of Sir GEORGE PREVOST, to possess these commanding pos! ms, at the time he invested Plattsburgh. This would have given him the command of the whole state of Vermont and the northern district of New York; from which districts resources for the maintenance of 20,000 men might be obtained. The water communication from this to Quebec being free, would have enabled the enemy with a powerful army to have threatened not only the interior of the country south, but the Atlantic shores; and aided by a fleet with a strong party in New-England, as he anticipated, might have prolonged the war; but which would have terminated not in the subjugation of the nation, nor division of its territories.

The expedition against Plattsburgh, with a view to the conquest of the country, would have been an act of madness, even with an army of 50,000 men, had not a diversion of some of the states been expected by the government of Great Britain in its favor.

Without strong assurances of such co-operation, would so important an object have been attempted with only 15,000 men?

Future historians, it is to be hoped, will be prepared to unfold a train of transactions veiled in mystery; the secret springs of which the public documents of individual states had commenced a development; and when fully exposed to the discerning eye of the people, the delusive, insidious charm, which bound their hands, would have been dissolved; their native spirits of independence would have kindled anew in their breasts; they would have burst from their mental inthralment; and while the internal foe sheltered his guilty head in coverts from public indignation, the enemy without would have felt the overwhelming power of their arms.

CONCLUDING OBSERVATIONS.

MANY casualties concur to enfeeble a soldier in the field; some of which have, in the course of these sketches, been noticed. When a man is animated with the object which duty urges him to accomplish, if his health is firm, and not rendered inactive by old age, he will endure extreme fatigues, and severe colds, when time is given him to take his common rations at seasonable hours. Long abstinence, watchings, and unremitted hardships, soon break down not only the spirits, but strength of an army. But when well fed, they cheerfully endure fatigues, colds, and expose themselves to the most threatening dangers, regardless of consequences. Familiar with death, the soldier soon forgets that the feeling of horror was once attached to its name. The love of country, honour, the pride of conquest, incite him to acts of heroism. When duty calls to confront the enemy, he obeys the summons with the same alacrity, as when invited by the alluring voice of pleasure to his amusements. Under these strong excitements, with a due proportion of nutriment, disease seldom assails the body. During long intervals of inactivity, the system becomes enervated. Then it is that the deleterious agents exhibit their influences upon animal life. Then it is that an army sickens from causes connected with their local positions. The soldiers are attacked with diseases in the field, which originate from their own filth and imprudence. In city cantonments, additional causes co-operate to enfeeble not only the body, but mind; productive of sickness and military apathy. During periods of active service, intervals of repose are necessary; but they should be short, and, during rest, unexposed to rain or snow. Profound sleep is increased by fatigue; during this state, the powers of life are either weakened or suspended. The cutaneous secretions are diminished in proportion to the waste or evaporation of caloric upon the surface.

The circumambient moist atmosphere favours the process, while diseased sensibility assumes the place of health. The sensations of cold and rigors succeed with obstructions of the capillary vessels upon the surface; which derangement, by a sympathetic association of parts remote from each other, disorders the more immediate organs of life. Hence arise fevers, rheumatisms, dysenteries and diarrhœas;—diseases, the forms of which are governed by the incidents of positions, or local causes, and seasons.

It is therefore favourable to the soldier's health, after a hard march, to be obliged to seek or cut his wood, to make a fire, and cook his provisions. By this gentle exercise a suitable action is preserved upon the several organs, while the perspiration on the surface is gradually evaporated, without the too sudden waste of heat; the powers of life do not sink, and are further supported by his soup, and a short period of rest. He rises refreshed, and is prepared to obey commands.

There are two principles which are necessary to form the efficient soldier. The first is a rigid military discipline, which operates on the mind of man with a force superior to the strongest apprehension of dangers. It is this which constitutes the courage and bravery of European armies, who have no object in view but to obey the commands of their superior officers. They fight the battles of a Prince without knowing whether the cause, in which he is engaged, is founded upon principles of justice; or whether he is actuated merely by capricious motives. Their soldiers, no ways incited by objects which they can appropriate to themselves, are but machines, while the courage which they possess is wholly artificial.

But there is a second principle which renders a man brave; a knowledge that he possesses a native property—liberty, independence, and a right of soil. These he will support and defend without compulsion. In defence of these, he instinctively assumes his arms and becomes a soldier. Added to this last principle the discipline of Europe, the armies and fleets of the United States have rendered themselves irresistible. And thus they will continue to be, while the principles of our government remain unimpaired; and the pillars of our federated constitution stand firm.

What besides this innate bravery has given superiority to our armies and fleets, over those of the enemy?

The unexampled heroic achievements of our fleets on the ocean; the attack on Little York, under General PIKE; and on Fort George, where Generals BOYD and SCOTT's intrepidity and consummate bravery were conspicuous; the defence of Sackett's harbour, under the command of Maj. Gen. BROWN; the several battles on the Niagara, at Chippawa, and Bridgewater; the defence of Fort Erie, and the subsequent sortie from that fort, by the army under the command of Major General BROWN; in which actions Brigadier Generals SCOTT, RIPLEY, GAINES, PORTER and MILLER severally, and the officers and soldiers of the army, generally, highly distinguished themselves, are ample testimonies of the above position. To add to the climax of brilliant victories, we record with peculiar pride the battles of New Orleans, and Plattsburgh, under Generals JACKSON and Mc'COOMB; and particularly the capture of two of the enemy's fleets on Lakes Erie and Champlain, by Commodores PERRY and MACDONOUGH. These demonstrate with what high toned courage, our soldiers and seamen defend and protect the rights and privileges of the nation; and evince that their superior valor is the effect of the principles of liberty and independence, associated with our forms of government—principles imbibed in infancy, a knowledge of which increases with growth, and becomes matured in adult age.

END OF CAMPAIGN 1814.

Gr
directl
miles
border
from t
ally ri
countr
vallies
of clay
The
Hudso
of the
this po
Lansi
they a
Unite
4000
inence
one h
are qu
dinate
in the
ly 20
The
the riv
pende
its sur

NOTES.

NOTE A.

GREENBUSH is a township on the east bank of the Hudson, directly opposite Albany. The town, which occupies eight miles square, has a diversity of soil and surface. Alluvial flats border the river. Hills present themselves in the rear, distant from the bank of the river from one quarter to one mile, gradually rising until they gain an elevation of 200 feet or more. The country exhibits an unequal surface, diversified with hills and vallies. The soil, in some parts, is clay; in others, a mixture of clay, loam and sand.

The cantonment is on an elevated plane, one mile east of the Hudson. It overlooks the city of Albany on the opposite bank of the river, and the adjacent country, five or six miles. From this position are seen, indistinctly, the beautiful villages of Troy, Lansingburgh and Waterford so contiguous to each other, that they appear as one. Here are barracks for the troops of the United States' army, sufficiently capacious to accommodate 4000 men, with adequate quarters for their officers. On an eminence 60 feet higher, is the hospital, which may accommodate one hundred patients. Attached to the hospital department, are quarters for the surgeons, offices and kitchens for the subordinates of the hospital. The wards of this hospital are too small in their dimensions, both for health and convenience; being only 20 feet by 16, and nine feet in height.

The elevation of the hospital is so great above the surface of the river, that the fogs, which, during the hot season, are suspended over the flats and villages on the banks, seldom rise to its summit.

Upon the alluvial flat opposite Albany, within six years has been laid out a village upon regular streets, which intersect each other at right angles; whose population has rapidly increased. At this time it contains about 70 houses. A sulphurated spring, about 100 rods from the landing at Greenbush, has attracted much attention. During the summer months, some resort here for the benefit of its waters; which, to my knowledge, have cured cutaneous diseases by ablutions and frequent potations. These waters would have more frequent visitors, if suitable baths were erected for the accommodation of invalids. Another beautiful village of 35 houses, called Bath, is romantically situated on the bank of Hudson, one mile above Greenbush.

The temperature of the climate on the Hudson is more regular than in the same latitudes on the Atlantic shores; where are experienced greater and more sudden transitions of weather than here. The cantonment, at Greenbush, has the reputation of being healthful; and the country in its vicinity salubrious.

The city of Albany, the capital of the state of New York, is situated one mile in length on the west bank of the Hudson. It rises from the river by a gradual ascent nearly 200 feet to the elevated plain. The width of this city is from one quarter to one half a mile. This city, with the diversified country in its vicinity, and the chain of the distant Catskill mountains, viewed from the elevated lands of Greenbush, forms a variegated, beautiful prospect. On the margin of the river, the lands are alluvial and rich; while those more elevated and uneven, are a mixture of clay and sand, and barren. That part of the city, on the alluvial flats, has the reputation of being less salubrious than that on the hill. The want of a rigid health police is manifested by the filthiness of some of the streets; more especially of the back yards connected with stables and kitchens. In a growing city, an apology for dirt may be offered, on account of unavoidable lodgments on the streets of materials for house building. As the increase of population introduces wealth and opulence; so these afford the best means to remedy the evils complained of. It is too frequent that people neglect their most important temporal concerns—those conducive to health; till, by repeated ep-

iaB
ch
ed.
ng,
led
ere
ur-
ns.
ths
au-
ted

gu-
are
han
be-

:, is
It
the
r to
i its
iew-
ted,
are
re a
, on
than
fest-
: the
ving
oid-
ling.
nce;
d of.
tem-
l ep-

idemic diseases and mortality, they are roused to adopt measures to obviate them. To an opinion that infectious distempers are of foreign, rather than domestic origin, the inhabitants of cities are mostly disposed to give credit; while it leads them into fatal security. Under this impression, at the moment when they view a formidable disease at a distance, it meets them unexpectedly at the threshold of their doors; the direful consequence of surrounding filth. With a good health police, Albany, from its local situation, may be considered one of the most healthful cities in the United States. With its natural advantages, it has, in a short period, increased in its population beyond example; and previous to the lapse of many years, will be classed as a commercial city among the first in the union. Agreeably to the census of 1810, the whole population of Albany was 9,356. At this time (1816) it may be not less than 13,000; who occupy more than 1,800 houses and stores, a large proportion of which are brick. There are also 10 houses for public worship; the capital or state house, built in a style truly elegant and highly finished, a new jail, three banks, with two banking houses, an alms house, a mechanic hall, a powder house for the state, and one also for the city, an elegant state arsenal, two market houses, a theatre, &c. [See Spafford's Gazetteer of the State of New York.]

The majestic Hudson, famous on the historic page, has often borne on its swelling tide, armies to defend its romantic banks, and the fertile territories through which it flows. The luxuriant fields, on its borders, from its mouth to its source, have been often crimsoned with the blood of freemen, in defence of their rights and privileges. The enemy has known, and still knows full well, the importance of this river to the possessors. The invading foe has always directed his march by this route; and has improved those advantages, which its waters give, to aid his movements both from New York and Canada. On the banks of the Hudson, BURGOYNE surrendered an army of veterans, to the undiscipl_aed yeomanry of the country. On the borders of lake Champlain, moving with an army to gain the source of this river-

24

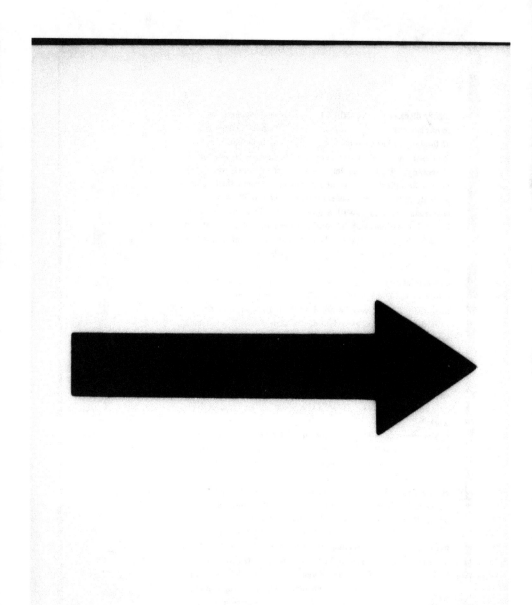

IMAGE EVALUATION
TEST TARGET (MT-3)

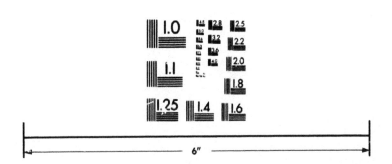

6"

Photographic
Sciences
Corporation

23 WEST MAIN STREET
WEBSTER, N.Y. 14580
(716) 872-4503

er, Prevost witnessed the defeat of his armed flotilla, and retreated with discomfiture and disgrace.

No section of the United States can bear testimony to more
hard fought battles, than the waters which intersect their most
northern territories. Time only will disclose, whether this district will become the seat of future wars—and whether a division of the states will again be attempted by this route. The
yeomanry of this district is a barrier, which is continually
strengthened by a rapid increase of population: and while directed by a Tompkins, will defy a foreign invasion. The state
of New York alone can bring with facility, more than one hundred thousand men to its defence; which forbids a belief that
an attempt to subjugate the nation by a division of its territories, at this point, will be again contemplated.

NOTE B.

Calomel and opium were found beneficial in chronic rheumatism; also Dover's powders. Blisters gave a temporary relief—their effects, however, were not permanent. When the
patient was kept in a gentle diaphoresis between blankets 24 or
36 hours, there was always a mitigation of pain. Later experience has demonstrated, that the Vapour Bath of Doctor Jennings is superior to any mode of removing rheumatism.

Without detailing that train of reasoning, by which he supports a theory, somewhat peculiar to himself, of the causes of
diseases, and their most appropriate mode of treatment, especially when supervening with most morbid symptoms, we shall merely select from his communication, the effects which have been
experienced by its employment.

Diseases attended with general coldness of the body, local, or
more universal pain through the system, torpor, and mental derangement; the patient, if not immediately relieved, expires in
two or three days, often within the first twentyfour hours. The

insuperable coldness, and torpor, which exists, has led the scientific physician to restore heat to the body by the application of artificial means. For this purpose, the warm water bath, billets of wood heated, hot ashes, bladders filled with hot water, have, according to the fancy of the prescribing physician, been applied in various ways to the body. In some instances, these warm and hot applications have been followed with success; while in others, they have failed; not because the intention of the application was incorrect; but because the intention was not completely fulfilled. The moisture which is attached to the body, and the surrounding clothes, frequently counteract all the benefit derived from the heat communicated, by favoring its speedy evaporation from the body; whereby the patient, in a short period, is found as cold and as torpid as he was previous to the employment of those heated applications. In these cases, internal stimulants, such as ardent spirits, have been resorted to, with effects more frequently dangerous than salutary, by inducing higher degrees of excitement upon the larger internal vessels, and some important viscus, already in a gorged state, without being capable of extending their influence to the extreme vessels of the skin. The substitution of Doctor JENNINGS' SPIRITUOUS VAPOUR BATH remedies the evils, which are necessarily connected with the usual application of heat; as its effects are more general, and as it diffuses throughout the system a more equal excitement, without the hazard of an exhaustion, which follows the employment of the water-bath heat, by its sudden evaporation.

The following extracts from Doctor JENNINGS' communications will give a partial idea in what cases the application of his Spirituous Vapour Bath is most suitable. A full knowledge of his treatment cannot be obtained except by reading the whole work, which is scientific and incomparable.

" Heat (says Dr. Jennings) is a very powerful medical agent, and admits of a more universal application than any other yet discovered. It is derived in certain seasons and countries, in part from the sun, but its principal source is from the lungs, in which it appears to be generated by the decomposition of pure air, and from whence it is conveyed by means of the circulation to every part of the body. But if the whole system is prostrated, the volume of heat, decomposed in the lungs, must be less than natural. In consequence of the feebleness of the excitement, it cannot be properly conveyed to the remote points of the system. It must, therefore, necessarily follow, that an external application of an appropriate portion will afford the most natural aid in this situation. In proof of this, it is always agreeable to the patient.

" Having tried the experiment an hundred times over, without meeting with one exception, I assert, that in every case of fever with exhausted energy, and in all cases of direct debility, artificial heat, in an appropriate degree, brings pleasurable sensation to the patient, and may be so managed as to produce cordial effects. In all cases of debility, whether directly or indirectly induced, there is a prevailing inclination to an introversion of excitement. Heat, applied to the skin, most effectually counteracts this tendency, and promotes a centrifugal determination.

" When the surface is abandoned through want of excitement, the skin collapses, and seems to lose its natural elasticity. Heat, artificially applied, corrects this inconvenience. In some instances it may seem at the first to produce a transient effect only; but by careful and well timed repetitions, it will at length become durable. The system artificially replenished with this principle, is presently enabled to generate a more competent supply for itself. But as an excessive portion of wine, or any other cordial, stimulates too much, and induces a morbid degree of indirect debility; so also an excessive application of heat will produce similar effects. In all such cases, therefore, special regard should be had to the feelings of the patient.

" There are some remarkable and important advantages attending the use of this cordial, which no other can possibly claim. In every case, where properly used, it produces a full effect, without imposing any improper stress upon the central vessels. So that in securing the most pleasant diffusion of excitement, it offers no injury to any of the organs of life; ordinary cordials, on the contrary, are dependant upon the struggle which they may excite in the heart and central vessels, for any and every centrifugal effect which they may produce.

" Again, at the same time that heat, by its stimulant power, invites excitement to the surface, it softens and expands the skin, in a way preparatory to receive the returning blood. Ordinary cordials must accomplish the effect, by compelling the feeble system, if indeed it can be done, to assume an action sufficient not only to resume all those branches which it had abandoned because it was not able to maintain them, but also to overcome all the resistance of an almost lifeless collapse of the vessels on the surface.

" It is true, that hitherto insuperable difficulties attended the use of this agent in many cases. But, by the aid of my portable apparatus, every difficulty is now perfectly corrected, and the application of heat can be made with such precision, as fitly to meet the most accurate intention.

" By raising an intense degree of excitement on the surface, every necessary effect can be produced with the utmost safety.

" Other powerful remedies, when once administered, are gone beyond the reach of control, and must have their full effect, whether judiciously or injudiciously administered. But if too much heat has been employed, it is perfectly within our reach to check its influence, by an immediate application of cold.

" In cases of gout, rheumatism, spasm, cholic, &c. when there is a morbid determination, or location of excitement, heat affords a safe agent by which to correct the determination of power, and maintain a sufficient degree of excitement on the surface, till the system can recover a balance.

" After debility has long prevailed in the system, by whatever cause it may have been induced, the collapse of the vessels of the surface becomes obstinately fixed. The skin, therefore, looses its elastic feeling—becomes habitually and obstinately pale, and through its privation of circulating blood, is disarmed of its power to resist the cold. Heat promises much in such a case.

" It may perhaps be feared, that a frequent use of heat may induce debility. My experience warrants the assertion, that the contrary is true.

" The bath produces no loss of vital fluid, and therefore any moderate degree of debility is quickly recovered. A pleasant expansion is given to the vessels of the surface, and by heat they are stimulated into increased action. The circulating blood is invited from the centre to the skin. The intestines, therefore, by being partially deprived of excitement, are, for a time, relaxed—But when the bathing is ended, the blood returns to its natural equilibrium, without any subsequent inconvenience.

" It is worthy of remark, that there is no danger of taking cold, especially in recent cases. The gass which is used, is as much freed from moisture as atmospheric air, insomuch, that it will dry a damp sheet."

Dr. JENNINGS is a respectable physician: he holds the use of his *portable warm and hot bath* by patent right. It is not to be placed among the ephemeral pretensions of those who deal in quack remedies. This new mode of applying heat, like all other useful remedies, should be employed under the direction of a scientific physician ; more especially, as its usefulness is circumscribed to states of morbid action, which require a knowledge of the animal economy, under all states of disease and health, to direct with precision.

NOTE C.

Cases of dissections reported by hospital Surgeon's mate, MARCH, exhibiting the appearances of the diseased organs of those who died with the pneumonia notha of the winter 1812-13, connected with the symptoms and general treatment of the disease.

CASE FIRST.

" JAMES CASSEN, 6th regiment infantry, was admitted into the hospital September 1st, 1812, sick with intermittent fever, from which he recovered by the ordinary treatment ; but continued weak, having some cough and diarrhœa until 1st November, when one eye was diseased, accompanied with pain, and a loss of clear and distinct vision, which terminated in eight days with a loss of sight. The pupil was white and opake, assuming the appearance of a cataract.

"November 10th, he was seized with violent pain in the breast and side, with common symptoms of pneumonia ; for which he was bled, and treated with medicines commonly employed in pneumonic fevere. He died on the 13th.

DISSECTION.

" Upon laying open the abdomen, the spleen was found uncommonly large, much resembling the kidney of an ox, and of a similar texture, and weighed 2 ℔ 2 oz. avoirdupoise.—The lungs were tumid, hard and inflamed ; adhering to the pleura costalis, in many places. A membrane of coagulated lymph lined the cavity of the thorax. A considerable quantity of effused lymph was found in its cavity."

REMARK.

The indurated spleen was probably the cause of his continued debility, after the intermittent fever was subdued. The state of lungs was such as were their appearance where the patient did not survive the first stage of pneumonia. In the above case, death took place previous to the suppurative stage, and the inspection evinced, that bleeding was not carried to the extent, which the state of the disease demanded.

CASE SECOND.

" —— SULLIVAN of the corps of artificers, 34 years old, robust, muscular, intemperate, and in a state of intoxication, took a large quantity of opium ; soon after, was seized with violent spasms, cramp in the stomach and breast, with vomiting. After recovering from the severe effects of the opium, was seized with pain in the side, for which a blister and diaphoretic powders were prescribed.

" I was called five or six days after his first illness to visit him, when he was found groaning at every breath, his hands alternately pressed upon his breast and head, and delirious. The whole of the symptoms indicated agonizing pains in the head, breast, and side. It was said he had been in the above condition three hours, and previously complained of a very severe pain in his head. With much difficulty eight ounces of blood was taken from the arm, and a blister applied. He continued in this distressed situation twelve hours, and died.

DISSECTION.

" The bowels on dissection appeared perfectly healthy, also the liver. The spleen was enlarged, darker, and of a softer texture than natural. When the sternum was raised, the lungs appeared in a high state of disease. The right lobe (the side affected) was much inflamed, adhering to the pleura, swollen so as completely to fill the cavity of the thorax. The left lobe was slightly inflamed—a fleshy substance similar to a gland was found detached from every part, in the abdomen.—This substance is now entire, preserved in spirits of wine."

REMARKS.

This robust patient, it is highly probable, was, in addition to the disease, in a state of intoxication. The state of the lungs required a full bleeding. Had thirty ounces or more been taken away, he might have been saved.

CASE THIRD.

" WILLIAM MURRAY, private of the light artillery, was admitted into the general hospital 1st December, 1812, with a pneumonic fever. The pain in the breast and side was very severe. He was of a robust and plethoric habit. The treatment was bleeding, cathartic, blisters, submuriate of quicksilver, and opium. He lived only four days.

DISSECTION.

" Upon examination, the abdominal viscera were sound; the lungs highly inflamed and surcharged with blood. A pint of yellowish, or whey-coloured lymph was effused into the cavity of the thorax. The inside of the thorax was lined with a thick membrane of coagulated lymph. The pericardium contained eight ounces of whey-coloured lymph, in which were floating coagulated lymph resembling cheese curds."

REMARKS.

The quantity of blood taken away is not stated, yet it is most certain, from the robust habit of the patient, and appearance of the lungs after death, that a sufficient quantity was not taken away in this case. At the commencement of this pneumonic disease, the lancet was employed with too great timidity in most cases.

CASE FOURTH.

" WILLIAM MOORE, 16th regiment infantry, was admitted a patient into the general hospital at Greenbush, October 17th, 1812, in a debilitated state of health, having pain in the breast, with a sore throat and cough—was bled once, took a cathartic, which relieved his throat. The cough continued; a diarrhœa soon supervened, which continued until death, which took place on the 1st December. Gentle cathartics were occasionally administered. His cough was generally attended with expectoration of muco-purulent matter, which denoted an ulceration of the lungs. An emetic of ipecacuanha was once or twice given to promote expectoration, and to determine the circulation to the surface. Paragoric was given to allay a dry tickling cough. The diet was rice, chocolate, milk, wine occasionally as a stimulus.

DISSECTION.

" Upon inspecting the chest, the lungs appeared large and hard, filling both cavities, and firmly adhered in several places to the

25

pleura. Both lobes, excepting a small part of the left, were of a dark purple colour. After making an incision into the substance of the lungs, and squeezing them, thick pus was forced by the compression out of the air cells. There were found also several hard lumps or tubercles.

"Upon examining the abdomen, the rectum, and sigmoid flexure of the colon were found of a livid hue, very much thickened in their coats. Those parts of the intestines which rested on the back or psoas muscles, assumed a dark and gangrenous appearance. In the cæcum, or caput coli, were found some hard lumps of hardened fæces, over which had passed the watery stools. These scybala are believed to be frequently the cause of our obstinate diarrhœas, especially where the stomach and intestines have lost their tone, so as not to perform their offices of digestion. The more solid parts are retained and keep up irritation, while the fluids pass on and produce a troublesome diarrhœa, which frequently continue a great length of time.

CASE FIFTH.

"THOMAS SETTLERS, private in the 2d regiment artillery, was admitted into the general hospital at Watertown, N. Y. (12 miles from Sackett's Harbour) about 1st April, 1813, with pneumonia. The pain in the breast and side was incessant and severe several days. Respiration was laborious, so that the patient was under necessity of sitting up in his bed most of the time, catching and gasping for breath—unable to make a long and full inspiration. Repeatedly bled and ...stered without effect. He died the 12th day after his first indisposition.

DISSECTION.

"On exposing the thorax, the lungs were found contracted, tough, compact, almost destitute of air vessels. The right cavity of the thorax was completely filled with serum, three pints in quantity; the lobe being so diminished as not to occupy but a very small space. In this case, the inflammatory symptoms had subsided, the patient died hectic, produced by absorption of pus, and from a hydrothorax. The latter was probably the chief agent of accelerating death."

CASE SIXTH.

" REUBEN SMITH, a private in the 9th regiment, 27 years of age, admitted into the general hospital at Watertown, 1st April, 1813, with the following symptoms : troublesome cough, difficulty of breathing, little appetite, and declining in strength, effects of a previous attack of the epidemic pneumonia. The lungs appeared the principal seat of disease. Small doses of calomel and opium were administered night and morning to promote expectoration, which had the desired effect. Intermediately was given a mixture of elixir, paragoric and antimonial wine ; a blister was applied on the breast to remove a dull heavy pain. Three days previous to death, the patient was attacked with hemo-phthisis ; and at the same time he expectorated a piece of the lobe of the lungs, a little hardened in texture, and partly ulcerated, which weighed over two ounces. The raising of blood continued, and he died while he was coughing blood."

DISSECTION.

" The cellular texture of the lungs, upon opening the chest, was yellowish ; the left cavity of the thorax was filled with yellow water. The lobe was large, hard, and adhered to the upper part of the cavity. The lobe on the other side adhered strongly and uniformly to the pleura covering the ribs ; it was large and appeared like the liver ; tender and easily lacerated with the fingers, entirely destitute of the spongy texture peculiar to healthy lungs ; in its superior part adjoining the clavicle and near the trachea, there was a large sphacelus. It was evident from its appearance, that a portion of this rotten part had been removed ; and undoubtedly was that which was raised by coughing. Pus was by compression squeezed out of the air cells. The substance of the lobe was easily broken and torn to pieces. The cavity of the abdomen contained at least two quarts of water similar to that in the thorax ; the stomach and liver appeared healthy ; the gall bladder was larger than usual, and filled with thinish bile."

" GEORGE WHEELIS, of the second regiment of artillery, was admitted into the hospital at Watertown 10th of March, 1813, in the last stage of the epidemic pneumonia; with short breathing and rattling in his trachea, which continued five or six weeks; troublesome cough, attended with expectoration of purulent matter; disturbed sleep, accompanied with delirious reveries upon being awoke. When first admitted, the patient coughed thick purulent matter in large quantities; became very feeble, emaciated and sweated profusely. Immediately previous to his being sent to the hospital, he was bled; after admittance, was blistered repeatedly on his breast, and took submuriate of quicksilver and ipecac. combined, in small doses with favourable effects. Other medicines were occasionally administered as symptoms demanded. About the seventh week he expectorated freely and largely, the calomel was discontinued, and camphorated tinc. of opium and wine of antimony were directed to ease the cough; sweating now began to abate, pain in the throat and breast had left him, breathing was more free, appetite better, cough was less frequent and expectoration less. The purulent matter which had been generated was thrown off, and less seemed to have been formed. The general symptoms were favourable, and a speedy recovery was expected.

" A severe dysentery at this time supervened from some cause unknown, which precipitated the patient in three days to the grave. The stools were very frequent, attended with severe gripes, tenesmus, rapid prostration of strength, sudden emaciation, sinking of the eyes and contraction of the features of the face. At the moment of dissolution, purple spots and streaks appeared over the body, particularly on the abdomen, which indicated mortification."

DISSECTION.

" The rectum and part of the colon, upon inspecting the contents of the abdomen, shewed strong marks of inflammation, being thickened in their coats, dark red, or nearly purple. The liver was sound. The lungs were full and appeared in a healthy condition, excepting one lobe, which had a small adhesion, and the other had depressed spots of a darker colour than the rest of the lungs; which evinced that these spots were once the seat of little ulcers or abscesses, but now healed and apparently sound as the other parts of the lungs."

CASE EIGHTH.

"LANDON C. BRUCE, sergeant in the 6th regiment of infantry, acting clerk to Doctor BLOOD, hospital surgeon, was seized with a fever about the first of November, 1813, of intermittent, inflammatory and pneumonic symptoms, with pain and soreness in the breast, and cough. Of these complaints he so far recovered as to perform the writing in the hospital, which occupied three or four hours in a day. During his convalescence he was in habits of intemperance. He still was troubled with some pain in his breast, and more or less cough, and often a diarrhœa accompanied the other complaints. These had increased by the first of March, 1814, to a considerable degree. About the middle of this month he became so emaciated and debilitated as to be unable to write in the hospital office. As cough and diarrhœa were aggravated, appetite failed. The expectoration at this time was mucus tinged with blood; pain in the breast, not severe. Little was taken by him except opium to check diarrhœa and alleviate cough.

"April 10th, a large blister was applied over his breast. The blister had little or no effect. Some calomel had been taken, but how long time it was continued, or much in quantity sufficient to produce a sensible effect, is to me unknown. 13th. He was so weak as to be unable to sit up, and at times a little delirious. 16th. He expired.

DISSECTION.

"The next day I opened the body. The abdominal viscera were not diseased, except the coats of some of the large intestines (rectum and colon) appeared to be a little thickened and inflamed in a small degree. Laid open the thorax. The left lobe of the lungs entirely filled its cavity, and adhered to the pleura costalis, diaphram, sternum, and pericardium, wherever it came in contact with these organs. Many specks of pus were discovered on cutting into the substance of the lobe; but no abscess. The right lobe had formed no adhesions; but some schirrous lumps were found in its substance. The heart and pericardium were sound."

CASE NINTH.

" JAMES KINNEY, 9th regiment infantry, was admitted into the general hospital 20th March, 1814, labouring under pneumonic symptoms in its advanced stage. On the 28th of the same month, he was placed under my charge, then complaining of pain in the breast, short and difficult breathing, scarcely able to articulate; with the above symptoms, and a diarrhœa, with which he was attended, had become emaciated and debilitated. A blister was applied, which relieved the pain in the breast; at the same time submuriate of quicksilver, opium, and tartrite of antimony combined, were administered in small pills night and morning; each pill containing one grain of the submuriate, one grain of opium, and one fourth grain of tartrite of antimony; occasionally a pill of opium, *per se*, when too great determination to the bowels was perceived. Camphorated tincture of opium was also given, when the cough was troublesome, to take off the irritation from the lungs. This treatment was pursued one fortnight. The pills produced a free expectoration, which was aided by soft diluents. About this time one gill of wine was allowed a day.

" The laborious respiration still continued. Small pains now and then returned, but confined to the left side. His general health failed, and he became more emaciated. Suspecting that there might be an effusion of lymph mixed with pus in the thorax, on the 20th of April an examination was made as to those symptoms which indicate an hydrothorax or an empyema. He had cold shiverings; no œdematous swellings of the lower extremities; nor had he dreamed of drowning; all of which occasionally occur. The symptoms which might lead to a suspicion of empyema were, he had a pneumonia; the left side of the thorax was visibly larger than the other; the spaces between the ribs on that side were more tense and distended than the other; in the left side there had been more pain than the other. The most unequivocal symptom of a fluid in the cavity was the fluctuation heard, when a sudden shake was given by turning him on the opposite side. The noise was not much unlike the agitation of buttermilk in a churn.

"By the advice of Hospital Surgeon BLOOD, I tried the effects of a large blister; the result was what was expected. It answered no good purpose. The effusion being the termination of a severe pneumonia, and the collection of long standing, and great in quantity, blistering was believed to be a very inefficient remedy in such a case. The inflammatory stage had subsided more than a fortnight. The operation of paracentesis appeared to be the last resort.

"On the 24th April, an opening was made between the sixth and seventh ribs, near where the external oblique muscle of the abdomen indigitates with the serratus major anticus; or, (which brings it to about the same point) at an equal distance between the ensiform cartilage of the sternum, and the spine. I made the incision through the skin and muscles with a common scalpel, and punctured the pleura with a lancet, a quarter of an inch long. The pus flowed in an uninterrupted stream. About one quart was taken away, at this time, when the patient began to grow faint, and I closed the orifice. This first discharge of matter procured him much relief in his breathing. He coughed less, slept better the ensuing night than he had done for three weeks previous. The orifice was opened again the next day, [25th] from which was discharged more than one pint of matter. Although his breathing was considerably relieved, yet his pulse became more hectic, and his strength failed. [26th.] Being weak and exhausted, and respiration not very laborious, no discharge was attempted. On the 27th, the orifice was again opened, and a pint and half matter taken away. The last discharge was of the fluid consistence of buttermilk, and of a greenish colour, very offensive, so as to contaminate the whole room with a nauseous smell. Pulse now, small, hard, frequent; he was restless, and had little or no appetite. At this period he took wine and soft nourishing diet, as much as his stomach could bear, with a pill of opium at night. From this time there was but little discharge, except when raised up. His breath became very offensive, and his pulse smaller and more frequent, until May 4th, when he expired."

CASE TENTH.

"THOMAS FARRING, 11th regiment, was placed under my care the last of April, 1814. Upon examination, he was found labouring under a chronic complaint of the lungs, consequent to pneumonia. At this time, his complaints were some pain in the left breast, hoarseness, troublesome cough, difficulty of breathing, little appetite. Previous to his present indisposition, he had an hemophthisis. He was bled moderately; a blister was applied to the affected breast; a pill of one grain of submuriate of quicksilver, one grain of opium, and one fourth grain of tartrite of antimony was administered every night, and was continued one week with some good effect, by promoting an expectoration; but his breathing was no better. Profuse night sweats supervened, with loss of speech, delirium and anasarcous swellings. He died ten days after I made my first prescriptions.

DISSECTION.

" May 6th. Upon opening the abdomen, it was found to contain about one and half pint of water. The intestines were much thickened and corrugated, bearing strong marks of inflammation. The caput coli and ascending part of the colon appeared to be free from inflammation, but much distended with wind. The stomach and spleen appeared sound. The liver, as in health and natural, except the ligamentum teres running along a fissure on the under side, passing through a foramen in the same place where the fissure should be. The foramen was free and open, and sufficiently large to admit my little finger by the side of the round ligament.

Upon raising the sternum, the lungs were found exceeding large in either cavity. The right lobe had some slight adhesions at the back and upper part of the cavity of the thorax. A small portion of the lobe immediately under the clavicle, and near the spine, had lost its natural spongy texture, and resembled that of the liver. Upon cutting into this part, a small quantity of pus was found in the cells.—The left lobe was very large, and distinctly divided by a fissure running longitudinally, dividing the front from the back part.—This fissure, or which was more like an incision made with a knife, was about an inch and half deep. The front division . this lobe appeared healthy and natural, without any adhesions; the back portion, (which was rather larger than the front, and by itself almost as large as a common lobe) adhered to the pleura in every part. It exhibited strong marks of inflammation, being of a dark purple colour, and considerably hardened. Upon cutting into every portion, particularly the upper and back part, every cell discharged thick pus in abundance. Indeed, wherever an incision was made, the wound appeared like a mass of thick pus, connected only by the thin membranous textur of the lungs; not much dissimilar to a honey-comb if filled with thick pus."

CASE ELEVENTH.

"DANIEL CATHBURT, 23d regiment infantry, was admitted into the hospital at Brownville, 10th March, 1814, with a pulmonic complaint. The greatest part of the preceding winter, he had been sick at Sackett's harbour, previous to his removal to Brownville. This patient had a bad cough, with slight pains in his breast, and difficulty of breathing, some diarrhœa, œdematous swellings of the legs, which were reduced by the spiral bandage. With the above symptoms he was much emaciated. Blisters were applied upon his breast; was ordered at night a pill of submuriate of quicksilver and opium; after taking the above medicine a few days, an expectoration took place; to assist this and quiet an irritating cough, camphorated tinc. of opium was administered with soft mucilaginous drinks. The diet was principally milk; and the patient was indulged with wine every day till his death, which was on the 10th of May.

26

DISSECTION.

"On opening the abdomen, the coats of the intestines were found very much thickened and corrugated, and appeared to have been highly inflamed. The stomach was contracted, the liver was whitish with a yellowish cast. The vesicula fellis contained but a small quantity of bile; its coats were much thickened, contracted, and appeared to have been inflamed. Having suffered from diabetes a considerable time, I was induced to examine the kidneys. To the upper part of that on the left side, there was an appendage, nearly as large as a midling sized auricle of the heart, and in resemblance somewhat like it, but in texture soft and tender as the liver or spleen. It was easily torn with my fingers. The right kidney appeared natural excepting the *ventricle* which empties itself by the ureter, was larger than usual.

"Each cavity of the thorax contained three pints of water, rather serum, limpid and glutinous, resembling whey in colour. The right lobe was contracted to half its natural size, the upper part consolidated and hardened, feeling and appearing like a piece of heart boiled. Adhesions had formed to the spine, ribs, clavicle and pericardium. The lobe was so much drawn to the spine, that no adhesion existed between it and the ribs of the anterior part of the thorax. In the upper part of the lobe immediately under the clavicle, there was an abscess as large as a goose egg. The substance of this part was destroyed. There was found adhering to the pleura and lungs, a membrane of coagulated lymph, and some similar thick pieces resembling what is commonly called mother of vinegar. The left lobe appeared little diseased; but, on cutting into the substance, drops of pus were squeezed out of its cells. There were slight adhesions, nothing more, it is presumed, than many have for years, who enjoy good health. The pericardium contained a fluid similar to that in the thorax, but more glutinous. This man was 25 years of age, light complexion, of a delicate constitution."

« were
red to
:d, the
: fellis
** much**
lamed.
induc-
on the
idling
like it,
vas ea-
iatural
:r, was

water,
colour.
upper
like a
e, ribs,
to the
the an-
nmedi-
i goose
re was
agulat-
is com-
l little
» were
othing
y good
: in the
of age,

NOTE D.

DOCTOR GALLUP observes in his treatise on epidemics, page 70, that " the winter epidemic of 1812–13, appeared among the soldiers at Burlington some weeks before it did amongst the inhabitants of that place. It appeared also among the soldiers at Plattsburgh and Sacket's harbour, and also in the camp at Greenbush, opposite Albany. No satisfactory account (he observes) has ever been given to the public relative to the diseases at Burlington. I have solicited information from resident physicians there, but have obtained none. By information from some of the most respectable inhabitants of the place, and also from others residing there at the time, I am warranted in stating, that for some time, it was common for eight to twelve to die in a day. The whole number is said to be not less than seven or eight hundred in four months. The number of soldiers stationed at this encampment was about twenty five or twenty eight hundred."

Thus far is Doctor GALLUP's statement; upon which (if any remark is necessary) we shall observe, that if the Doctor had applied to the surgeons of the hospital at Burlington, rather than citizens, for information respecting deaths in the army, he would not have committed so considerable an error respecting numbers. The troops at Burlington, in the winter 1812—13, did not number over sixteen hundred, and the deaths did not exceed two hundred. The mortality was greatest during the month of December, while stimulants were the principal remedies employed. The antiphlogistic regimen was commenced under my direction the first week in January, when uncommon mortality ceased, although cases of new attacks were not less frequent.

Doctor GALLUP is correct where he considers " the exposures and fatigues of a camp, life to men unaccustomed to it, might have a share in rendering the soldiers the first victims of the disease." It being true " that it appeared among the troops two or three weeks earlier than among the citizens," who eventually suffered with no less severity from it, but in some instances much greater. In the month of February, the number of deaths agreeably to the official report of Doctor LOVELL, did not exceed three in a hospital, which contained more than one hundred patients through the whole time; when during the same month, there were seventy three deaths of citizens in the small village of Burlington. This last fact was communicated to Doctor LOVELL, by a highly respectable clergyman of the town. The remark in a medical view is especially important, that while the soldiers were under an antiphlogistic practice, the citizens were treated by stimulants.

" A depression of mind from a repulse immediately before, under General DEARBORN, in an attempt to invade Canada," (as conjectured by Doctor GALLUP) could not have existed ; when there had been no repulse which this division experienced. Neither did General DEARBORN immediately command the army on the lines of Canada; which had an invasion been intended, he would have headed in person. After General VAN RENSELEER's disastrous battle at Queenstown, and failure of General SMYTH's expedition, no hostile movement against the enemy was contemplated at that late season of the year. The officers of the army well understood that General BLOOMFIELD's movement towards the lines of Canada was only a feint to draw the attention of the enemy from Upper Canada, to aid General SMYTH in his expedition.

No person can more respect the opinions of Doctor GALLUP than myself; especially as to the nature and treatment of epidemic diseases, particularly the pneumonia notha of 1812—13. A similar treatment had been pursued by the surgeons of the army, in opposition to the sentiments of very respectable physicians in that part of the country. A concise view of which was published, at that period, in the ARGUS at Albany, and with some additions may be seen in the MEDICAL REPOSITORY for 1813 and 1814, printed at New-York.

NOTE E.

In a late American edition of Goldsmith's History of England, by the Reverend Manly Wood of Exeter College, Oxon. is a summary of events to the year 1815, published by a professor of Harvard University at Cambridge, (who has acknowledged himself the author,) from which the following abusive statement is extracted.

" The border war against his majesty's North American Colonies, produced no important results; but was incalculably distressing to the inhabitants of both frontiers. In the course of the season, several considerable battles were fought. Little York, the capital of Upper Canada, was taken, *sacked, and the public buildings wantonly destroyed,* in the former part of the campaign, by troops under General Dearborn; but the Americans were soon forced to abandon it with considerable loss."

What base pusillanimity is represented in the above paragraph! *"forced to abandon the place,"* when an enemy was not within the distance of 90 miles! A more astonishing and impudent mistatement never was before published, directly in the face of correct official documents.

It is much to be lamented that any one, but more especially a member of the Massachusetts Historical Society, holding a highly respectable place in an important public institution, established for the advancement of science, morality and religion, should be so lost to a just sense of his situation, as to have given vent to such virulent party feelings—as to betray a disregard of facts, as well as common decency.

NOTE F.

In justification of measures pursued by General BOYD, while he commanded the army at Fort George, we state, that the gallantry of no one, on that memorable day, when Fort George surrendered, was more honorably mentioned than his was, after the action; in which he not only led his brigade up the bank, defended by a line of the enemy eligibly posted for defence; but by his animating address to his troops while in the heat of battle. It is in my power to state, being on the battle ground immediately after the action, near four hundred men, including those of both armies, either killed or wounded, extended on the high bank, intermixed, a length of 200, and breadth of 15 yards. This alone demonstrates the ground was disputed nearly at the point of the bayonet, until the enemy's line broke.

From information given by officers, some sections of our army actually engaged the enemy at the point of the bayonet.

The following extracts of letters from Officers of high grade, express the sentiments of the officers, generally, of the army, respecting the conduct of General BOYD on that occasion. Extract of Major General LEWIS' letter to the Secretary of War.

" Of General BOYD, I feel it a duty to do justice to his intrepid conduct at the landing of our troops on the Canada shore, at Niagara. His brigade made the landing under a heavy fire of musquetry. It was instantly formed, and he led it up the bank with great gallantry, and was the first himself to gain it."

Extract of General P. B. PORTER's letter to the President of the United States.

" AT the taking of Fort George, on the 27th May, the American troops landed in succession—1st, the advance on the right, under the command of Lieutenant Colonel Scott—2d, Boyd's brigade—3d, Winder's, and lastly, Chandler's. The landing of General Boyd's brigade, was effected (as well as that of Scott's command) under a heavy shower of musquetry from the enemy, who lay on the margin of the lake. But such was the promptitude and order with which the troops were formed and led into action, that the enemy was beaten by the time Winder's brigade began to debark.

"General Boyd and his brigade participated largely in the well earned honors of the day; and the expedition and order with which his brigade landed and formed, and the personal gallantry, were spoken of throughout the army in terms of the highest commendation."

Extract of General Miller's letter to a General in Boston.

"I served in his brigade (General Boyd's) at the capture of Fort George on the Niagara. Lieutenant Colonel Scott led the advance and struck the shore first, followed immediately by our brigade, which landed in succession from right to left, and formed under a most destructive fire from the enemy who lined the bank for some hundred yards. The contest was principally, or all over, before any other brigade landed.

"General Boyd was the senior officer on shore. I have ever considered his conduct on that occasion brave, animating, intrepid, and officer like."

General Miller, speaking of the capture of Fort George, says—

"General Boyd inspired the whole by his zealous and animating conduct. He rushed up the steep bank at the head of his brigade, when after about fifteen minutes sharp fighting, the charge was given, and the enemy fled. General Boyd was senior officer in the battle, and proclaimed the victory by three cheers—to him and Scott, the army acknowledged a preeminent claim to the honors achieved.

"This conquest I have ever considered one of the most brilliant achievements during the war, the sortie at Fort Erie excepted."

The following document exhibits the orders by which General BOYD was governed subsequent to that period, when General DEARBORN was ordered from the command of the army at Fort George.

"*War Department, July* 7, 1813.

"SIR,—General DEARBORN being about to withdraw from the command of the army, until his health shall be re-established, this trust will devolve upon you, as the senior officer, until the arrival of some person *to* whom it will be specially assigned. During this period, you will pay the utmost attention to the instruction and disciplining of the troops, and engage in no affair with the enemy that can be avoided. The orders of Generals HAMPTON and LEWIS you will obey.

"I am, with great respect, your most obedient servant,

JOHN ARMSTRONG."

The above documents have been already published, and coming from officers of most respectable standing, when more generally known, will remove every aspersion which has been cast upon General BOYD by the public, while he commanded at Fort George.

The aggregate of the army at Fort George and its dependencies was about 5000. From an estimation of numbers sick in general and regimental hospitals, it was my persuasion, but little more than one half of the army were capable of duty, at one period during the summer months. The officers equally suffered with the rank and file. This has been already expressed in page 66. It was repeatedly stated to myself by officers, that they were on duty every other day.

Wherein the comparative strength of the two armies, as to aggregate numbers, is noticed, page 91, it is not designed to impute to General BOYD a want of courage; no officer was ever heard to suggest that he would not have attacked the enemy in their lines, if he had been at liberty to have acted offensively. If he was unfortunately placed under circumstances by *superior* authority, which operated to his injury in the public mind, a full exposition of which, prudence, at the time, forbade; the injustice is to be attributed to those orders, which restrained his native energies, and prevented him the acquisition of those high military honours, for which, in early life, he assumed the profession of arms; for which he always thirsted, and for which he has, at all times, displayed the highest ambition to expose his life.

While enumerating the several causes of disease, to which the army was subjected at Fort George, the sinks were noticed in pages 66 and 70 as ONE. No neglect on the part of General BOYD is here intended. The officers of the army, in all things connected with cleanliness, were governed by their perceptions. To the eye the encampment appeared in fine order, and very clean. Nevertheless, offensive effluvia from the sinks, (when the wind was from that quarter, from which it blows four-fifths of the time during the summer months) were noticed by myself and others, who occasionally visited the encampment from a position surrounded by a purer atmosphere. A report of the existent fact, however, is not intended as a censure on any *one*. The observation is made, not in a military, but a physical point of view, to show more generally, what every physician knows, and all the world should know, that persons may be surrounded with poisonous gasses, without being conscious of them through the medium of any of the senses. Had I been placed two weeks under similar circumstances, it is presumed the unpleasant effluvia would not have been noticed by myself, more than by those whose sensitive organs, from habit, were not annoyed by them.

27

SURGERY.

AMPUTATIONS, AND CASES OF WOUNDS.

The opinions of Larrey, chief surgeon of the imperial guards, and inspector general of the medical staff of the French armies, respecting amputations and gun-shot wounds, are well deserving the attention of surgeons. It is generally believed, they are correct, and with some exceptions, should be adopted. He observes, " when a limb is so much injured by a gun-shot wound, that it cannot be saved, it should be amputated *immediately*. In the army, many circumstances enforce the necessity of primitive amputation."

" 1st. The inconvenience which attends the transportation of the wounded from the field of battle to the military hospitals on bad constructed carriages.

2d. " The danger of remaining long in hospital. This risque is much diminished amputation; it converts a gun-shot wound into one which is capable of being speedily healed, and obviates the causes that produce the hospital fever and gangrene.

" 3dly. In cases the wounded are of necessity left on the field of battle ; it is then important that amputation should have been performed, because when it is completed, they may remain several days without being dressed, and the subsequent dressings are more easily accomplished.

" The necessity of primitive amputation is enforced by statements of a number of cases illustrated by examples.

CASE FIRST.

" When a limb is carried away by a ball, by the bursting of a grenade or a bomb, the most prompt amputation is necessary. The least delay endangers the life of the wounded."

After the battle of Lake Champlain, two cases of this discription fell under my observation. A simple dressing was applied to the ragged stump. In this situation they were brought to the hospital. The wounds, having the appearance of being dressed, did not call our first attention, when many presented, which required an immediate operation ; and not being painful, were neglected on the day of the action. The following morning one was found dead, and the second having been exhausted by loss of blood, survived amputation only a few hours, although he did not loose half a gill of blood during the operation. The above cases might have been saved by an immediate amputation.

CASE SECOND.

" When a body is projected from a cannon, and strikes a limb so that the bones are fractured, and the soft parts violently contused, extensively torn and broken up, amputation should be instantly performed." I am persuaded that several of the above description lost their lives in consequence of wounds received by the explosion of the magazine at Little York, who might have been saved by immediate amputation.

CASE THIRD.

" When a large portion of the soft parts and the principal vessels of a limb are carried away by a ball, and the bone is fractured, amputation should be immediately performed."

CASE FOURTH.

" When a large ball strikes the thick part of a limb, breaks the bone, cuts and tears the muscles, destroys the great nerves, and yet leaves the principal artery entire, immediate amputation should be resorted to. It is rendered necessary by the destruction that has taken place in the limb, and by the concussion that has been given to the whole substance."

At the engagement of Plattsburgh, Lieutenant Duncan of the navy, was wounded by a cannon ball, which passed in a direction of the scapulo-humeral articulation. The superincumbent muscles of the shoulder with part of the subjacent were destroyed, leaving a small portion in the axilla connected with the principal artery, which received no injury. The acromeon process and clavicle were fractured. The head of the humerus was broken, and four inches of its substance forced away by the ball, leaving an inch of its extreme head attached to its socket. In similar cases, Larrey recommends immediate amputation. From the destruction of the parts, my opinion was that to save life amputation was absolutely necessary. I had previously read Larrey's statement of similar wounds cured only by the operation; of which he triumphantly says, "the truly intelligent, bold and experienced man can alone know and appreciate the wonderful effects." Lieutenant Duncan objected to amputation, saying he had rather lose his life than his arm; the loss of which he did not wish to survive.

The fractured pieces of the bones, and ragged portions of the muscles were removed by the attending surgeons, Doctors BROWN and WALKER, after he was removed to Burlington, distant twenty five miles; by attentive and careful attention to his wound his arm was saved, and in addition to appearance, is of some use.

Two wounds of a similar description were received from cannon balls by two seamen of Commodore MACDONOUGH's fleet, on the eleventh September, 1814, in Plattsburgh bay. Upon both I applied the first dressings. Fragments of the humerus, clavicle and acromion process adhering to the lacerated muscles were removed, as well as such portions of the muscles as appeared to be deadened by the ball; the end of the fractured humerus which presented itself through the wound, was removed as low as possible with the saw; the superior extremity of the humerus which remained in the socked was detached by dividing its ligaments. The sound muscles which remained with the skin were secured by straps of adhesive plaster in as close contact as possible, without giving pain; the arm was permitted to retract to favour this contact. Large sloughings succeeded for some considerable

of the
direc-
nbent
stroy-
h the
n pro-
merus
by the
ocket.
tation.
o save
ly read
opera-
lligent,
te the
itation,
which

of the
BROWN
twenty
und his
e use.
om can-
fleet, on
n both I
clavicle
es were
eared to
is which
as pos-
us which
gaments.
secured
le, with-
vour this
siderable

time; the patients were supported with a soft generous diet, wine in moderate quantity and bark; and eventually recovered. A maimed arm is preferable to no arm, if only for its appearance. Where the loss of skin is as extensive as the wound, and little or none can be had for flaps, the cure, in the above instance was nearly as soon effected as it would have been had amputation been performed. Larrey exults, that by the operation nine cases out of ten will succeed.—But it will be understood, a loss of a limb and consequent deformity succeeds. Whereas I am convi. d that ten out of ten may be cured, where the patients have good health; the limb saved, with the small deformity of a too sudden sloping of the shoulder.

CASE FIFTH.

"If a spent or a rebounding ball strikes a limb obliquely, without causing a solution of continuity in the skin, as often happens, the parts which resist its action, such as the bones, the muscles, tendons, the aponeuroses, and the vessels may be broken and torn. The extent of the internal injury must be ascertained, and if the bones be fractured under the soft parts, and if there be grounds to suspect the vessels are lacerated (which may be known by the enlargement, and a kind of fluctuation) amputation should be performed without delay. But sometimes the vessels and the bones have been spared, and the muscles alone have been totally disorganized. Then an incision should be made in the skin; by this means the thick, black blood may be permitted to escape, and the consequences may be predicted."

CASE SIXTH.

"When the bursting of a bomb, or the stroke of a ball has fractured the orbicular extremities, more particularly those which form the knee, or the ankle joints, and when the ligaments which surround these articulations have been torn or broken up, immediate amputation becomes indispensably necessary. The same indications will present, if the foreign body bury itself in the thickest part of one of the orbicular extremities."

Doctor HALL, the translator of the works of LARREY, is opposed to his last opinion, and says "this advice should not be followed in all cases; where the ball is made of lead, and is no larger than a musket ball, it may remain many years in the joint, and perhaps during life, without causing much inconvenience after the first symptoms." The observation of Doctor HALL we believe correct. Wounds made by musket balls through the articular extremities have been cured without the loss of the limb. Besides there can be no inconvenience or hazard of life by attempting a cure, compared with the certain loss of the limb. A patient is willing to submit to extreme distress for the sake of a limb, if there is a distant prospect of saving it.

CASE SEVENTH.

"Has a ball or the fragment of a bomb passed through a limb, and denuded a large portion of its bone without fracturing it? In this case, although the soft parts may appear as if they might be saved, yet amputation is not less indicated. Yet, before a decision be made, all the symptoms should be attentively considered."

It is believed the above case seldom requires amputation in the first instance, especially where the ball is no larger than one projected from a musket. It is more advisable to wait, and be governed by consequences; and depend upon consecutive amputation if necessary.

CASE EIGHTH.

LARREY "adds another case in which primitive amputation is requisite; that is, when a great ginglymoid articulation, such as the elbow, and especially the knee is opened by a cutting instrument to a great extent, and a sanguineous effusion takes place in the joint. In these wounds the synovial membrane, the ligaments, and the aponeuroses inflame from the injury received and the contact of the air.

"Tumefaction and erethismus of the parts soon ensue, and acute pain, abscesses, deep fistulas, caries, fever from absorption, and death follow. I have seen a great number perish from this species of wounds, because the operation has been postponed from a hope that the limb might be preserved."

Doctor HALL, the translator, does not admit as conclusive evidence, the necessity of amputating when large joints are wounded. Of the cases adduced by LARREY, " one was brought to the hospital two days after he was wounded ; and in the second, the soldier walked two miles after having the knee opened by a sabre. Is it then surprising," adds Doctor HALL, " that fatal inflammation should ensue, where p⁃ ⁃ us, every necessary cause is combined to produce it? What d have been the result in these cases, if their wounds had received immediate surgical attention in the comfortable and temperate wards of a hospital ?"

A soldier of the 33d regiment was admitted into the hospital at Burlington, having received a wound through the knee. The ball entered at the external condyle of the femur, just under the upper edge of the patella, and passing obliquely downwards and backwards, made its exit where the inner condyle meets the tibia. Amputation was proposed. This was objected to by the patient. Six weeks after, this case came under my observation. The integuments of the knee joint were extremely swollen, the swelling extending up to the trunk. The leg and foot were enlarged and ædematous ; pus mixed with synova issued from the wound. Upon examination, a sinus extended from the external opening up under the muscles of the thigh, also between the muscles and femur on the internal and posterior parts. The capsular ligament appeared to be thickened and distended with matter. The patient, extremely emaciated, had suffered exceedingly from pain. Amputation was again proposed, but his first resolution was still adhered to. The sinuses were laid open up from the external, and from the internal wounds ; and a more depending opening was made on the back part between the two openings. A spiral bandage was applied upon the limb from the foot to the trunk. After ten days, the discharges from the sinuses lessened ; the swellings throughout the thigh and leg had much abated ; the wounds assumed a better appearance. Finally they healed and the limb was saved, but with a stiff joint.

The above wound not made by a cutting instrument, was

more hazardous. The case demonstrates that LARREY was too precipitate in making up his opinion.

The following case is similar to the last position, wherein LARREY recommends immediate amputation. A soldier received a sabre-wound on the knee, which divided the common tendon of the extensors of the leg, near its union with the patella, obliquely downwards. The patient was immediately put into bed, his leg extended, was largely bled, purged, and put on a vegetable diet. The lips of the wound were immediately brought into apposition by straps of adhesive plaster. This wound was cured by the first intention without suppuration.

In many cases it is difficult to determine, most correctly, whether it is best to amputate immediately, or defer it, to see if the limb may be saved—and if it cannot be saved, to operate at a future period. When an opinion is formed that the chance of saving a limb is greater than the risque of losing life by deferring an amputation until an experiment is made to save it—to defer the operation is proper.

While taking this into consideration, due weight should be given to all the circumstances which may tend to promote, retard, or prevent a cure.

When a case is of such a nature as would render a cure dubious under the best attendance, and most eligible situation—if circumstances do not admit of these, the operation should not be deferred; because a case, which is doubtful in the first instance, becomes, from unfavourable circumstances, not only hazardous, but fatal, under their influence.

The circumstances, which might determine the chances favourable and unfavourable, are many and various.

Where the wound is extremely hazardous from its nature, and the patient must be necessarily exposed to cold, wet, bad diet and lodgings; to defer amputation would be certain death; because the only chance for life would be to render his condition more comfortable by removing a part of the causes which enfeeble life, that life may be supported so as to overcome the remaining causes which endanger life.

When a wound, which may require amputation, is in its nature dubious, under all the comforts of life; if received when under a state of debility from bodily infirmities, the only chance will be to remove the limb immediately.

When a wound, which may require amputation, is received, under an epidemic state of atmosphere, or when an infectious disease prevails; to defer the operation would deprive the patient of every chance of life.

The above observations are particularly applicable to field practice.

Although there are cases which require immediate amputation on the field of battle, and without which life cannot be saved; yet we have to observe, that after the battles of Little York and Fort George, a less number survived primitive than consecutive amputation. From reports it was understood, that three or four died immediately after the amputation was performed on battle ground; whereas there was not a single case of death during the campaign, after consecutive amputation, occasioned by this operation.

Several amputations, performed immediately after the first symptoms were passed, were followed with success. Three were made by myself between five and seven weeks after their wounds were received, all of whom recovered. The amputation of these was delayed in the first instance, in expectation of saving the limb; but unavoidable exposures, on board transports, to wet, and motion of the vessels during a storm of several days, rendered amputation necessary after the wounded were landed on the Niagara. I also performed an amputation at Lewistown, upon a Canadian volunteer, belonging to the corps of Colonel WILCOX, twenty-one days after the wound was received, with success.

A musket ball shattered the femur about five inches below the great trocanter. This man remained with his corps and was attended by its surgeon, until the day previous to the operation, when he was received into the hospital at Lewistown, extremely emaciated and debilitated, with total loss of appetite. Sinuses were formed down the thigh its whole length; the leg was also extremely swollen and œdematous. In order to avoid a si-

28

nus running up, the amputation was made as near the trunk as possible. The first six days his case was doubtful. In consequence of great distention of the lymphatics, large discharges from their open mouths, followed the operation a number of days. After which his appetite was restored; the wound was entirely ealed in five weeks.

I performed an amputation in a similar case, at Plattsburgh, upon ———— WILLIAMS, a soldier of the 10th regiment from Virginia. This man was admitted into the hospital twenty-three days after the wound was received. The ball fractured the femur half way between its articulation with the tibia and the great trocanter. The thigh and leg were much enlarged; an œdematous swelling extended to the groin. Sinuses were formed through the muscles of the thigh in all directions—so that it was necessary to make the amputation as near the trunk as possible; and then it was discovered that a sinus continued up above the place of incision. This man's wound healed completely, and he was on his crutches in sixteen days after the operation.

When a wound is of such a nature, that, from the first, no cure may be calculated upon, no delay for the first symptoms to pass off should be admitted; an amputation should be immediately performed. It is acceded to by all, that the primary symptoms of a wound, which requires amputation, are more severe than those which succeed primitive amputation. Wherefore nothing is gained by waiting until the primary symptoms are over, but much is hazarded. The patient, convinced that amputation is necessary to preserve his life, has less hesitancy to the immediate operation, than the consecutive when it becomes necessary.

I have seen cases, where an amputation, performed immediately after the wound was received, might have saved life; and where the same limb might have been preserved by suitable means; and life eventually lost by neglect of proper management. Instances like these should not be brought as examples to demonstrate that delay was improper; they show the necessity of applying the means of cure most assiduously; and where these means are not at command, no delay of amputation should be permitted.

LARREY mentions four cases where consecutive amputation is required.

CASE FIRST.

When there is mortification on a limb; "if gangrene be *traumatic*, no time should be lost in removing it above the sphacelated part. The amputation will succeed, when the deleterious principle has not been copiously absorbed. There are many facts to support the doctrine."

EXAMPLE.

Report of a Case of Amputation, by J. B. WHITRIDGE, M. D. Hospital Surgeon's Mate, now a resident in Charleston, South Carolina.

"SIR—Permit me to offer you the following report of the case of JAMES PARKER, of the 13th regiment United States' Infantry, belonging to Captain PAIGE's company; who was wounded at Sandy Creek, and received into the general hospital at Sackett's harbor, on the 11th of June, 1814.

"This patient was wounded about six days previous to his being sent to the hospital, and received little or no treatment during that time, not even the common attention of nursing; of consequence his case was a very unfortunate one.

"I feel peculiarly interested in this case, as it is the only fatal case of simple amputation, which has occurred to me in the course of an extensive surgical practice, during the present war.

"A common musket bull, of nearly one ounce weight, and three buck shot, entered upon the inside of his right leg, near the edge, and at the superior portion of the gastrocnemius muscle. They passed in a direction obliquely upward, through a portion both of the tibia and fibula; the ball and two shot made their exit at the articulation of those two bones; extending the fracture into the articulation of the knee joint.

"The fracture was very extensive, and several large portions completely detached, while a large mass of the bones were reduced to very small fragments, approaching even to powder.

"When this patient was received into the general hospital, from Sandy Creek, transported by land, a distance of eighteen

miles, his leg was in a state of complete sphacelation, as high as
the wound.

" From a history of the case, it appeared that there had been
much hemorrhagy from the wound in the first instance, and during the first day of the accident; from this circumstance, and
from the course of the ball, it is probable the peroneal artery, or
perhaps the tibialis postica, was wounded; which, however, was
not particularly demonstrated after the operation.

" On the first day after his reception, carbonic acid gas, was
applied, in the form of a fermenting cataplasm to the whole limb.
Bark, (cinc. offs.) wine, and opium were given him. The evening following, a tinct. meloes vesicat. was applied to the gangrenous part, and the fermenting cataplasm re-applied over the
whole, with the hope of restoring the heat and circulation; but
in vain!—The bark, wine, and opium, and the fermenting poultices, were continued until 4 o'clock the day following; when a
consultation was called. Four hospital surgeons, and a number
of other medical gentlemen, both of the army and navy, being
present, (from the declension of his health,* and urgency of the
symptoms,) an immediate amputation was agreed on, though
under circumstances, not the most favorable.

" The inflammation and swelling about the knee, and along
the muscles of the thigh, having measurably abated, and the
progress of the mortification being checked—circumstances, which
were thought to warrant the operation; the limb was amputated about five inches above the knee joint; the skin below the
place of operation, having a somewhat livid appearance.

" The whole thigh still considerably swollen,§ and the integuments and muscles very rigid. After the integuments were divided, and the flap dissected up with a scalpel, the swelling and
rigidity were such, that it was with much difficulty reflected.

" It is remarkable in this case, that the muscles when first divided, shew very little disposition to retract.

* See DORSEY's Surg. Vol. 2d. p. 246.
§ Vide Mr. C. BELL's Operat. Surg. Vol. 1st. p. 270.

"I performed this operation by the triple incision, (something in the style of the celebrated M. Louis,† a French surgeon,) in the manner mentioned by Mr. S. Cooper‡ and recommended by Doctor Warren, jun. of Boston.

"Very little, however, was gained by this complicated mode of operation in this particular case. The superficial muscles, though first divided, retracted so little, that perhaps not more than a quarter, or three eights of an inch was gained by this second incision: by the third incision the deep seated muscles were divided, and the retractor applied without much effect, in consequence of the inflammation and swelling of the muscles, at the place of operation.

"The bone was sawed as high as possible, with the ordinary retraction; this, however, was very little above the division of the deep seated muscles.

"After the ligatures were made upon the blood vessels, the edges of the wound were placed in contact, which fit very neatly together, so as to form only a longitudinal line; and secured in that situation by adhesive plaster. The stump was then dressed, and the patient placed in bed. He rested very well the night following, and appeared to be very much relieved by the operation.

"The local arterial action for the first two or three days after the operation, was inconsiderable; but the general action something above the healthy standard; so that he would bear no stimulus above his ordinary food, and for that he had not much appetite.

"On the fourth day, in consequence of the bandages becoming foul, it was thought advisable to dress it. On removing the dressings, it was observed, although the lips of the wound were perfectly in contact, no union of any consequence had taken place. As soon as the adhesive straps were removed, the lips of the wound fell immediately asunder: no granulations had formed; suppuration had not taken place; the muscles were shrunk and contracted, and had assumed a pale and almost col-

† For his method consult Mem. de l'Acad. de Chirurgie.
‡ See Cooper's First-Lines, p. 426.

ourless appearance ; but which was pre-eminently the case at
the subsequent dressings. There seemed to be a want of action
in the parts; as it afterwards appeared, there was not action
sufficient to excite adhesive inflammation.*

" By the medical gentlemen present, this first dressing was
thought premature : had it not been dressed so soon, perhaps adhesion might have taken place. The parts were then placed in
contact, and the dressings applied as before. Cinc. off. was
administered in as large quantities as the stomach would bear.
As much wine was given as the patient could be made to take,
and occasionally a few drops of the tinct. opii.

" By the advice of the faculty, the dressings were not again removed until the third † day following ; at which time it had become very foul. On remov'ng the adhesive straps, it appeared
no union had taken place ; the lips of the wound fell immediately apart as before : no granulations had taken place from the bottom, and very little suppuration. The muscles had contracted
still more, and left the bone quite bare ;‡ they were shrunk and
pale, and indicated a total want of action. The stump was thoroughly washed with a strong solution of soap. Bark in powder
was then introduced in large quantities, into every part of the
wound, to endeavour, by its co-operation with the stimulus of the
soap, to excite it into action. The parts were then placed in
contact, and the wound dressed as before.

" At this time diarrhœa supervened, which occasioned the
use of an additional quantity of the tinc. opii.

" The anorexia and debility increased. Nourishing food was
given him—such as rich soup, milk porridge, panada, &c. in such
quantities as he could be made to take. Bark, wine, and laudanum were also continued in large quantities.

" Tuesday, the 21st. It was dressed as before : medicines
continued—had the patient sponged all over with St. Croix
rum, and the stump frequently wet with it—substituted milk-
punch, instead of wine for common drink. The patient now be-

* See Bell's Operat. Surg. vol. 4st, p. 246.
† See Dorsey's Surg. vol. 2d. p. 251.
‡ Vide Bell's Operat. Surg. vol. 1st. p. 290, Amer. Ed.

came somewhat lethargic and stupid, with a slight diseœa. Though restless and uneasy, from the time of the operation, complained of no pain in his leg, but pain in his back and hips from fatigue of lying, and would frequently roll from side to side, regardless of the stump; instead of resting it on the pillow upon which it was placed, would suffer it to hang without any support, or lie any way he happened to turn.

" Wednesday, 22d. Though the integuments covered the bone handsomely, the muscles had retracted so much that it was evident a cure could not be effected without a removal* of a portion of the bone, either by a natural or artificial process. The process of exfoliation is so tedious, that it was thought advisable, to remove it by means of the saw. The crureus muscle was re-divided by the scalpel. Not apprehending any difficulty from the hemorrhage of the blood vessels of this small muscle, though provided with a tourniquet, I did not take the precaution to apply it, until reduced to that necessity by the hemorrhagy. A retractor was then placed on, and by powerful retraction I was enabled to remove an inch and a quarter of the os femoris.

" I proceeded to secure the blood vessels : they were, however, so small, and the muscular fibres so tender, that they could not be taken up by the tenaculum. I passed a needle round a plexus of vessels which appeared to bleed most, without having much effect upon the hemorrhagy. I passed it round a second and a third time, without completely restraining it. It appeared to bleed from the whole surface of the divided muscle.

" The fact was, the debility of the divided muscle, and the parts adjacent was such, that there was not sufficient power in the blood vessels to retract themselves. The blood, though probably oozing from minute branches of arteries, appeared to be completely deoxygenized, and had the appearance of venous blood.

" The stimulus of cold was not alone sufficient to produce that contraction necessary to restrain the hemorrhagy. I therefore applied cold, undiluted spirits, which immediately produced

* See Mr. C. Bell's Operative Surg. vol. 1st. p. 263, 264, and 290.

a retraction of the vessels, and the hemorrhage ceased. The stump was then washed all over with spirits, and dressed as before. Milk-punch was given him freely, and the whole body sponged with rum three or four times in the course of the day. The anorexia and debility increased, pulse quick, small, and frequent. Bark, wine, and laudanum continued.

" Thursday, the 23d. No action had taken place; the stump was dressed as before. The same treatment continued, with the greatest possible energy. The patient became more comatose; the disecœa increased, and all those symptoms supervened which are the precursors of death.

" He survived until about one o'clock in the morning of the 24th, when the cold and pallid hand of death visited him, which terminated the tragic scene !"

" With sentiments of esteem, and the highest respect,

your very humble servant,

J. B. WHiTRIDGE."

Dr. James Mann, Hos. Surgeon.
"Sackett's Harbour, June 28th, 1814."

The following cases of gun-shot wounds, where the operation was delayed to preserve the limbs, and a consecutive amputation became necessary, is here detailed at full, as reported by hospital surgeon's mate, March, to show, that in similar cases, immediate amputation should be made; as well as to describe the feelings of a young surgeon, when performing his first amputation.

" Jacob Blunt, a private in Capt. Van Vechten's company, 23d regiment, 24 years old, in the action at Sackett's Harbour, 29th May, 1813, received a grape-shot in his leg, which shattered the tibia and fibula. It soon inflamed and became much swollen. Cloths wet with diluted spirits were continually applied. By the fourth day the limb was so much swollen as to induce Doctor Trowbridge to make several incisions through the integuments, from just below the knee to the ancle. At this time mortification had considerably progressed. The leg assumed a mixed colour of yellow and purple; the cuticula was raised in small blisters.   The leg and thigh were continually wet with cold rum and water, until the tenth of June, when the mortification had ceased.   Inflammation had disappeared from both leg and thigh so much, that an amputation was determined upon.   Upon the 11th of June I performed the operation in the following manner just above the knee.   I gave the patient, 30 minutes before the operation was commenced, two grains of opium, when he was placed on a high table.   After the application of the tourniquet, Doctor TROWBRIDGE, my operative assistant, grasped the thigh with both hands, and kept the integuments steady, while the first incision was made down to the fascia; after which he retracted the integuments as much as possible, while I dissected them up from the muscles with a scalpel.   Having dissected the skin with the cellular substance about an inch and half up, and turned them back on the thigh, at this point, I made a second incision with a steady and firm stroke of the knife around the thigh down to the bone.   [NOTE. It requires considerable strength and firmness to carry the knife through the thick muscles and firm tendons, at one stroke.   If we are not aware of this, we shall fail in our first attempt.   At the moment the incision is made, the venous and arterial blood gushes out in such torrents, as to alarm the young surgeon, performing his first amputation, fearful that the tourniquet was not sufficiently secure.   But soon I found the blood issued from the veins and arteries below the incision, when apprehension of danger ceased.]

" The muscles being divided down to the bone, the operative assistant applied the retractor, made of new strong linen, (preferable to leather,) and drew back the divided muscles, while I dissected the muscles from the bone one inch or more, when the bone was divided with the saw, and arteries taken up with the tenaculum.   In this case they were five ; more in number than usual.   After sponging the stump with warm water to clear away the clotted blood to search for other bleeding vessels, and finding none, I turned down the integuments over the stump, and secured them in apposition, with strips of adhesive plaster, and dressed in the usual method.

29

" Upon the 4th or 5th day, the dressings were removed ; the adhesive straps had not adhered with sufficient force ; the lips of the integuments had separated to the distance of an inch or more. New strips were applied, and the lips brought together as near as possible without using force. This man was afterwards dressed by others, and confined in a room with many, both wounded and sick with typhus. He, in a few days, was also seized with the fever, and died in about thirty-six days after the amputation.

" Had this patient been removed from a foul, crowded hospital, as soon as the limb had been taken off, and received that attention his case required, there is little doubt but he would have recovered in a reasonable time. But, without charging the surgeons and nurses with negligence, it is not to be expected that 150 wounded men could receive every necessary attention which their sufferings demanded."

REMARKS.

This case was attended at Sackett's Harbour, where the author was not at the time. He has heretofore observed, that no infectious disease was generated at those points where he performed duty. The above patient, agreeably to the statement, lost his life in consequence of being placed in a foul hospital. If an hospital is foul, no person but the director can be censured. When patients die in foul hospitals, the surgeons are as culpable for their deaths, as if they had been improperly treated by medicine or wholly neglected. A foul hospital is no excuse for want of success in practice.

The following case reported by hospital surgeon's mate MARCH.

Upon the 6th July, 1813, SIMEON GRANT, of Castine, District of Maine, a sailor belonging to the schooner Scourge, on Lake Ontario, commanded by sailing-master OSGOOD, being in a saw-mill, his hand was caught by the saw, and was separated at the wrist joint, the carpal bones were torn asunder by a stroke of the saw; no hemorrhage succeeded. An immediate amputation was performed about half way between the wrist and elbow, by semicircular and angular incisions; their angles meeting on the outside of the ulna and radius. The dressings were removed the fourth day; it was not found necessary to remove the adhesive straps until the day following, when the lips of the wound were nearly in contact, and the integuments united by the first intention. After the 6th day the ligatures were solicited, but were not removed until the 12th and 15th. In four weeks the cure was finished.

REMARK.

Union of the integuments, over the stump of an amputation, succeeds immediate amputation more frequently than consecutive.

CASE SECOND.

When there is a convulsive spasm in the wounded limb. "If a limb be amputated as soon as tetanus appears, all communication between the origin of the disease, and the general system is cut off. This division removes the nervous pain, by separating the local irritation from the rest of the body; if this is performed before the general system partakes of the diseased mobility of the muscles, caused by their sympathising with this wounded part, tetanus will be obviated. But if tetanus has become general, it is doubtful whether amputation will succeed to remove the spasm. The momentary pain produced by the operation, cannot augment the existing irritation. The pains of tetanus, over-balancing those which arise from the operation, make it more supportable, and diminish the intensity of pain, especially when the nerves of the limb are strongly compressed."

During the campaigns, no instance of tetanus, either from wounds or any other cause came within my observation.

CASE THIRD.

"*Vitiated suppuration.*—It often happens in gun-shot wounds, complicated with fracture, that in opposition to the best directed care, suppuration becomes putrid, and the bony fragments are

enveloped in pus, and have no disposition to unite. Hectic fever
and colliquative diarrhœa weaken the patient, and in this extremity amputation has saved his life, and by removing the source
of matter absorbed, the above evils are obviated." The wound,
from being complicated, becomes simple. The system recovers
from its languid state, as soon as causes opposed to healthy action are removed." I have witnessed cases of the above description, where cures progressed astonishingly quick after amputation was performed.

Gun-shot wounds of the thigh, complicated with a fracture
of the femur, may, in most instances, be cured by the immediate
application of DESAULT's splints, constructed for extension and
counter-extension of the limb. Doctor PHYSICK of Philadel-
phia, has improved DESAULT's plan. Some within my knowledge have had their limbs saved by them; while many have
not only lost limbs, but lives for want of their seasonable employment.

CASE FOURTH.

Bad state of the stump.—The cure of stumps is arrested by
fevers, and exposures to cold. Subsequent to the battle of Little
York, the wounded were exposed in tents, on the Niagara, in the
month of May, wanting warmer accommodations. The integuments preserved to cover the surface of the stump, did not unite
for want of adhesive inflammation; large vitiated suppurations,
a retraction of the muscles round the bone, which left it projecting beyond the surface of the wound, from one to two inches,
supervened. These projecting ends of the bones were amputated. The cures of several were retarded by exposures to cold
and unhealthy situations. After the sick were removed to Lewistown, the weather became more pleasant; the wounds assumed
a better appearance and finally were healed.

We coincide with LARREY in opinion, that " under any circumstance, amputation should be the last resort. But when
there is a decided necessity for performing it, there should be no
hesitation nor delay. The operation should be performed before the invasion of the primitive symptoms. If they have tak-

en place when the surgeon is called to the assistance of the wounded, he should wait until the first inflammation is removed." LARREY establishes it as a principle, where a ball has fractured the femur at the condyles, to perform the amputation immediately. Wounds of the thigh with fractures, are always dangerous, and if not immediately secured in a state of extension by DESAULT's or PHYSICK's method, the limb cannot be saved. Where the radius is shattered, and ulna fractured near the elbow, LARREY divides the aponeurosis, removes the splinters, and dresses the wound with a view to preserve the limb. All sphacelated limbs in consequence of gun-shot wounds, as well as extensive lacerations, require immediate amputation.

Gun-shot wounds through the trunk, are not always necessarily mortal. Men frequently survive wounds through the lungs, by musket balls and the bayonet, also through the abdomen. It cannot be always ascertained to what extent a viscus is injured; whether an intestine or an important blood-vessel is lacerated. When either of these last have taken place, the event will soon determine. But in cases where the membranous coverings of the viscera are only wounded, and the extreme danger arises from consecutive inflammation, the intention is to obviate its excess by liberal blood-letting. A ball passed through the left lobe of the lungs, the man fell on his face, and fainted from loss of blood. His position on the ground favored the egress of blood from the wounded chest. After two hours, he was found with scarcely the symptoms of life, was taken to the hospital and eventually recovered. In this case, there is no doubt, the excessive loss of blood was a cause of recovery, by obviating high inflammation. Repeated instances of similar cases may be related, where wounds from the same cause had a favorable termination. The more blood expended the better, in wounds of the viscera, provided life is not exhausted, when hemorrhage is stopped.

A soldier at Greenbush was wounded by a bayonet, which entered the left of the spine, passed through the trunk below the diaphragm. This man was attacked with puking, and suffered extreme pain. He was bled immediately; the operation was repeated as pain indicated, until he lost two quarts in thirty-six hours. Anodynes were administered. The bowels were kept open by injections. Within three days the puking ceased, when the man became composed. At the expiration of three weeks, the wound healed without suppuration; at the same time he was seen to bring a bucket of water in each hand, sixty rods. It is good practice to bleed in all cases of wounds by musket balls, or bayonet, where there is but little loss of blood from the wound.

An officer at Little York, was wounded by a bayonet, in the axilla, which divided the artery; he bled until he fainted, when the hemorrhage ceased. This wound was cured without any unpleasant accident, the consequence of excessive loss of blood. Bleeding from a wounded axillary artery, may be stopped by a compression immediately under the clavicle. Sometimes it has been found necessary to dissect down through the integuments, over the artery under the clavicle, and secure it at that point with a ligature.

When loss of blood is accompanied with deliquium animi, hemorrhagia frequently ceases spontaneously, and life is preserved, provided stimulants are not hastily administered. Temporary faintness may be obviated by them, while their effects are permanently injurious. In these cases the patients should be supported by soft nutritious vegetable diet, at first only sufficient to support life, afterwards by milk. Animal nutriment should be prohibited, until symptoms indicate that the wounds of the viscera are healed. Gun-shot wounds through the lungs are always accompanied with more or less cough and expectoration. These are increased by indulgence in the use of stimulating drinks and diet. To allay irritation opium is necessary. The external wounds always heal before the lungs become sound. Instances have occurred, where upon the closing of the external wound, the lungs have exhibited increased symptoms of danger, which have been obviated by removing the cicatrix and making an opening into the chest, at the most depending wound. Chinchona, which is too frequently and indiscriminately administered in gun-shot wounds, is of no use in wounds of the lungs. On the northern frontiers we had full evidence of the truth of the above position. In cases of amputation, the bark was but seldom necessary.

I have frequently observed evils originate from the liberal administration of bark and wine in gun-shot wounds, especially in cases of amputation. I amputated a leg in consequence of a caries of the tarsal bones, produced by a wound from a sharp instrument. The patient at the time had a cough, accompanied with hectic fever. The complaint on the lungs was thought to be symptomatic, and it was believed by removing the diseased foot, the complaint on the lungs would disappear. But we were disappointed. The amputated wound assumed a favourable aspect. For the cough and hectic symptoms were adminstered camp. tinc. of opium and antimonial wine. After the first week the patient was dressed by a young assistant, who immediately proposed bark and wine; to which I objected. At the expiration of four days, the wound upon examination was found in a bad state; the hectic symptoms had increased with loss of appetite, when it was made known that the bark and wine had been administered contrary to my orders. Then the case was taken into my hands. An emetic was prescribed. After which the camp. tinc. of opium and antimonial wine were again resorted to. In two days the cough and hectic symptoms subsided, appetite returned, the appearance of the wound improved. With a continuance of the last medicine, a soft nutritious diet and wine in small quantities, in a few days the wound was cicatrized, and cough and hectic fever were removed.

I have never experienced any benefit from chinchona and stimulants, where amputations were immediately performed, after the wound was received. They induced, in most instances, inflammations, abscesses and ill conditioned sinuses.

In consecutive amputation, even when the patient is much emaciated, bark is injurious until the suppurative stage has supervened. In army practice, amputations, where the superficies of the wounds is covered with the integuments, seldom heal by the first intention. Primitive inflammations, the consequence of gun-shot wounds, with fractures, extend generally throughout the limb, which in twelve or fourteen days becomes edematose,

if not obviated by emollients. The swelling commences where
the bone is fractured. When the swelling is not remedied by
permanent extension and spiral bandages, extensive sinuses are
formed between the muscles; which demand amputation of the
limb to preserve life.

PHYSICK's improvement on DESAULT's method of extension
and counter-extension in compound fractures by gun-shots, obviates many unpleasant symptoms. By this support, the fractured
extremities of the bones are preserved in their natural position;
irritation, a cause of inflammation, extensive suppuration and
deep-seated sinuses are obviated. Extension and counter-extension obviate the contraction of the muscles, which shorten the
limb, when a portion of the bone is destroyed and removed.
Where there is no loss of bone, with a diagonal fracture, by
means of PHYSICK's splints, the limb may be retained at its full
length; while pain is mitigated, as irritation from the sharp ends
of the bones is prevented. Too many attempts were made to
preserve a limb, in cases of compound fractures, without the use
of PHYSICK's splints. It was urged by those opposed to the
method, that extension could not be endured by the patients.
To my knowledge, their conditions were infinitely more tolera-
ble with PHYSICK's splints than without them. At the commencement of the war, only a few surgeons of the army had
witnessed their benefit. Time and experience were necessary
to remove prejudices. PHYSICK's improvement is to be preferred to DESAULT's; the extension being completely under the
command of the patient.

A surgeon may operate well, still he may not be a proficient
in his art. After an operation, if he is not well acquainted with
the animal economy, he cannot cure the wound. A clean
wound upon a healthy person will readily heal by retaining its
sides in contact; yet a different practice is necessary, or more
is required, where the constitution is impaired; a knowledge of
which is only acquired by inspection, and practice of dressing.
Scientific surgery is so intimately connected with a medical education, that to be a proficient in the healing art, he should be a
practical surgeon. By practical surgery—an attendance on

dressings of wounds and ulcers, the nature of the living body is more thoroughly investigated, and habits and temperaments more correctly acquired. External inflammations, with their most suitable treatments, lead to a knowledge of internal affections of a similar nature. As much information may be gained of the internal states of the human body by the appearance of ulcers, as by feeling the skin and pulse. The effects of external applications are allied to internal. Practical surgery familiarizes us with the active principles of life in all temperaments. More attention is often paid to operative surgery than to scientific. Some ulcers require stimulant applications, while others demand emollients. This knowledge is only acquired by practice. An amputation may be well performed by one little skilled in medicine; while to cure a wound and preserve a limb require the talents of the most experienced practitioners. To become a good surgeon a man must be a good physician. These professions are inseparably connected. The aspect of a wound frequently points out the state of the body, and indicates the most suitable remedies. A correct method of practice is founded on practical facts and observations, not on speculative opinions. The first are stable, the last fluctuating. Experience directs our reason, and impresses on the mind facts, in a manner which language cannot. Curative indications are founded upon an acquaintance with the laws of animal life both in health and disease. In cases of wounds, to form an opinion how they will terminate, more depends on the habit of the body and part injured, than on the application of a dressing. Upon a robust patient, an inflammation will supervene proportionate to the injury done, or other concomitant casualties; upon one weak and feeble, a wound may be succeeded by spasms and convulsions. These morbid dispositions are to be obviated by different and opposite remedies, known only to the practical, scientific surgeon. In incised wounds where the skin, cellular membrane and muscles are divided, it only requires to bring the divided parts in contact, and secure them in that position by straps of sticking plaster, with a pledget of any mild soft ointment to exclude the air; when, if the patient is of a healthy habit, a re-union of

30

the divided parts will follow, and in a few days he will be cured
by the first intention. Here inflammation only sufficient to effect adhesion takes place between the sides of the wound. But
a bad habit of body, or irregularities of life will prevent this happy and speedy termination of the wound, and will require such
medical treatment as appearances may indicate. Where there
is much inflammation, bleeding and emollient applications are
demanded ; perhaps cathartics, as neutral salts, or castor oil, as
well as antimonials. Where there is debility, tonics and stimulants are necessary. An incorrect practice of securing the sides
of divided muscles by stitches or sutures should be avoided,
when a few strips of adhesive plaster of linen will better fulfil
the intention, without causing irritation and inducing inflammation and pain. A suitable application of plasters and bandages will generally secure divided muscles in apposition ; and
even where wounds are contused and lacerated by blunt instruments, a retention of their sides in as close union as possible by
straps of adhesive plasters, obviates great suppuration, and ex-
pedites their filling up with new granulations, and accelerates
cicatrization.

It has been already noticed in the preceding sketches, that
many soldiers, after their passage down lake Ontario and river
St. Lawrence, were afflicted with edematose swelled legs. In
many instances, the swellings were accompanied with both fun-
gous and callous ulcers ; the consequence of long exposures to
cold, wet and inclement weather ; also, a want of exercise of
the lower extremities while on their passage down in open boats,
confined on their seats ; supported with coarse, and in some instances damaged rations, irregularly administered, or after long
periods of abstinence. Under these circumstances a small scratch
soon enlarged, and by frequent exposures in water, deteriorated
to a most formidable ulcer, in extent from six to twelve inches
up and down the legs.

The following treatment was adopted ;—after the ulcers were
washed clean with water, in which a little soap was dissolved,
adhesive straps were applied across them so as to support the
pendent muscles on the side opposite, as well as the integuments

cured
to ef-
But
is hap-
e such
there
ns are
oil, as
stimu-
e sides
oided,
r fulfil
inflam-
d ban-
n; and
instru-
ible by
nd ex-
elerates

es, that
id river
gs. In
oth fun-
ures to
rcise of
n boats,
ome in-
ter long
scratch
riorated
e inches

ers were
issolved,
port the
guments

at the margin of the ulcers. Over the straps was applied dry lint, instead of pledgets armed with ointment. To remove fungosities, the nitrate of silver was applied; and when the ulcers shewed little, or no disposition to granulate, the surface was occasionally stimulated with merc. precip. rub. Over the whole dressing was applied a spiral bandage, commencing at the toes and extending above the knee; and where the swelling had attacked the thigh, the spiral bandage was continued up to the trunk of the body. Cathartics were occasionally administered. When the ulcers continued ill-conditioned after the above means were employed, the chinchona was directed to give tone, but seldom with any benefit excepting in cases of sphacelus. A laudable digestion and healthy granulation was better promoted by calomel in small doses. When the patients were restrained from ardent spirits, and confined to a milk and vegetable diet with light soups, their recovery was astonishingly rapid. During the winter 1813—14, there were in the hospital at Burlington more than one hundred of the above described cases.

The following case of anthrax admitted into the hospital at Malone, is worthy of being recorded in detail. A small swelling appeared immediately over the vertebræ of the neck, equidistant from the occiput and the first dorsal vertebre, not unlike, at first, a small phlegmon, but as it progressed it was characterized with marks essentially different. It commenced with shooting pains through the tumor, which at first was red, and after a few days livid; when were noticed upon its surface small vesicles filled with a thin yellowish matter. The tumefaction continued to extend from its centre to the circumference in every direction. When the vesicles burst, the subjacent cutis was found perforated, exhibiting small ulcerations throughout the tumor, scarcely large enough to admit the blunt end of a probe; through which issued, when the tumor was compressed, a small quantity of purulent matter. At this period the tumor felt spongy in its texture, deep and firmly attached to the subjacent parts, and assumed at its centre a black appearance; then dry, hard and depressed, while its circumference continually enlarged.

The gangrene progressively and rapidly extended from its centre to the circumference.

This patient when admitted into the hospital at Malone was extremely emaciated and debilitated. The sympathetic fever, which usually accompanies phlegmonous inflammation did not exist; the tongue was dry and of a dirty yellow. A soft nutritious diet with wine was prescribed during the first state of the disease. An emollient poultice of the bark of slippery elm was applied over the swelling. On the fourth day appeared the small vesicles; on the fifth the chinchona with an increased quantity of wine was directed; on the eighth day the tumor was sphacelated throughout its whole extent; when the mortified parts were separated from the sound by Doctor VANHON, hospital mate. The diameter of the open ulcer then was not less than five inches. The wound was washed with diluted muriatic acid, and filled with chinchona in powder. The bark in substance was administered in quantity as much as the stomach could bear with wine. The eleventh day the mortified loose parts which were attached to the wound sloughed off from the sound, and exposed to view some of the processes of the vertebræ of the neck. The dressings of bark were continued a few days, until new granulations were seen rising from the surface of the wound; when the usual dressings of lint and a pledget spread over with cerate were applied. As the wound filled up from its base, it contracted in its dimensions, and in a few weeks was reduced from a deep, extensive, fetid, gangrenous, to a healthy, superficial ulcer, the size of half a dollar; and was, a short period after, completely cicatrized.

A soldier, —— BROWN, was admitted into the hospital at Lewistown in July, 1813, who had previously been reduced by fever and diarrhœa. When admitted, his extremities and face were extremely emaciated, and his abdomen much swollen and tense. It was, on first inspection, apprehended that the swelling was dropsical. From his general emaciated appearance and extreme debility, it was believed he could survive but a few days; and not being a subject for active medicine, the only indication, which his miserable condition pointed out, was such support as soft nutriment and wine, with opium to procure ease, might afford. After three weeks the attending surgeon, to my astonishment, reported him still living; when he proposed to perform the operation of paracentesis on the abdomen. At this period being confined to my tent, and not having seen this patient after the first examination of the case, the operation was performed in the presence of no surgeon. The following day upon enquiry, it was learnt that the opening was made in the region of the liver; and that a discharge of pus followed the operation. The patient still lived; at the expiration of three weeks the case was examined by myself, when it was very evident that the trochar not only penetrated the parietes of the abdomen, but into the cist of an abscess in the liver; the discharges from the opening had gradually enlarged the external puncture to the size of an inch and quarter in diameter. Notwithstanding all the unfavourable circumstances of the case, the general health of the body was improved; the appetite was better, the stomach was capable of receiving more nourishment than at first; milk being the principal diet. Now bark and wine were administered with good effect. His health continued to improve, so that he was able to leave that frontier. The winter following he was seen either at Greenbush or Burlington hospital in a good state of health; the opening into the liver having entirely healed.

OF HOSPITALS.

THE social affections have enlarged their sphere of operation, as the arts and sciences have progressed. No longer confined to a small circle, they embrace not only nations, but the human race as one family. Dissentions and their bitter consequences are nevertheless excited between nations. As in the small family contested interests engender strife; so in the large, contentions more extensive and permanent are productive of destructive warfare, merciless devastations and a miserable waste of human life.

In proportion to the value, a people estimate their property and privileges, the defence of them will be sanguinary. The most valuable of all possessions are liberty and independence. In support of these, the lives of thousands are sacrificed. To maintain these, wars the most vindictive have existed. Still under the highest excitements of inflicted injuries and violated rights, the soothing influences of civilization ameliorate the evils attendant on these national calamities. They render the condition of the conquered less severe, as they soften the ferocious temper and disposition of man.

Uncivilized man inflicts upon his captive the most dreadful tortures, or death. If, in any instance, life is preserved, it is to subject him to ignominious slavery. The sick and wounded prisoner never excites a feeling of compassion in the breast of his savage conquerors, but is generally doomed to suffer.

The wars of civilized nations to the conquered are less dreadful than of savage. To become a prisoner to the first is not the wor   evils. The captive soldier is no longer viewed as an enemy. He receives from the victor every attention which humanity dictates, and circumstances allow. The healing balm is applied to his wounds, and his dispirited heart is revived by the cordial draught. Instances, however, there have been, where the conqueror, divesting himself of the fine feelings which characterize the human heart in civil society, has satiated his thirst for revenge, by inflicting misery and distress when the fortune of war has placed his enemy in his possession. Crimsoned with the blood of a defenceless prisoner, the victor, although educated in civil life, is but a savage.

In ancient wars pestilence and disease were more destructive to armies than the sword of the enemy. Ignorant of their causes, the Gods were believed by the multitude the immediate, or secret agents of pestilential calamities. To avert their mortality, prayers and incantations were resorted to, instead of more appropriate measures—cleanliness and ablutions. Prophylactic means were neglected; putrid gasses, mefitic airs, and marsh miasmata had no place in ancient nomenclatures; while armies were wasted by diseases, generated by them and their own filth. In proportion as superstition has yielded its influence upon the mind to general science, so have philanthropy and benevolence prevailed, and human calamities been overcome, or their causes obviated.

Medical philosophy investigates the disease, and points out its preventive and curative means; while ingenuity is called into action in war, to furnish the instruments of human destruction.

In modern times, systems of military operations, plans of attacks, and methods of slaughter, are not the only preparatory measures for warfare. Accommodations for the sick and wounded of an army, are among the first considerations of military expeditions.

Hospitals are established, to which a medical staff is assigned, distinct from that immediately attached to the line of army. The medical department is not its least important appendage, and when well appointed, may, by its efforts, ensure strength, and give energy to its movements; not merely by attention to the sick and wounded, but by recommending precautionary measures, to secure to the soldiery, health, and obviate diseases, to which, in the tented field, men are subjected.

The good of service requires that the medical staff of an army be not only well appointed, but respected by the officers of the line. Without due respect, advice, given by surgeons however correct, will not be regarded, especially by young inexperienced officers. Invested as they are with authority, they often affect to despise counsel offered by surgeons; who, under the present establishment, have no rank nor command in the army.

The medical department will never command that degree of confidence and respectability from officers of the line, necessary to promote its greatest usefulness, until it is more immediately protected by government. It was frequently the case, during the war, that commissioned officers, of inferior grades, intruded themselves into the hospitals, without consulting the attending surgeons, and without their knowledge ordered out of the wards the convalescent men; and when detected in such unmilitary conduct, justified themselves by claims of superior rank. Officers commanding regiments, who had been long in service, were guilty of similar misdemeanours. Interferences of this description, at the commencement of the war, were extremely vexatious to the surgeons. In one instance, a Colonel ordered his Quarter-master to take possession of barracks already occupied by the sick, who, weak and infirm as they were, left their beds, and preferred to expose themselves without doors, on the ground, to being crowded and overrun by healthy rude men. At another time, a sergeant regularly appointed to perform the duty of Steward in a hospital, was, at the moment of making issue of stores to the sick, taken from his duty by a file of men under arms, by an order from the Commandant of his regiment, for the alleged crime of neglecting to join his regiment, upon his order.

Irregularities like these were remedied only by a special order of the Commanding General. Whereas, had the surgeons been invested with explicit and distinct powers, in their own department, and these inserted among the rules and regulations of the army, troublesome collisions would have been avoided.

That the medical staff of the army was not respected in proportion to its importance, was evinced by facts which are not justified upon any principle, civil or military. They were engaged in more unpleasant rencounters with officers of the line, than those officers were with each other. As many of the surgeons of the army sacrificed their lives in support of what was falsely called their honour, as of commissioned officers of the line. These fatal evils occurred at periods when medical assistance was most in demand.

The first transition to which a recruit is exposed, when he quits domestic employment for a camp, is a change of diet. Vegetables, excepting bread, are not a part of his ration. The meat allowance is more than he requires were vegetables made a part of his ration; and where it might be convenient to commute a part of the meat for beans and peas, it would conduce to his health. But, in active services, the proposed commutation would be impossible, as the transportation of animal food, being less bulky, is less expensive. The beef ration of an army frequently travels with the troops.

A change of lodgings from dry houses to tents, exposed to atmospheric damps, and evaporations from the ground, predispose men to disease, by obstructing perspiration. This, in some degree, may be obviated by woolen shirts, at all seasons, on the north-western frontiers.

The sick and wounded of an army, when suffered to continue with their corps, impede military operations. It has, on this account, been found expedient, in modern wars, to select some convenient post for the establishment of hospitals. Positions not too remote from the scenes of action, nor where they may be exposed to depredations of an enemy, should be chosen. A cultivated country, where milk could be procured, as well as vegetables, is preferable to towns, or thick settled villages. The situation of hospitals should be at such points, which least interfere with extensive military movements of an enemy, and his opposing army. Although, agreeably to modern warfare, hospitals are respected by an enemy; yet, established within the compass of active movements of armies, they are exposed to be deprived of such necessary supplies, as are furnished by the circumjacent country.

Elevated lands, which command a free circulation of air, and an abundance of good water, are preferable to plains, for the site of hospitals. They should be erected at a distance from extensive woods, where it is possible; in an open country, remote from marshes, or swampy lands; and beyond the influences of winds, whose currents of air are infected with miasmata generated on sunken lands; and are known to convey with them the seeds of disease.

A military hospital which is considered temporary, built of rough materials, should never be but one story in height.

The attendants of a second story have additional duty to perform; the sick in the wards beneath are incommoded by the necessary noise of walking on the floors over their heads. In the upper wards the observance of cleanliness is with difficulty enforced. Attendants, rather than give themselves the labour of descending a flight of stairs to execute their duty, take liberties of throwing filth from windows above, to the annoyance of patients below, without possibility of detection.

The wards of a military hospital should have an east and west aspect, with windows on each side. On the west, a closed passage should extend the length of the hospital 12 feet wide, into which the doors of the several wards open. The passage should be furnished with windows, which correspond with those of the wards. This passage will be commodious for the patients able to walk, where they will be secure from cold and wet. In front of this should be an open piazza projecting ten feet, where the patients may walk unexposed to the rays of the sun in hot weather. By means of two walls and the roof of a piazza, heat will be excluded the rooms, which is at its highest in hot seasons, after the sun has passed the meridian. These walls will also secure the wards from cold, during the severe frosts of winter.

Wards of an extensive hospital should be thirty feet by twenty four in dimension, and not less than eleven feet in height; which may accommodate twenty patients, if not sick with contagious diseases. This number in a ward requires only two nurses, when their diet is prepared in kitchens. The wards of Burlington hospital, (which had the reputation of being under the best regulations of any in the northern district) are twenty four feet by twenty, and nine feet high. These rooms were found by experience to be too low. The windows of the wards should be constructed so that the upper sash may fall, and the under rise at pleasure; that when ventilating them, the air may have free access to the rooms, without passing in currents immediately over the beds of the sick.

Convenient rooms should be appropriated for offices. One to contain hospital stores under the charge of the steward of the hospital; one for the use of the ward master, under whose care is placed the furniture and bedding; one to be improved as a dispensary; one room for a kitchen, and one for washing.

The hospital department should be furnished with spare clothing as well as bedding, for men who are frequently admitted destitute. During the war it was frequent that the wounded lost their clothing in battle. Many, after the action at Little York, were received without an article except what they had on their backs, who, in consequence, were not only dirty, but covered with tribes of lice. As soon as their circumstances were reported, the commander in chief ordered cloth for shirts, but they could not be furnished before the men suffered for want of a change of garments.

Each patient should be provided with a separate bed in a moveable bunk. When bunks are attached to the walls of a room, as has been sometimes the mode, they are not easily cleansed. The proper dimensions of a bunk are 6 feet 8 inches in length, and 2 feet 8 inches in breadth.

Various methods have been proposed to ventilate the wards of a hospital. A hospital having east and west aspects, with single rooms, is easily ventilated; especially where the windows are made with double sashes, which rise and fall.

Chimnies are of themselves good ventilators; no dwelling house should be destitute of them, even in climates where fires are unnecessary to warm them. A wind-sail suspended over the top of a chimney by two posts and a cross piece, and its funnel

let down from the top as low as the fire place, will throw a column of fresh air into a room, which will expel the impure air
through the open doors and windows. These can be employed
only during the warm seasons.

Doctor TILTON, Surgeon General of the army, with a mind
possessing correct principles of philosophy, desirous of introducing a system of economy creditable to himself, suggested hospitals upon a novel plan. They are built one story in height with
round logs, having a fire place or hearth in the centre, without
a chimney, the smoke ventilated through an inverted wooden
funnel affixed to an opening in the roof; the floors of the rooms
earth, in the true aboriginal stile. He thinks them an improvement as they respect health. Hospitals of this description, he
believes, obviate diseases which have their source from impure
air of crowded rooms, which is generated from animal filth.
The Doctor is believed to be correct in his observations, so far
as wooden floors retain infectious principles, while earth floors
absorb or neutralize them. Examples are not wanting to demonstrate, that infectious principles attached to wood retain their activity during a long time. An improvement, which is truly philosophical in theory, cannot be carried into practice under all
circumstances. The plan proposed may, in southern districts, or
milder climates, fulfil the benevolent intention of its learned pro-
jector. These hospitals are for winter months. During the hot
seasons, tents are the best military hospitals. When snow covers the earth to a considerable depth, it dissolves next the surface. The water irrigates under the bottoms of the timber
which composes the outer wall of the hospital; by which the
earth floors are rendered uncomfortable from moisture, and the
beds dirty. In a hospital on the above plan, the smoke, in its
ascension, may convey with itself infectious principles; but it
aggravates coughs and complaints of the breast, which accompany the winter diseases on the northern frontiers.

These hospitals are more expensive than those built with
framed timber and plank, excepting when the timber stands in
the vicinity of the spot where erected. Upon a fair calculation
made by the assistant Q. M. General at Plattsburgh, where it

was necessary to draw the timber one mile, the expense of erecting log hospitals upon Doctor Tilton's plan, was greater than with planked, or boarded sides. The consequence was, the Q. M. General absolutely refused to give his assistance to erect them upon the plan proposed by the Surgeon General. The experiment to demonstrate their usefulness was but partial, at French Mills, where the army remained only a short time. No other attempts were made within my knowledge to prove them, excepting at Brownville, under the direction of Hospital Surgeon Blood, who, it was said, reported favourably of them.

The nature of infection and the means of obviating it were so little known by Sir John Pringle, that he viewed large military hospitals as the graves of an army. The same opinion continued in Europe and America, until the philanthropic and humane Howard explored the hospitals in many of the kingdoms on the eastern continent, " penetrated the dark cells of despair, the wretched prisons of man, where the seeds of disease long matured, diffused their pestilential effects ; and with a success unrivalled, divested them of their deadly powers."

The soldiers of the army, at the commencement of the war, possessing all the prevailing prejudices, reluctantly consented to be removed into the military hospitals ; from which, after recovery, they as reluctantly departed, having once experienced them as comfortable asylums.

This was noticed at Lewistown, on the Niagara, where it was known deceptive arts were often resorted to by the soldiers, to induce the surgeons to permit them to remain in the hospital, after restoration from sickness, and able to perform their duty in the field. Similar deceptions were more frequently practised by the men at Burlington hospital ; which, in point of cleanliness, had claims to be ranked among the best established hospitals in the United States.

The following regulations were adopted in the General Hospital at Burlington ; where in no instance from its first establishment, even when the monthly reports counted from six to nine hundred men, was an infectious disease generated, or propagated.

The washing of the floors and walls with soap and water, or lime water, was of the first importance. This was frequently repeated, especially during hot weather. In cold weather, when the wards were occupied by the sick, washing them was not only inconvenient, but hazarded the health of the patients. A coat of sand half an inch thick or more, renewed on the floors every day, was never attended with ill consequences, but was refreshing to the sick, while it superseded the necessity of washing. White-washing the walls with lime and water never incommoded the sick; it sweetened the rooms and corrected infectious principles. By daily sanding the floors they were preserved not only clean but perfectly white. The opportunity of washing them was improved, when the number of sick was reduced so as to admit their removal from one ward to others. The wards were thus alternately washed and thoroughly repaired. Bunks, as soon as they were unoccupied, were removed from the wards, and after cleansing, returned. The straw of the sacks was burnt as soon as the bed was vacated. The sacks were washed once in two weeks and the straw changed. Blankets were always clean, and frequently changed. During hot seasons the windows and doors of the wards were continually open. In cold seasons the windows were opened, for a short time, repeatedly in the day; care being taken that the sick in their beds were not exposed to the direct currents of air. No person was permitted to spit on the floors of the wards. Spit-boxes were furnished every bed, and filled with fresh sand twice a day, sometimes oftener where the patients expectorated largely. Close-stools, bed pans and urinaries were removed as soon as employed. No culinary process was performed at the hearths of the sick wards. Attached to each ward was a closet, where the table furniture, after washing, was deposited in neat order. Each ward was furnished with a large table, constantly covered with a clean cloth of linen, the better to ensure its cleanliness; on which was placed a box with a number of little apartments, wherein were set in order the vials and medicine for the patients, each vial and parcel labelled with directions, so as to obviate mistakes.

Attention was paid to the distribution of the sick. The wards appropriated to infectious, or contagious diseases, were less crowded than those occupied by patients with less important complaints. Surgical cases had rooms separate from the febrile. Venereal and itch patients were assigned to their separate wards, and not intermixed with men of different diseases.

To guard against infection, or obviate its generation, was of the highest importance. An infected ward was not seen at these points, where my observations were made; but it required unremitted application of the means which were experienced most efficient to prevent infection—such were the daily sanding the floors—ventilating the wards—and frequently washing the walls with lime and water.

Personal cleanliness was also a mean which promoted health, and obviated the generation of new diseases. At Burlington hospital, the sick, previous to admittance, were washed in tepid water, in an apartment appropriated to this use; then placed in a clean bed with a clean shirt. Daily ablutions of the hands and face were ordered. The sick with febrile diseases under the immediate direction of a surgeon, were occasionally washed or spunged with vinegar and water, at some seasons. The patients in the hospital were shaved every other day, and shirted twice in a week.

The beds throughout the hospital were always in order whether occupied or not. If a patient left his bed ever so frequently in the day, if only for five minutes, it was immediately put in order; so that the wards were always in a condition to be visited or inspected by officers of the army.

The inspectors, generally, gave a few hours notice of their regular inspections. This was done more with a wish that the surgeons might be present at the time, than to give opportunity for preparatory arrangements. For the hospital department was not ignorant that domiciliary visits, or private inspections were frequently made without the knowledge of the surgeons; also, confidential reports to government by inspectors, as a part of a system of *espionage* instituted at the war department. This was told in my hearing by an officer, when reproving one for ne-

glect of duty. With this system we were not dissatisfied, and
no officer will object to it when carried into effect without preju-
dice, and solely with a view to promote good discipline. But
when entrusted to men who might seek their own preferment by
a premeditated disgrace of others, the system was dangerous in
pits oeration, by compelling the most efficient officers to leave
the service of the army.

The gentlemen of the hospital were not a little amused and
pleasantly entertained at one time, by the conduct of an assistant inspector of the line, so little acquainted with the management and arrangements of a hospital, that he was ignorant of
what were most fit ; but willing to exhibit his talent as a critical
observer, captiously censured practices designedly adopted by
the director of the hospital, and recommended different methods
most improper. If a department require improvement, the officers of police, as well as inspection, should possess a competent
knowledge of every thing pertaining to it. It cannot be expected that officers of the line of an army, have a correct acquaintance with all the appendages of a hospital ; it seems necessary
then, that a surgeon be associated with an inspector of the line,
when he executes his duty of examining the hospital department ; especially when the establishment is extensive.

The hospital at Burlington, during five months in succession,
when under my immediate direction, was not one hour in a state
so bad, it would not meet the approbation of an inspecting officer who knew his duty. This hospital was visited repeatedly
by officers of the line, when under the direction of Doctors
WHEATON and HUNT, and during every period after August,
1813, was always seen in the best possible order; and deservedly merited the high encomiums it received, not only from inspectors of the army, but private citizens.

The more than useless parade of prescribing in a dead language, should be dispensed with in hospital practice. Physicians
of all nations, except the British, write their prescriptions in
their own languages. No cogent reason can be assigned, why
we should continue to imitate a practice, which originated at a
period of general ignorance, when learning was confined to a few

men, who wore large gowns and full wigs. But since these appendages of the scientific professions are justly ridiculed, even in Great Britain, where most in use, and are not adopted by gentlemen of our learned professions, it is time that other practices, equally ostentatious and unnecessary, should be treated with equal contempt.

Prescriptions and directions in hospital practice, should be plainly written in an intelligible language, on a book left with the nurses in the several wards; by which, during the absence of the attending surgeon, they may govern themselves, after the prescriptions are made up. By this improvement, all unpleasant accidents may be avoided.

During the winter 1813–14, there was attached to the hospital under my immediate care at Malone, a faithful sergeant; with whom was intrusted the medicine for fifty patients, with directions for each in plain english. This sergeant, without any assistant, administered the medicine daily for six weeks; and executed this duty with the greatest precision and punctuality.

It would be convenient that stewards and ward masters were acquainted with the materia medica, and the several compositions employed in practice. Such aid during the war was most acceptable, when the hospitals were crowded with numbers greater than the surgeons present could, with all their industry, properly attend. In two or three instances, such appointments were made. It is not unfrequent, that students in medicine, who have acquired a partial medical knowledge, are found willing to accept such appointments, for an opportunity of further improvement. Such industrious, ambitious young men, are highly useful in extensive hospitals.

At the commencement of the war, a young gentleman, who had received a medical education, accepted the appointment of steward; not being able to obtain a better at that period. He acquitted himself, in that office, with so much honor and fidelity, that, at the opening of the second campaign, he received the appointment of hospital surgeon's mate; wherein his services were meritorious, and met with approbation.

32

A registry of every patient should be kept, noticing rank, time of admittance, company, regiment, casualties, when discharged service, when returned to duty, and death. This regulation was adopted at Burlington in the winter 1813–14; previous to which, no sick records were found at that hospital. The hospital records on the Niagara, were under no order. The pressure of duty was so heavy and unremitted, that all our time was employed among the sick. Besides, in many instances, they were sent from their regiments, in an irregular manner, unaccompanied with their description rolls; and this neglect of duty continued in some cases, even until the close of war.

It is necessary that surgeons should preserve a record of their prescriptions, as well as a correct history of diseases which fall under their immediate observation. These assist memory, improve practice, and establish method and order; which are highly important in an extensive hospital. At Burlington and some other posts, this regulation was adopted. An abstract of important cases is equally important; but was only very partially attended to by the surgeons of our army. The above regulations will not be carried into practice, until the surgeons feel that a neglect is an abandonment of duty.

During the winter 1813–14, at Burlington hospital, Vermont, there were, at one period, between 7 and 800 patients, distributed in 40 wards, nearly equally divided among eight hospital surgeons and mates. These young gentlemen felt themselves highly responsible for the state of their respective wards, and condition of the sick; who were not a little benefited by a competition excited to excel each other in their duty; which was manifested by daily improvements, in respect to cleanliness and accommodations of their patients.

During four months, my own task was unremitted; every ward was daily visited, and an equal share of the prescribing duty was performed by myself; not a day was granted for relaxation; every hour in the twenty-four, except when taking refreshment and natural rest, found me at the hospital.

The location of this military hospital is most eligible, situated on the highest bank, elevated sixty or seventy feet above the water. The soil of this spot is sand mixed with gravel, dry and hard at all seasons of the year.

During the campaign 1814, a convenient garden was laid out, under the direction of Doctor HUNT, hospital surgeon, for the benefit of the convalescents and invalids, which by their labour was kept neat and in good order.

The interior of this hospital has been already noticed, the exterior was not less attended to. In an adjoining house, the surgeons were accommodated with comfortable rooms, where one or more always remained.

The wards of this hospital were regularly swept and put in order by sun-rise through the year. The wards were visited by their several surgeons in the summer months, at eight o'clock in the morning, in the winter at nine. Previous to these hours, the patients had breakfasted. The rooms were not only in perfect order, but every patient was found in his own lodging. While the surgeons were making their prescriptions, silence was preserved. The prescriptions were taken by the attendants to the dispensary, where they were immediately made up by the apothecaries. During the winter 1813-14, four apothecaries were constantly employed in their appropriate duty.

FLYING HOSPITALS.

IT has been found necessary, during active operations of an army, to attach to it flying hospitals, so denominated, because they are subject to repeated removals during a campaign. As, at all times they should be in preparation to receive and accommodate the sick and wounded, so they have or should have annexed to them a complete corps of the hospital staff, with an adequate number of attendants, enlisted solely for that employment. Instead of which, on the Niagara, we were under the necessity of selecting stewards and ward-masters from the line ; and were dependent, in the first instance, upon details from the army for our attendants, who, unfortunately, were men of incorrect habits, and bad dispositions. It was understood, when the details were made, such were designedly selected for this (which was considered) permanent duty, as were obstinate and ungovernable; men upon whom no dependence could be placed. So illy disposed were they to perform, and totally unqualified to execute the duty assigned, they were immediately ordered to rejoin their several corps. Thus disappointed, no further requisitions were made on the adjutant general of the army for attendants during the war; but they were selected from the convalescents, who were retained for this service. From among these we were always able to obtain men of happy dispositions, who were kind to the sick, and whose unremitted attention was a constant pledge of their fidelity.

Large tents were improved as field hospitals during campaigns, each of which was sufficiently capacious to accommodate 16 or 18 patients. From the 1st of June to the last of September, hospital tents were comfortable accommodations for the sick, in the northern district; far preferable to common dwelling-houses. Tents require but little care and attention, to preserve them in a state of cleanliness.

It is of importance that a suitable position be chosen for an hospital encampment. The ground should be gravelly, hard and dry. Such were the lands on which the hospital was established in 1813, at Lewistown. Drains or ditches should be cut to take off the rain water; and the tents should be removed as often as two weeks from the old ground to fresh. Frequent changes prevent the generation of infection. Ground floors should be daily scraped and swept. On the Niagara, these duties were rigidly enforced. The flying hospital at Lewistown, was continually preserved in so healthy and pure condition, that, where the monthly reports exceeded, at one period, 600 men, no new disease supervened. Among some hundreds of convalescents, who were discharged the hospital for light duty; only three were returned to the hospital from the first of July until the last of September. Such were the state of the hospital and healthy situation of that encampment.

After selecting suitable ground and pitching tents, the first care is to dig sinks, at a proper distance from the hospital, most nec⹁ ⹁ary receptacles for all kinds of filth, and which should be daily covered with earth.

Kitchens are most necessary appendages to a field hospital. They are expeditiously constructed with stones or sods of earth, in shape of the fire-place of a chimney. The opening in front and sides is defended from wind by a barrier composed of pliant branches interwoven with stakes fixed in the ground, and roofed over with boughs or bark of trees to protect the cooks from the rain and the sun's rays.

Ovens are also conveniently constructed with stones, if at hand, or earth supported by round timber in a square form of suitable dimensions, locked into each other at the corners. The floors of the ovens are of flat stones, or clay, which are shaped by small dry wood covered with bark of trees, and plastered over with a thick coat of clay, worked to a consistence which is necessary for bricks. In this state they are suffered to remain, defended from rains by bark roofs, until hardened by wind and the heat of the sun. Fire is then set to the wood within, which supports the coat or covering of the ovens; which, by burning, becomes hard and durable. To Colonel PINKNEY I feel myself indebted for the above expeditious method of erecting field ovens, important to be known in an army, more especially when suitable stones for their formation are not to be found in its vicinity.

Large barns may, at a small expense, be made the most commodious field hospitals, during the heat of the summer months, from the first of June to the last of October. At Lewistown, in the vicinity of the hospital encampment, two barns, forty feet square, were fitted for hospitals. Floors of inch plank were laid on joists raised on a level with the cills of the barns. In each of these were placed one hundred men; but they were too much crowded. As soon as tents were furnished, more room was given by removing a part of them to tents; so that sixty patients were comfortably accommodated in each barn. These were the most eligible summer hospitals which I saw during the cam-

paigns. The sick and wounded, here, were as comfortably lodged as they would have been in a dwelling house; and much less
incommoded by the heat of the weather, which was very oppressive, at times, during the months of July and August. Through
the spacious and lofty rooms, by means of large double doors on
each side of the barns, a free circulation of air was admitted;
which was not only grateful, but salubrious.

Bunks were furnished the sick; but as bunks made of boards
are not conveniently transported, at even a short distance, the
movement of a flying hospital would be facilitated, if it were furnished with canvas bed-bottoms, constructed with loops on the
sides, through which pass poles for their support. The bed-bottoms are supported by stakes drove into the earth with a fork on
the top to support the poles, to which the bottoms are attached.
These beds may be put up in a few minutes. They are less expensive than bunks of wood; which, when the hospital removes,
are generally left. Furnished with these, no other bedding, or
straw, except two blankets, are necessary in hot weather. During the campaign of 1813, I furnished myself with one of these
bed-bottoms, upon which, lodging was easier and much co_.er
than on a sack filled with straw in a bunk of wood.

As the events of military operations are doubtful, to facilitate
the movement of the hospital department attached to an army, it
should be furnished with a number of waggons and teams, so as
not to be immediately dependent on the Qu".ter-Master's department, when requisite either to take the wounded from the field
of battle, or transport the sick in case of a retrograde march, or
remove invalids after having recovered from wounds to a remote
hospital. The flying machines, called *volantes*, drawn by hor-
ses, (an improvement of LARREY, chief surgeon of the French
army) are useful in open countries, where a corps is assigned to
accompany them on the field of battle, upon LARREY's plan.

Flying hospitals, during campaigns, are often temporary.
Three new establishments were made on the Niagara in 1813,
in consequence of removes. These removes and establishments
are attended with trouble, anxiety, and much labour to the surgeons, as well as distress and pain to the patients, especially over

bad roads. The movement of 250 sick, from Lewistown to Williamsville, a distance of 40 miles, was painful to the spectator—it aggravated the disorders of many, and caused the death of some. This was performed the last of October. There were but two alternatives, either to erect hospitals from the rough timber of the forrests in the vicinity of Lewistown, or occupy the barracks built at Williamsville (eleven mile Creek) by General SMYTH's division. The first required too much time to complete, at this advanced season of autumn; the last was considered the most eligible, as the men would have less ha. hips to endure by a remove to houses already erected, than by necessary exposure, while new huts were building. The barracks at Williamsville wanted considerable repairs; but in a short period were rendered comfortable. During this remove Doctor WHITRIDGE was my only assistant.

The February following, in most severe weather, the removal of 450 sick, from French Mills and Malone to Burlington, distances of 75 and 93 miles, through a dreary wilderness, with few improved spots, was a scene much to be deplored.

To establish an hospital, and render it a comfortable asylum for the sick and wounded, is a work which requires considerable time; and while in preparation, their sufferings, frequently, are extreme. To support it in good order, requires unremitted duty and rigid attention. It often happens as soon as an establishment is completed, it is ordered to be broken up, the sick removed to a distant position, where the business of forming a new establishment is repeated. Such was a part of our duty from the commencement of the first campaign to the close of the war. It were unreasonable to expect that such temporary infirmaries could be made to assume, in a few days, that order and regularity which are seen in old established hospitals.

It is much less difficult to frame a system in the closet for the well ordering of a department, than put it into execution in the field; especially in a country where materials for its organization are with difficulty obtained; where ingenuity and industry, as well as science, are called into requisition to give their aid. Surgeons and physicians may write admirably well upon wounds and diseases, and describe correctly modes of treatment and methods of practice, who are unable to perform the simplest operation, or prescribe with judgment at the bed side. Men who have never witnessed an action, nor seen an encampment, can with adroitness manœuvre an army on paper, beat his enemy and claim all the honours of war. Take a man educated in a city, and locate him in a wilderness, he would starve. As examples make stronger impressions on the mind than precepts; so the manner in which a thing has been executed, is more durable on the memory, than systematic rules and regulations; which, under all circumstances and at all times, cannot be followed.

The Physician and Surgeon General to the army directed, that in all instances where the hospital department was not supplied with a sufficient number of the hospital staff to execute its requisite duties, the directors of hospitals should require a detail from the regimental surgeons for assistants. The above regulation was made without reflecting that the increased duty in hospitals immediately attached to the army, did not lessen that of regimental surgeons in their respective regiments. There were times when the hospital mates were ordered to perform regimental duty, while at the same period the hospital department was deficient of medical aid. From Lewistown, two hospital mates were ordered to Fort George by the commanding general, which reduced the number of mates attached to myself to two, at a period when the hospital returns of sick and wounded counted between six and seven hundred. Remonstrances against the impropriety of the order had no influence to countervail its execution. It was assigned by the Commander in Chief as a reason for this procedure, as the army expected an immediate action, it was important the destitute regiments should be furnished with surgeons. At another period, when the sick in the general hospital numbered 730, the only mate present, capable of duty, was ordered into the line of the army, when I was left to perform the whole duty. This last circumstance occurred immediately subsequent to directions from the Physician and Surgeon General to demand from the line additional medical aid; these directions were the consequence of my reports to him, that the hos-

pital department, under my immediate charge, had not sufficient
assistants to prescribe for the sick and do them justice.

These were embarrassments resulting from existent regulations, which located the P. and S. General, with whom was
lodged the sole authority of distributing the hospital staff of the
army, at a distance of five hundred miles from the scene of actual service; who, consequently, could not have been fully acquainted with the real state of the hospitals; and could not
have known when medical aid was most necessary, nor the
changes the department was subjected to, in consequence of unforeseen movements of the army. Every new disposition made
by the commander in chief could not have been anticipated at a
remote distance from the army; nor could it have been known
that a division of the army, upon suddenly changing its position
by taking up its line of march to a distance of two hundred miles
or more, would take with it the principal part of its medical
staff, and leave 931 sick under the charge of one hospital surgeon
and one mate capable of duty; and only one surgeon to two regiments of the brigade which remained; and which, momently,
expected an attack from a vastly superior and overwhelming
force of the enemy.

These evils did not spring from an injudicious distribution of
the hospital department, but from a defect in the general system.

Established hospitals should have had surgeons permanently
located to them, who should not have been subjected to a removal from one post to another. The moving army should have
had a distinct hospital staff attached to it, to accompany it in
all its movements; which should have been furnished with the
means of establishing a field hospital as soon as the army took a
position; and necessary transportation to advance, or retrograde,
as circumstances might require. An arrangement upon the
above plan would have obviated confusion, and would not have
left the sick destitute of medical aid, at any point.

It has been already observed, that soldiers in the hospital, frequently, attempted to impose on the surgeons, after they were fit
for duty. Such impositions were easily detected by a little observation. Some of these artful men had the power of assuming

33

a countenance of extreme distress, and even despair, whenever
they pleased. The best method I experienced was not to treat
the men with severity, but to put them off, with a view to take
their cases into consideration, and visit them in their wards at a
time they least expected; when, being taken off their guard, deceptions were more easily detected. I have seen a man come
to me limping and always appeared lame, in and about the hospital, but when permitted to depart from it a mile, could walk perfectly well. The following case is here published at large on account
of its singularity.

During the month of September, 1812, an enlisted soldier, who
had been admitted into the hospital on account of some indisposition, presented himself to me, requesting a certificate of inva-
lidity to perform duty, in order to obtain his discharge from service. His countenance not exhibiting marks of disease, led
me to enquire the reasons he should make such a request, especially, as he had not performed any duty in the field, and had
not been previously enlisted more than three months. For some
time he hesitated to reply; at last said he was not a man. Upon examining his countenance with more attention, I observed to
him he could not be a woman. He said he was not, but would
shew me what kind of a being he was. Upon examination, it
was discovered he did not possess the characteristic marks of either the masculine or feminine gender; therefore I was under
the necessity of considering him as one of the few of the animal
creation, as belonging to the neuter. An hermaphrodite is an
animal, which, agreeably to its import, unites both sexes—this
person had not the characteristic marks of either. The testes
and penis were wanting; in place of the scrotum there was a
fleshy excrescence which was not pendant, but appeared similar
to the scrotum of a child; in place of the penis there was a
fleshy elongation similar to the teat of a cow, about two and
half inches in length, destitute of a urethra; immediately under
which was the urethra of the bladder. There was no such part
to be found as a vagina. When I conversed with him respecting venereal passions and sexual intercourse; of the first, he said
he had none, of the last, he had no knowledge except what he

had occasinally learnt from those better experienced than himself. Upon examining his countenance more particularly, (although he had a thinly scattered beard, being over the age of thirty) it exhibited neither the expression of masculine nor femnine. It wanted the bold front of the man, and the soft features of the woman; the spirit and animation of both. There appeared about him nothing revengeful, but every thing inoffensive; something of low cunning and deceit. This being was filthy in his general appearance, and to me extremely disgusting; more especially after his character was known.—A being abhorrent to human nature; having nothing about him which could excite the passions of either sex. He had, however, sufficient address to impose upon the officer who enlisted him; willing to receive a premium, but as willing, after having obtained his bounty, to exhibit pretensions, whereby he might be discharged the service. With his physical defects, a moral turpitude, as want of honour and rectitude, was very conspicuous.

The distresses incident ·to an army, however bad, and frequently as great as can be endured, are always exaggerated at a distance from the scenes of action. High coloured representations produce on the public mind sensations as varient, as are political views respecting measures pursued. Those, who have not the means of obtaining a correct knowledge of facts, are among the first to censure; while one sincerely laments, another rejoices at every disaster. Could all become eye-witnesses how much with spare means is executed, the tongue of slander and detraction would be converted to vehicles of praise and admiration. For the reputation of the establishments where orders have called me, it is my duty to state, that visitors from remote parts always expressed astonishment, on finding the condition of the sick far more comfortable than was expected from representations received; while it gave me much satisfaction to improve every opportunity to undeceive all, who were prejudiced by misrepresentations.

It is with peculiar pleasure that I call to mind the gentlemen, with whom I had the honour to serve, at various points, on the frontiers during the war. Particularly, the names of WHEATON,

HUNT and LOVELL, of the highest grade of surgeons; the first of
whom, my predecessor at Burlington, directed that establishment
very creditable to himself; from whom the hospital came under
my charge in high order.   To Doctor HUNT, who succeeded me
at that post, the most liberal encomiums are due.   My acquaintance with the last gentleman being more extensive, gave me an
opportunity more fully to appreciate his merits as director of
that establishment; which, from its infancy to the close of the
campaigns, had a claim to pre-eminence.

I have had frequent occasion to respectfully mention Doctor
LOVELL in the course of these sketches.   His frequent reports,
one of which is communicated at large, bespeak an accurate and
discriminating mind.   As an operative surgeon, he is inferior to
none.

In a particular manner, my acknowledgments are here expressed to the medical gentlemen of the second and subordinate
grades, with whom I was associated at various periods.   Among
the first are Surgeons DAY and WILSON; by whose exact system
of police, the hospital establishment at Burlington was, in the
first instance, reduced to order.   Surgeon's Mates WHITRIDGE,
VAN-HOVENBURGH, PURCELL, MARCH, WALKER, WALLICE, VAN-
HOY, RUSSEL, TREVET and RUSSEL, severally claim my high
regards.   To all these gentlemen I shall ever feel attached by
the strong ties of friendship.   To their aid and assistance, industry and economy, close application and unremitted duty, the
hospitals, at every point, where orders called my attention, owe
their celebrity.

I recognize with pleasure the urbanity of Doctor BULL, Hospital Surgeon; although not immediately associated with him in
duty, yet his scientific knowledge entitles him to my high respect.

It is with peculiar satisfaction, I recollect the good state of
some of the regimental hospitals, particularly that under the
charge of Doctor BRUNOUGH, now Hospital Surgeon; and those
of Doctors DUNHAM, of the light artillery, and LAWSON, of the
6th regiment, at Plattsburgh.

There are many meritorious gentlemen of the medical staff, both of the hospital department and line of the army, whose names have not been recognized in these sketches. These gentlemen have not been particularly noticed, because my circumscribed observations, embracing only those associated with me in their duty, at different periods, precluded me from that critical knowledge so necessary to appreciate their superior claims. Of their services, the army has reaped the benefits; of their merits, the nation will long have a recollection.

In justice to Doctor LE BARRON, Apothecary General of the army, whose civilities will always be preserved in grateful recollection, it is with pleasure we acknowledge, he executed his duty with promptitude and fidelity. I have the fullest evidence, that the defect of supplies for the hospital department on the Niagara in 1813, was not occasioned by his neglect; as they were diverted on their route, from the Niagara frontier to Sackett's Harbour, by superior authority. For the deficiency, at French Mills, he was not censurable; no person could have anticipated the unaccountable waste of property on the St. Lawrence. To Doctor Low, Assistant to the Apothecary General, who was attached to the division of the army, where orders called my services, many encomiums are due. In addition to his appropriate duty of issuing stores, he, at all times, volunteered his services in the hospital; and was considered, in point of abilities, among the most efficient surgeons of the army.

OFFICIAL LETTERS,

WHICH ARE ILLUSTRATIVE OF OBSERVATIONS, ADDU-
CED IN THE PRECEDING WORK.

NUMBER I.

General Hospital Malone, January 31, 1814.

To Doctor Le Barron, Apothecary General of the
Army.

Sir—Your letter of the 20th instant was this day received. In answer to which I have to state, that your assistant, surgeon Low, upon reporting himself to the Commander in Chief, with his instructions from you, was directed to perform duty under my orders at this place. As the hospital stores addressed to him had not arrived, and having but one mate doing duty with me at this post, his services were necessary in the hospital. Since which, having been advised the hospital stores had arrived at French Mills, Doctor Low was released from duty here, and ordered to take charge of the stores and medicines, in conformity to your instructions; and is now at the Mills issuing stores and medicine to the several regiments. As soon as the regiments have received their supplies, more especially, as soon as the sick at the Mills can be accommodated at Malone, Doctor Low will be ordered to this post, where he will have an opportunity to do hospital duty. This is agreeable to his wishes, as well as mine; as he is very attentive to his duty, and a young gentleman of pleasing manners.

The Commander in Chief has selected this place as being the most eligible situation for a general hospital; especially as the army may not remain a long time in their present cantonment at the Mills; and upon retiring from that post, the sick must be transported to a more secure position, remote from the excursions of the enemy.

In consequence of my frequent removals at the close of the last year, the reports of sick, and estimation of supplies for the present year, were to have been forwarded to the surgeon general of the army, by Doctor Ross from the Mills, and by Doctor Pentegrass from Plattsburgh.

From some cause, the hospital stores, which accompanied the expedition down the river St. Lawrence, were not properly secured. They were either consumed by the troops, damaged, or lost. Many articles were not to be found, which were put on board the flotilla, and were not accounted for, when the army arrived at French Mills. It is now ascertained, that no person was charged with the care of them; it appears they were promiscuously placed on board the boats, wherever room for their reception could be found. It has been said, the quantities lost were amply sufficient for the army through the winter. (This estimation is not incorrect, judging from the invoice of stores ordered on board the flotilla, which was shewed me by Doctor Ross.)

I wish to impress upon you, the necessity of furnishing the hospital with a larger supply of rice. This article, in a particular manner, is adapted to the forms of the prevalent diseases of the army, diarrhœa, and dysentery.

Very respectfully,

your humble servant,

JAMES MANN,

Hospital Surgeon.

NUMBER II.

General Hospital Malone, February 1, 1814.

To Major General Brown, at French Mills.

Respected Sir—It is my duty to state to you, the sick, sent
to this place yesterday, were not all accompanied with the regular reports required by the rules of the hospital department.
Consequently, the surgeons, annexed to ——— regiments, are
reported as having neglected their duty. Similar neglects and
inattentions have been often overlooked. The service requires
a more punctual attention to duty. Being unacquainted with
the names of the surgeons attached to those regiments, I am unable to point out, at this distance, the delinquents. Those gentlemen are undoubtedly known to you. It is important that the
surgeons of the army strictly obey the rules and regulations
pointed out by the Surgeon General; and, during his absence,
those which may be enjoined by the senior hospital surgeon
present.

Yesterday, I had the honor to state to you, no provisions have
been made for a larger number of sick than we have at present.
The A. Q. M. General will not take upon himself the responsibility of quartering them upon the inhabitants. All the sick
now here, are not as yet made comfortable. It is my duty
further to state, that out of the number sent here yesterday, four
literally died with cold; having not a sufficient quantity of
cloathing and blankets, to render them, in their debilitated condition, comfortably warm. Many of them are destitute of apparel. The reputation of either our government, or the officers, who have the immediate command of the troops, is daily
suffering among the citizens, in consequence of the distresses to
which the soldiers are subjected. Humanity shudders at the
appearance of these unfortunate men. Cannot the officers of
the line be stimulated to pay some attention to their sick?

Do surgeons of regiments exercise all their talents to alleviate the wretched condition of those intrusted to their care? It seems as if their only anxiety was to pass them off their own hands, indifferent to the manner, regardless of ill consequences, provided they do not make themselves, immediately, accountable for the deaths which follow.

Doctors LOVELL and WOODBURY are the only surgeons of regiments, who have sent with their sick regular reports. It is expected that all the sick sent to the hospital be furnished with their descriptive lists; noticing their diseases, time when taken down, and the general method of treatment.

With sentiments of high respect, I am, Sir,
your most obedient and very humble servant,
JAMES MANN, *Hospital Surgeon.*

NUMBER III.

General Hospital, Malone, February 4, 1814.
To MAJOR GENERAL BROWN.

RESPECTED SIR—The regimental surgeons have neglected to send with their sick their bed-sacks. All we can procure here have been already issued to the sick in the hospitals. Destitute of bed-sacks, the men must suffer extremely during the severe weather. Information has been received, that there are no sacks in the Quarter Master General's store. Blankets are also wanted. One hundred and fifty received from Chateauguy Four Corners have been long since issued. Less than three blankets will not render a man sick in hospital comfortable.

With sentiments of high respect, I am,
your most obedient and very humble servant,
JAMES MANN, *Hospital Surgeon.*

P. S. Eighty sick have this day been received, consequently, as many sacks and one hundred and sixty blankets are wanted for these men. J. M.

34

NUMBER IV.

General Hospital, Malone, February 5, 1814.

To the Commander in Chief.

Respected General—During the month of January, accommodations were provided for about two hundred and fifty sick. This number was received, and comfortably lodged. The second of this month, the A. D. Q. M. General at this post was directed to make additional provisions for the sick ordered here from the Mills. A house capable of receiving one hundred men was procured. Upon the evening of the 4th, two hundred men, in addition to those already in the general hospital, were sent on. It is impossible to render their situation comfortable, with the means in our possession. Every house in this village, which can be procured at this time, is appropriated to the use of the sick. They may possibly receive four hundred. It is not possible to do justice to these unfortunate men, destitute of bed-sacks, and wanting additional blankets. These men were sent on without attendants or nurses, without kettles, pans, and cups; destitute of even an axe to cut their own wood. These evils are accumulating; while writing this, several loads of sick have arrived in a deplorable condition. It is now understood, the sick of the army are all on their way to this place. And if information be correct, and it is presumed some opinion may be formed, from returns already received, the number ordered here, exceed one thousand. In what manner these invalids are to be covered from the weather is not known. And if secured from the inclemency of the season, how are they to receive medical aid? This is not the first time since the war, the hospital department has been flooded with numbers. In the month of July last, when the general hospital was established

at
sic
we
It
hei
ent
arn
giv
bei
per
fori
ing
bla.
hav
sha
to i
the
less
ticl
ing
was
duty
shu
cau
S.
ed t
tion
eral
imp
ty
wan
istei
A
cine
assii
shift
of tl

at Lewistown, on the Niagara frontier, five hundred and forty sick were received at one time, from Fort George, when there were only three of the hospital department present at that post. It was impossible then to do justice to the sick. There are now here more than can be attended by the hospital surgeons present. When it is found necessary to remove all the sick of the army to the general hospital, (the hospital staff being too few to give them necessary attendance,) would it not conduce to the benefit of the service, that regimental surgeons be directed to perform hospital duty? For while surgeons of hospitals are performing severe duty, surgeons of regiments have little or nothing to attend to. Many of the sick want not only sacks and blankets, but common clothing. It may be alledged, these men have received all their clothing due. Admitting this as a truth, shall men be left to suffer? Cannot some measures be adopted to remedy evils resulting from loss of their apparel, whether their wants are the consequence of unavoidable casualties, carelessness, knavery or folly? Of the means of cleansing such articles of clothing as we have on hand, we are destitute; not having a sufficient number of men in health to perform the labor of washing. Women in this part of the country will not do this duty for others, although they may for themselves. Humanity shudders at the appearance of distress, whatever may be the causes.

Sensible as I am, that high degrees of responsibility are attached to my office, I am unwilling to suffer the evils above mentioned to rest concealed within my own breast. To you General, as Commander in Chief of the most respectable, as well as important division of the army of the United States, I am in duty bound thus to state them; persuaded that nothing will be wanting on your part, that the appropriate remedies be administered.

At present we have at command a supply of stores and medicines. With more extensive accommodations, more medical assistance, an additional number of nurses, more bedding, and a shift of clothing to enable the men to be cleaned; the gentlemen, of the hospital department attached to me, would be ambitious to give a high character to their several wards; and while bestowing the balm of life to the distressed, would acquire additional honours and a well deserved praise. That they possess the talents and disposition to execute (if they had the means) all which may be required of them, I have the fullest evidence to believe. With the highest respect, &c.

JAMES MANN, *Hospital Surgeon.*

NUMBER V.

General Hospital, Feb. 14, 1814.

Extract of a letter to Doctor TILTON, *at Wilmington, Physician and Surgeon General of the Army.*

RESPECTED SIR—Inclosed you will receive a proposed system for the re-organization of the medical department of the army. How far it will meet with your approbation we do not know. With me it is doubtful whether it will comport with the views of government, even if it should be approved by the committee to whom it is addressed. If, however, you should think it worthy their attention, it is our request it may be laid before them.

This is a fact, and a serious one too, that the surgeons and mates of regiments, under existing encouragements, have no inducements to continue long in service. Curiosity alone will induce them to sacrifice the term of one year in service. This being gratified, its exciting powers lose their effects. The pay and emoluments of Surgeons and mates of regiments do not give them a support, especially on the frontiers of Canada, where the articles of life are procured at the most extravagant prices.

With the highest respect, &c.

JAMES MANN, *Hospital Surgeon.*

REMARK.

During this session of Congress, the pay and emoluments of the regimental Surgeons were increased.

Left margin fragments:
be-
iddi-
isess
) all
e to

i.

14.
sician

ystem
army.
know.
ews of
tee to
vorthy
1.
is and
no in-
e will
This
ie pay
ot give
ere the
i.

eon.

ents of

NUMBER VI.

General Hospital, Burlington, April, 1814,

To GENERAL SMITH, BURLINGTON.

RESPECTED SIR—There are a number of men in the General Hospital at this post, who are fit subjects for discharge. It is necessary the hospital surgeon be possessed of their descriptive lists, to enable him to make correct certificates. The regulations of the General Hospitals are, that every man admitted be furnished with his description roll upon his admittance; these are put on file, to be used if necessary. In many instances, these rolls have not been forwarded; in some, refused by officers of companies. To remedy the evils arising from these irregularities, the interference of the commanding general is necessary.

With high respect, &c.

JAMES MANN, *Hospital Surgeon.*

NUMBER VII.

General Hospital, Burlington, April 21, 1814.

To COLONEL SMITH, 20th REGIMENT, AT PLATTSBURGH.

SIR—Inclosed you w. l receive the written orders directed to two men of your regiment in my hospital, to join their regiment immediately, or be considered as deserters and treated as such. No man regularly admitted into the general hospital can be considered as a deserter while in the hospital. No officer has authority to order a man out of the general hospital, until he is reported fit for duty, or by an explicit order from the Commanding General. In either case, it is expected that so much respect, at least, be shewn to the hospital department, the application for discharge from the hospital be made to the senior surgeon present, not directly to the man himself. This last procedure is calculated to induce irregularities in the hospital. Men must not leave the hospital without the knowledge of its officers. Evils too much abound in our department, without measures to create more. In addition, I have to state, that general orders were in force, which prohibited men from joining their regiments at Plattsburgh, even if capable of duty. The men demanded by Lieutenant H———— were, however, not fit for duty.

I am, with much respect, &c.

JAMES MANN, *Hospital Surgeon.*

NUMBER VIII.

General Hospital, Burlington, April 28, 1814.

To BRIGADIER GENERAL SMITH.

SIR—It is with pain, I am obliged to state to you, that three men of ———— regiment, have since the 25th instant, found their way, or been brought into the general hospital in an irregular manner. It has been reported, these men have had no medical aid, previous to admittance. Had it not been for the call of humanity, they would not have been so received; but their condition was deplorable. One, brought last evening in a dying state, lived a few hours only. The sick are not so numerous, at this time, but that they may be faithfully attended by the surgeons of regiments. If the last man had been seasonably reported, his life might have been spared. The last part was the duty of the surgeon to attend to; and where there is no surgeon, it becomes the duty of the immediate commanding officer of company. Of what use can it be to send a dying man to the hospital, except to give the hospital department the credit of *killing*, and trouble of *burying* him! If men are sent, in cases where they cannot be attended or cured by their own regimental surgeon, it is desirable to have them reported before they are in a moribund state.

Very respectfully, &c.

JAMES MANN, Hospital Surgeon.

NUMBER IX.

General Hospital, Plattsburgh, August 17, 1814.

To Colonel Cummins, Adjutant General.

Sir—There are in the general hospital at this cantonment, more than one hundred men, who require medical aid. These are under my sole care. In addition, Doctor Wheaton takes charge of the hospital in the village, in which are thirty patients. The several surgeons in this cantonment have each in their respective hospitals from fifty to ninety sick. Doctor Wheaton and myself are the only surgeons of the hospital department present, capable of duty; hospital surgeon's mate Purcell being confined with an intermittent fever. In addition to my duty of prescribing, of making up my prescriptions, attending to the police of the hospitals, I have yet to provide for the accommodation of one hundred more recently sent up from the lines of the army at Chazy, without any hospital assistants; having no Steward, no Ward-Master, no Orderly, capable of making out provision returns, (Steward and Ward-Master being sick) nor even an attendant capable of preparing the diet in a suitable manner.

This statement however, is not made with a view to censure any officer; but that you will order hospital surgeon's mate Russell, who has lately reported himself at your office, to perform duty at this post. I have no doubt the Commander in Chief, in all his transactions, will consult the good of the service; yet duty compels me to state, that with every exertion, full justice cannot be done the sick.

Very respectfully,

JAMES MANN, *Hospital Surgeon.*

NOTE.

On the 1st September following, the hospital returns counted more than seven hundred, with one assistant only.

NUMBER X.

Extract of a Letter addressed to Doctor TILTON, *Surgeon General of the Army, dated Plattsburgh, Hospital Department, September 2, 1814.*

RESPECTED SIR—You will at one view perceive this division of the army, is not sufficiently furnished with medical aid. I have only one assistant, on whom much dependence can be placed, this is surgeon's mate RUSSELL; PURCELL is out of health.

General IZARD, when he left this post with his army, ordered with his division, hospital surgeons HAYES and BRUNOUGH; and mates WALLACE and WALKER. The sick of the division, were placed under my charge. Hospital surgeon WHEATON, had previously obtained leave of absence, on account of bad health. Hospital surgeon HUNT is at Burlington, with TREVETT, as his assistant. You will perceive there is placed on me, more duty than it is possible for me to perform.

September 3.

The sick and convalescents have been ordered to Burlington Vermont; but for want of transportation, are removing to Crabb Island, two miles and a half from the fortifications at Plattsburgh.

Such of the convalescents as can perform garrison duty are ordered into the forts. More than five hundred have already arrived at Crabb Island, a barren uninhabited spot. Hospital tents to cover them have been furnished. Doctor PURCELL is now my only assistant, and he sick. RUSSELL is ordered into one of the forts. Doctor Low, assistant to the Apothecary ·General, has volunteered his services, and is also attached to one of the forts.

Crabb Island, September 10:

We have received the wounded of the army, about forty. Four hundred, with the assistance of Commodore MACDONOUGH, have been sent to Burlington hospital from this place. I am left destitute of any assistant; except the services of Doctor BROWN, and two medical students, who have volunteered themselves, my situation would be most unpleasant and distressing.

Respectfully your humble servant,

JAMES MANN, *Hospital Surgeon.*

NOTE.

On the morning of the 11th of September, the remainder of the sick were all sent to Burlington.

―――――――

NUMBER XI.

Plattsburgh, November, 1814.

Extract of a communication to Doctor TILTON, *Physician and Surgeon General of the Army.*

RESPECTED SIR—If we may be allowed to draw conclusions from the present aspect of our political affairs, the prospect of peace is remote; while, should the war be continued, to me it

35

seems highly important, the medical staff of the army be placed on a more respectable basis, than its present establishment. To judge of the conduct of some officers of the line, towards the medical staff, particularly that branch attached to hospitals, it appears they are considered in no higher light than warrant officers. It is well understood, the medical staff have no command out of the hospitals, indeed they ask for none; they wish only to be respected in their own department. There is nothing in the rules and regulations of the army, to deter commissioned officers of the lowest grade, from intruding within hospital bounds, and assuming authority to order their men in and out of it *ad libitum.* Intrusions of this nature too frequently occur, to pass without notice; but when they have been reported to the commanding general, redress has been obtained by a special order in the case. This does not place the hospital department beyond the reach of vexatious interferences.

In all services, except our own, the medical staff of the army is respected, because it is protected by government. Even where it is clothed with any powers, it is not placed in an attitude to exercise them. The senior surgeon of the army is, *ex officio,* constituted director of hospitals, and is made superintendant of their building. At the close of this campaign, orders were issued to erect hospitals for the sick, in which the director was not known; and although the rules and regulations of the army designate, the sick of the army be the *first* accommodated, yet the present season, they are the *last.* The regiments have their barracks nearly completed, as have also the artificers; while the foundations of the hospitals are but just commenced. The sick consequently are in tents, and will remain in them until the cold becomes severe. The sick with typhus, can hardly recover at this season, exposed as they are to cold and moisture. Medicine, under such circumstances, can have but little good effect. If men die, the skill and assiduity of the surgeon are called in question, without considering the real fatal causes; while it is frequently the case, the most judicious are censured, and accumulated disgrace unjustly attached to them.

In events of high impartance, it is seldom the medical staff are noticed. This is discouraging to the ambitious young surgeon of the army. It may be alleged, tho surgeons being non-combatants are out of danger. This however is not always the case. During the investment of Plattsburgh by the enemy, the surgeons were constantly passing from fort to fort, or block-houses, to dress the wounded, exposed to a cross fire of round and grape shot; while the greater part of the army were covered by fortifications. The cool bravery of the surgeons were, in private conversation, noticed by the Commander in Chief; had half as much been reported to the War Department respecting them, they would have felt themselves amply compensated. While making this observation, I do not include myself; because I was snug on duty at Crabb Island, out of much danger, while our fleet continued master of the lake. If reports, honorable to officers, are founded upon good conduct and cool bravery, who, more deserving than the non-combatants? They have fewer motives to excite them, and are equally exposed to danger as officers of the line, whose minds as well as bodies, are constantly exercised by their commands. If any officer has hardships attached to his office, it is the surgeon who executes his duty with fidelity and assiduity.

I feel myself bound to report with much respect, the conduct of all the medical gentlemen attached to this army, who have at all times this campaign, performed their duty; and who, for their particular services, during, and after the investment of Plattsburgh by the enemy, merit the applauses of their country.

To discriminate, would be an act of injustice. Doctors LAWSON and MASON, surgeons of regiments, WARMSLEY, BEAUMONT and HUGO, surgeons mates, have all deserved well of their government. I would particularly mention RUSSELL, hospital surgeons mate, and Low, Assistant Apothecary General, who volunteered his services, for their attention and professional abilities, at a time, when the wounded of both fleets and army were placed under my charge; on whom were performed, immediately after the action, more than thirty capital operations. It is with much pride, this opportunity is improved to state, that the medical gentlemen of our army and navy, were not inferior, but superior to the medical gentlemen of the British navy; several of whom were made prisoners of war, and assisted to dress the wounded of their own fleet. This circumstance is very flattering to our infant medical institutions; and is good evidence, they are not less respectable than the ancient schools of Europe.

    With the highest respect, &c.

        JAMES MANN, *Hospital Surgeon.*

NUMBER XII.

—

General Hospital, Plattsburgh, November 6, 1814.
   To ELBRIDGE GERRY, VICE PRESIDENT.

HONORABLE SIR—Permit me to intrude upon you, while employed in the highest concerns of the nation, and invite your attention to a subject, which by me is considered of no small importance—no less than a more comfortable provision for such soldiers, as have become decrepid in the service of their country. There are many of this description rendered unable to provide by manual labour a subsistence; broken down by severe duty and hardships, during unfortunate and unseasonable campaigns. Many of this description, at this time, are strolling about the country, subsisting upon the charity of individuals to the no little disgrace of the nation. Orders have been issued this autumn, to discharge from service all incapable of bearing arms in the field; many of these have not been mustered for months, having been absent from their corps in hospitals; and who, consequently, have not received pay during these periods. A large proportion of these men have not the necessary documents furnished by officers, to enable them to receive their pay justly due. To cast these disabled men upon the wide world, will place them in a distressed situation; in which, hereafter, they will not be able to exhibit, and prove their demands upon government; and being thus liberated from their connection with the army, will, by their complaints and unfavorable representations, render the service unpopular, and discourage the recruiting of our armies. Men already discharged, under the above circumstances, have, I am persuaded, injured the recruiting service.

Some of these invalids have incumbered our hospitals, a year and more, for want of necessary documents, by which they may be honorably discharged. Officers last winter were called upon to furnish the necessary papers; but these are withheld by them, it is presumed, from sinister views, at a time the regiments were about to be consolidated. Hence it is, while the rolls of the army at the war department, appear strong as to numbers, they are, comparatively, weak as to efficient force.

Many invalids, although incapable of field duty, may be serviceable in garrisons, where they are able to defend the lines of fortifications. These men also, may be employed in fixing ammunition; some may be employed as artificers.

If it would not be considered that I assume too much, a suggestion is made to government, to place these men in a comfortable situation, in which they may be made useful to the nation, instead of travelling through the country as vagrants. Many, when discharged, return to the bosom of their families; but it should be known, that many of these decrepid men are foreigners, having no homes, and must depend on charity for subsistence. Offer them a home, especially such as may accept it. Let a corps of invalids be established. This corps should be considered honorable, as being composed of veterans, disabled in service. 'It should be considered as the *most honorable* military institution in the nation; where not only the *war worn* soldier, but the *decrepid* officer may find an asylum, in which he may enjoy the comforts of life, with a heart overflowing with gratitude; that his government duly estimates his valour and patriotism, and here receive a just but inadequate recompense for the toils he endured, the dangers he encountered, and the wounds he received in the service of his country.

With the highest respect, I am
your most obedient and very humble servant,
JAMES MANN, *Hospital Surgeon.*

NOTE.

To this communication, a reply was received, signed by the Honourable Mr. GERRY, the day previous to his death.

APPENDIX.

A DISSERTATION ON DYSENTERY,

WHICH OBTAINED THE BOYLSTON PRIZE MEDAL FOR

1806.

To WARD NICHOLAS BOYLSTON, *Esq.*

SIR,

THE first honours of your benevolent institution for the promotion of medicine, and the sciences connected with the healing art, were conferred in 1803. The fortunate dissertation on CHOLERA INFANTUM was impressed with a token of your approbation, by permitting its author to dedicate it to yourself. This dissertation on dysentery is so intimately connected with the former, that the author was induced to become a competitor for the prize, which was adjudged him in 1806. Various circumstances have conspired to prevent its publication until now. Among the most potent was, that in reviewing the dissertation, it was found to embrace no new principle in theory, nor improvement in practice. A determination was adopted, not to expose it to the eye of the world. But, since the adjudication was publicly announced, repeated applications have been made by friends for a copy, excited probably more by curiosity than an expectation of acquiring any new ideas on the subject. To gratify a curiosity thus excited is one reason now offered, why the author assents to its appearance in print. If the dissertation

IMAGE EVALUATION
TEST TARGET (MT-3)

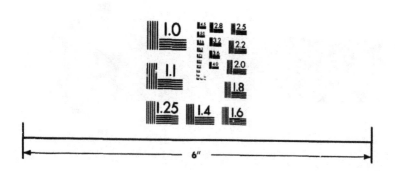

6"

Photographic
Sciences
Corporation

23 WEST MAIN STREET
WEBSTER, N.Y. 14580
(716) 872-4503

has any claims to merit, it will appear as comprising in a compendious form, the most approved practice in the United States.

Diseases of the bowels are among the most formidable disorders to which armies in the tented field are exposed; produced by hardships, bad provisions, insalubrious climates and unhealthy positions. As these, on the northern frontiers, appeared under forms different from those in domestic practice; the additional observations respecting the disease among soldiers will not be unacceptable. In proportion as the usefulness of this dissertation is more enlarged, so the object of your benevolence is promoted. Your views, similar to your good and great prototype, the immortal Howard, are not circumscribed within narrow limits; they embrace not only states and kingdoms, but the whole human race.

No further apology is believed necessary, for the publication of this dissertation, connected with the diseases of the army.

The author deprecates *wars*, as well as the causes which excite nations to arms against each other. From a state of barbarism, by the instrumentality of a few, the horrors of a field of battle have been progressively ameliorated; penal laws are rendered less severe, and our prisons converted to comfortable asylums for the wretched; wherein penitentiary hours for reflection and reformation are granted; and while under the salutary discipline of retributive justice for evils inflicted on society, criminals may, by solitary labour, make a partial atonement for their sins. These improvements are the glorious and happy effects of that spirit of divine love, imbibed from the doctrines of Christianity. These doctrines, in proportion to their diffusion, have, in some degree, softened the calamities of war, and averted its attendant evils.

While philanthropy invites to her aid the benign arts and sciences, which improve the state of society, and meliorate the condition of man; she causes to be inscribed upon the historic page—a monument more durable than marble or brass—the names of those philanthropists, the worthies of every age and country, who have devoted their lives, fortunes, or time to her cause.

Harvard University with pride enrols the name of BOYLSTON among her most liberal benefactors. The medical college of that university will long remember him among its principal patrons; while the rapid improvements in the healing art in New-England bear testimony, that to his munificence they are highly indebted, for their increasing extension and wide diffusion.

May he long survive his establishment, to enjoy the sublime satisfaction of witnessing the multiplied benefits resulting from his liberality, is the sincere wish of his most obedient, and very humble servant, **THE AUTHOR.**

ADJUDICATION.

At a meeting of the Committee upon the Boylston prize question (as published the 13th March last) at Boston, December 31st, 1806.

PRESENT, ISAAC RAND, M. D.
LEMUEL HAYWARD, M. D.
JOHN BROOKS, M. D.
BENJ. WATERHOUSE, M. D.
AARON DEXTER, M. D.
JOSIAH BARTLETT, M. D.
WILLIAM SPOONER, M. D.

" A dissertation on the first question, relative to mortification, and one on the second question, relative to dysentery, having been read and duly considered, the question was taken whether they were respectively entitled to the premiums offered, and it was determined in the affirmative, on condition, that neither of them should be published, unless revised and abridged by the authors.

" On opening the papers accompanying the dissertation, it appeared that the one on mortification was written by GEORGE CHEENE SHATTUCK of Templeton, in the county of Worcester; and the other on dysentery, by JAMES MANN of Wrentham, in the county of Norfolk.

36

" *Voted,* That the chairman be requested to write to Doctor Shattuck and Doctor Mann, and also to the President of Harvard College, informing them respectively of the doings of the Committee, and that the adjudication be published in the Columbian Centinel, and Independent Chronicle."

ADVERTISEMENT.

Agreeably to the recommendations of the adjudicating committee, the following dissertation has been revised and abridged.

No alterations have been made in respect to the causes and the general treatment of the disease, excepting some observations have been added, which were made on the northern frontiers, on the disease as it appeared in the army.

In consequence of an objection adduced to the author's hypothesis, that materials under the form of gass are one cause of dysentery, the consideration of that subject is more fully attended to, and for the sake of elucidation, some observations are added.

It has been urged, the author employs inefficient cathartics. This objection will be removed, when the reader understands, that liberal evacuations from the intestinal tube are strenuously enjoined in all cases of dysentery. Will it be a question, by what kind of cathartic medicine this is effected, if the intention is fully accomplished? May not the less irritating cathartics, in large doses, fulfil the intention, as well as the more drastic, with less hazard of an hypercatharsis? During the last war there were experienced a few cases only, compared with the number attacked, which required very active medicine. Drastic purges are sometimes required for patients of robust habits. The practice in this dissertation is applicable to dysentery as it appears under every circumstance of age, habit, temperament, and climate.

A DISSERTATION

UPON THE CAUSES OF THE VARIETIES OBSERVED IN DYS-
ENTERY, AND THE METHODS OF TREATMENT ADAP-
TED TO THE CURE OF THESE VARIETIES.

—◦+◦—

PATHOGNOMONIC OBSERVATIONS.

IT may not be improper to observe, that the appellation, dysentery, is derived from the Greek language, denoting a bad state
of the intestines. Hippocrates, the father of medicine, gives the
following definition : " When the body is heated and there are
acrimonious purgings, with bloody stools, corrosion and ulceration of the intestines, the disease is called dysentery." His co-
temporaries and more immediate successors adopted an opinion
that ulceration and corrosion were necessarily connected with
the other symptoms ; but physicians of the present age consider
these morbid affections within the intestines the consequence of
the disease, not the immediate cause of the symptoms constitu-
ting the several phenomena.

The various nosological descriptions of dysentery, as being
little applicable to practice, we decline to notice ; but shall proceed to point out its most prominent symptoms, as described by
physicians of the present day.

Dysentery should be distinguished from diarrhœa and other
diseases of the same organs ; which, although they may change
from one to the other, require in several respects very dissimilar
methods of treatment.

In dysentery the evacuations are small, accompanied with
gripes and tenesmus, evincing that there is some obstacle to the

free discharge of fecal materials lodged in the intestinal canal. In diarrhœa the flux is copious without tenesmus, sometimes involuntary; wherefore gripes and tenesmus are considered the pathognomonic symptoms of dysentery. In the first onset of the disease, the tenesmus which accompanies the complaint is aggravated by fecal congestions; but it is certain that the tenesmus which exists after the disease is of some duration, is not a consequence of congestions, but increased sensibility and irritability of the villous coats of the rectum, the effect of inflammation and ulceration.*

In its progress through its several stages the disease appears often under various forms, generally ushered in with slight rigors, accelerated pulse not full, with slight pain in the head and back; after some hours increased heat and soreness upon pressing the abdomen. The disease is sometimes accompanied with coldness of the extremities, small pulse, diminished heat, nausea and vomiting, even at its first attack. The last form takes place mostly on persons advanced in years; in cases also, where the patient had been previously exhausted of the vital principle by cold, fatigue and bad provisions. This combination of causes among the soldiers was productive of a most formidable disease.

The most common evacuation in the disease is mucus streaked with blood. The immediate cause of this appearance is inflammation; the sensibility of the coats of the intestines is increased, while the mucus designed by nature to defend them from injury is voided by violent efforts, and the more substantial feces retained by spasm, or stricture. This form constitutes the ideopathic dysentery.†

When the disease is not cured in its early stages, a bloody

---

* It was the case that when tenesmus succeeded profuse diarrhœa, as it appeared among the soldiers on the northern frontiers, that states of ulceration and inflammation were demonstrated by many dissections of those who died by the disease.

† The tenesmal diarrhœa, which destroyed many during the war, in most cases succeeded simple diarrhœa, the consequence of continued exposure to the primary causes of the last complaint, and required a treatment very opposite to the ideopathic form.

vanies, or materials not dissimilar to the dregs of red wine are
dejected. These discharges demonstrate a morbid secretion of
the inflamed surface of the inner coat of the intestines, and deficient venous absorption.

In the last stage of the disease, especially where it has continued a long time, part of the discharges are not unlike cheese
curds, similar to the apthous incrustations often observed on the
tongue, and which line the throat, stomach and intestines
throughout to the rectum; and when they are separated from the
little ulcerations to which they are affixed, are evacuated with
other fecal materials.† These apthœ are formed from the coag-
ulable lymph, and have probably for their cause, says DARWIN,
an increased action of the secerning system from increased sensation, with a decreased action of the absorbent system from decreased irritation.

Balls of indurated feces, called by medical writers *scybala*, are
sometimes evacuated. The fecal materials retained within the
foldings of the intestines are moulded into balls, which having
their more fluid parts absorbed or evacuated become hard, and
by irritating the extremely sensible coats of the intestines, aggravate the gripes and tenesmus. It has been observed by
medical authors, that when these congested feces have been
evacuated, that the patient has been relieved from the torturing
pains and tenesmus, which have induced a belief that they were
the cause of the disease, which has frequently induced a continuation of purges to the no small aggravation of all the violent
symptoms, which they were intended to obviate.*

The villous coats of the intestines, in consequence of excessive inflammation, are detached from their contiguous parts after
a similar manner the cuticula, in cases of sphacelus, is from the
cutis. The intestines are liable to gangrene and mortification

---

† These appearances succeed ideopathic dysentery; no instances existed within my observation, where they were exhibited among the dysenteric patients of the army.

* Scybala have been noticed but seldom in domestic practice by myself,
and never in hospital practice, where the disease is seen under all its various forms.

from excessive inflammation as well as other parts of the body ; and as it has supervened and been noticed by physicians, they have formed an opinion that dysentery is a gangrenous disorder at its commencement ; and governed by this persuasion, have in their practice prescribed medicine to obviate gangrene, rather than the real state of the disease. Hence we find stimulants prescribed, instead of the more appropriate antiphlogistic regimen, at the first attack of the disease.

Pus has been noticed in the evacuations in the last stage of dysentery. Hence arises the preposterous and inert practice of administering traumatics to the exclusion of more efficient remedies at the commencement of the disease.†

The fecal materials voided are, at times, brown or black; upon which has been established an erroneous pathology, that bile, or its vitiated state, is the formidable cause of all the evils attendant on the dysentery, as well as other diseases.*

In some states of disease there is a copious evacuation of blood from the intestines. This has never been noticed by myself when it was accompanied with genuine dysenteric symptoms, as gripes and tenesmus. It is mentioned however by authors. MOSELEY says he has seen blood evacuated in dysentery in torrents, as from a wound. Whenever I have observed discharges of pure unmixed blood from the intestines, by pints and quarts at one evacuation ; this profusion evinced it did not es-

---

† It has been ascertained by many dissections in the hospitals of the army, that the purulent discharges in dysentery are secretions from ulcers within the rectum, the consequence of inflammation.

* Notwithstanding all the light which has been given upon this subject by modern writers, yet bile is still charged with all the deleterious effects of diseases, and is believed to be more productive of plagues *hot* and *cold ;* of fevers *spotted, yellow,* and *scarlet,* through all their varying shades and shapes, down to that produced by *rum* and *whiskey.* That salubrious and inoffensive liquor denominated bile, for whose bountiful secretion one of the most capacious organs of the human body is wisely appropriated, is, even at this enlightened period, believed to be more prolific in destructive diseases which afflict mankind, than was the celebrated *Pandora's box* among the ancients.

cape from the blood vessels of the intestines; these being too small to supply the quantity voided. Hence it was inferred, this astonishing flood of blood could have no source but the liver; from thence the blood is supposed to pass through the ductus choledocus into the duodenum. The state of this important organ so necessary to digestion and healthy action of the intestines, when in that condition which permits its vital fluid to pass off in torrents, will be hereafter explained.

Whenever in the course of the disease the evacuations from the bowels exhibit natural appearances, there is a remission of all the violent symptoms. Severe gripes and tenesmus sometimes abate while the evacuations assume the form of diarrhœa, or a lienteria, wherein the nutriment is voided in the same state as when taken into the stomach, and slides through the intestines so quickly, that it appears indigested or unchanged.

These various appearances, formerly distinguished by different appellations, as being different diseases, are influenced by climate, season and constitution upon the disease in its different stages and degrees of existing disorder.

The danger is always estimated from states of severe pain and debility induced by morbid effects of the disease. Unremitted gripes with most frequent and ineffectual efforts to evacuate the contents of the intestines; swollen, tense abdomen, cold extremities, indicate death, or imminent danger.

CAUSES.

Previous to a consideration of the causes which we believe active in producing dysentery, we think it expedient to concisely notice the opinions of writers upon this subject; and shall, at the same time, take the freedom to controvert such as appear objectionable; and with much deference to high and distinguished authorities, offer reasons for our dissention which to us appear important.

SYDENHAM supposes that dysentery is the fever of the season turned in upon the bowels. This sentiment has been often referred to by writers upon this subject. As this disease most generally prevails in those seasons when autumnal fevers are epidemic, it is inferred by that accurate observer of the nature of diseases, and their changes depending on transitions of seasons and weather, that dysentery and these fevers have one common cause. Among others who have adopted the above opinion is MOSELEY; who has adduced an additional observation to support the sentiment, "the stools are more frequent, and every symptom of the disease aggravated at those hours when these fevers are in their exacerbation." "This fever of the intestines like most other fevers," adds MOSELEY, "is caused by obstructed perspiration, not confined to cold, wet or dry seasons, particular food, water, or fruit, chiefly depending on some influence of the atmosphere, or sudden transitions of the air, and such other causes as expose people to have their perspiration stopped." In order, however, to assign a reason why one part of the body becomes affected at one time, and a different part at another, from the same cause; MOSELEY finds it necessary to have recourse to a conjunct cause, otherwise "obstructed perspiration," to use his own language, "the parent of so many diseases, would always produce the same." MOSELEY further remarks, "as he has practised in the opinion that this fever of the intestines is caused by obstructed perspiration, so he universally found it relieved by turning back the discharges to their natural channels."

If obstructed perspiration be the principal cause of dysentery, it may be asked, why does not the application of cold, or a sudden transition from heat to cold, by abstracting heat (caloric) from the body, whereby the pores are closed or contracted by spasm, produce this disease, at every season of the year, as well as the autumnal?

From the accuracy of Moseley's observations upon most subjects, one would suppose several circumstances as productive causes of dysentery would not have escaped his notice; viz. heat, moisture, filth, and vitiated food; except for the purpose of supporting a favorite doctrine. Perhaps we all are disposed to give too much weight to a simple agent, when it is discovered to be deleterious; and lose sight of a combination of causes most productive of violent epidemics; sometimes an effect is assigned a cause of disease.

Heat and moisture, filth and vitiated food conjoined, or even severally, may be demonstrated to have been more active in the generation of violent forms of disease, than any agent, which is only capable of obstructing perspiration. It is among soldiers in the field and quarters, that filth and bad provisions abound. It is among that class of men, that dysentery appears with all its hideous forms; and it was among these that Mosely collected the most of his facts upon which his observations are founded.

Cullen says, that "dysentery often arises from the application of cold, and, often contagious; that by propagation of such contagion, independent of cold, or other exciting causes, it becomes epidemic in camps and other places," and adds, "that specific contagion is the remote cause of dysentery." That "dysentery is a contagious disease, passing from one to another in camps, and from soldiers to the inhabitants of the neighboring villages," is also an opinion of Sir John Pringle, who further observes, "this disease, *cæteris paribus*, prevails mostly among such, as are of a scorbutic, that is, of a putrid habit; or among the poorer people, who, from foul air, bad diet, and nastiness, are most liable to putrid diseases."

If it can be made evident, that this disease may be produced by causes independent of contagion, where is the consistency or rationality of having recourse to the supposed contagious nature of the disease, to account for its prevalence in those seasons, even when it is epidemic? A supposition more philosophical is, that the same causes, which produce an epidemic disease, and give its form to a single patient, may continue active in producing a similar state on others. Formerly epidemic diseases were apprehended to have been propagated mostly by contagion: the doctrine had become so general, that even common coughs were called by some contagious. But in cases, where a disease originated without a concurrence of known communication with an infected person, to account for its existence physicians resorted to cold, heat, nastiness, putrid effluvia, marsh miasmata, obstructed perspiration, or some secret agent of darkness; but the disease having been fairly introduced into community, all the assigned causes of its first existence are forgotten, and no longer

37

mentioned. The multitude hope to escape disease, by avoiding the sick; while at the same time they cherish about themselves many of the active causes, and hug to the last the most fatal.

" The doctrines of *contagion* and *infection*, and the scientific distinction between them were not formerly, it is apprehended, so well understood as at the present day. This interesting subject has been recently treated with so much clearness and perspicuity, in that valuable collection of communications, the MEDICAL REPOSITORY, and is therein exhibited in so luminous a point of view, that we deem it necessary only to refer the reader to the definitions of those terms, therein found, " which," says the author, " although they have been used in a synonimous sense, appear to a mind, in the habit of noticing nature, in her diversified forms, to convey very different and distinct ideas."

Diseases, known to be contagious, as small pox and measles, are propagated at all seasons of the year, without regard to temperature; whereas, diseases, which depend on an infected air from putrefaction of substances in a state of decay, or on local position for their existence, are endemic only at one season. Dysentery prevails during the summer months, and does not become endemic until the heat of the weather is so high in degree, as to generate putrefaction on animal and vegetable substances, in a state of decay; this disease abates or disappears, as soon as the heat of the season decreases to the line of frost. Dysentery may also exist during winter, in crowded prisons and hospitals, where a putrefactive process is generated from filth and animal excretions. [NOTE. The last observation is added since the author was conversant with the disease during the winter months, in the military hospitals. Under these circumstances, the disease was considered consecutive, not ideopathic. It was the consequence of habitual diarrhœa, continued from its first appearance by the agency of those causes which produced it, until the rectum became excoriated and ulcerated. If dysentery is generated during the winter months, it is where the patient is surrounded with animal filth, and in a confined state.]

Diseases are considered epidemic, when they spread over a considerable extent of country. They have common symptoms, which constitute their pathognomonic characters. Similar causes, under similar circumstances, are productive of the same effects. Different additional causes may, and do often co-operate to diversify the forms, under which diseases may appear.

From considerations to be adduced, we presume to say, that one immediate cause of an epidemic dysentery is the production of putrefaction in a subtile form, or gaseous state acting immediately upon the alimentary tube. Should it be controverted, that invisible gasses are active agents, when in contact with irritable fibres, we enquire, what form " that vitiated product of living vascular action" assumes, which excites, through the medium of the air, a disease like that by which itself was produced, but gasseous ? What is the material, expired from the lungs of a person under the measles, which is capable of communicating to a person in health a similar disease, except gas ? What is that agent which abounds in unventilated prisons, in dirty hospitals, in foul ships, in large towns and populous cities, filled with filth, in houses stored with fish, beef, and corruptible articles, which have been known to have been active in the generation of disease, but the production of either putrefaction, or animal decomposition, or animal excretions in the forms of gas ? Do the emanations from substances in a state of putrefaction assume the form of gas ? Are offensive productions of animal excretions gasseous ? The olfactory nerves of every one will determine the question. To convince ourselves, that more active agents cannot be found to generate diseases, than the production of putrefaction and animal excretions, it is unnecessary to review the history of diseases further back than the late summer and autumnal epidemics in cities and in the field. In all cases where critical examinations have been made, it has been demonstrated by clear elucidations, that the prevalent diseases had their sour from gasseous materials, eliminated from either the animal kingdom, or vegetable substances in a state of decay.

Cold and sudden transitions of weather from a hot to a colder state of atmosphere, are considered as exciting causes of dysentery, co-operating with the more efficient, which give the form of the disease. Great variations of weather co-operate with all the hurtful agents, during every season of the year. But the cold seasons do not generate epidemic dysentery, independent of other causes. Is it remarkable, that dysentery succeeds sudden variations of weather, without the co-operation of other active agents? It has been observed, that this disease is mostly epidemic in that season, and those years, when there is the least variation; when the hot season continues during a long period, with little variation.

Heat may be considered an immediate exciting cause of dysentery, as well as mediate. An *immediate exciting cause*, by increasing the irritability of the body, or rendering it more susceptible of active stimulants, and thus co-operating with deleterious agents. An over proportion of caloric induces morbid excitability; to support the health of the body, due degrees of that powerful agent are necessary.

It is to be observed, that heat, also, is a *mediate*, or more remote cause of this disease, by a combination with moisture, acting upon vegetable and animal substances in a state of decay, favourable to a putrefactive process.

During the hot seasons of the year, an extensive section of a country may abound with deleterious agents, productions of putrefaction, so as to generate dysentery; which, from its general prevalence, may be denominated endemic. From the records of endemic diseases, evidence of the above position may be drawn. A diseased action of the organs of digestion, effects of intemperance, may induce in the alimentary canal morbid agents liberated by the process of putrefaction, and produce inflammation and all the symptoms of dysentery. Provisions in a tainted state, " replete with the poison of putrefaction," may be eaten by numbers, and who, at the same time, may be attacked with this disease. These last conditions will be denominated sporadic. The disease may originate from a combination of the above causes, infected air, impaired digestion, human excretions, and corrupted provisions taken as nutriment; and prevail under forms the most mortal. Thus generated, it frequently appears in camps, in besieged cities, in prisons and hospitals.

A question may be asked, in what manner gasseous poisons introduce themselves into the body from the atmosphere? The air impregnated with these volatile materials may be conveyed to the stomach with the saliva and nutriment in the act of deglutition; thence into the intestines. It is most evident, that these organs are primarily diseased, as if some poison had been swallowed. All the symptoms of morbid action, nausea, vomiting, and gripes demonstrate it; more particularly inflammation and ulceration of the intestines, when the disease is not cured in its early stage. The increased heat upon the surface, and obstructed perspiration, which are among the first symptoms, are the effects of association, not the causes of the disease. Such is the connexion between the internal viscera and the skin, that the diseased actions of the last are intimately connected with the morbid condition of the former.

If, as has been adduced, epidemics are all caused by the same exciting agents, it becomes a subject for enquiry, how the same cause, at one time is productive of *fever*, at another time *dysentery*, and at a third, *diarrhœa.*

We reply, that when the hurtful agents are absorbed into the pulmonic vessels, through the thin membranes of the lungs with the oxygen, and there united with the blood, thence conveyed to the heart, they become a direct stimulus to that organ and the arterial system; when a *fever* will be the effect. When the poisonous cause of diseased action is conveyed to the stomach and intestines, by deglutition, or in the act of swallowing our saliva, a *dysentery* may be the consequence; while a fever which accompanies it will be a secondary effect. But when the disease-generating-principles in their progress through the intestines, stimulate the gall duct, a flow of bile is thereby produced, and meeting the offending cause, a salutary *diarrhœa* may follow, which in its progress may wash from the canal the foul materials; when a natural cure may be effected.* It is further to

* Medical Repository.

be understood, these hurtful agents, under some circumstances, find access to the important organs of life, through all the avenues of the animal system.

Dissections have given us a clearer view of the diseased conditions of the intestines. In some cases they have been found ulcerated, or in high states of inflammation; in others, in a state of gangrene and mortification.

These morbid states, connected with the several forms and symptoms of the disease, direct us to the nature of the offending causes, which are lodged within the alimentary canal. From the morbid effects produced, they are believed to be of a caustic, or irritating quality. That their irritating property depends on acidity, is presumed from the well known beneficial effects of neutralizers of acids in this disease; and for a curative indication it is immaterial whether the offending principle, denominated acidities, is cause or effect.

From the diseased state of the alimentary organs in dysentery, and the combination of morbid actions, as symtoms associated with it, our indications of cure are obvious.

TREATMENT.

Having delineated the several forms under which dysentery appears, and concisely stated, what are believed to be the causes of the varieties, under which this disease commences; also, what are supposed the general causes; and as it is apprehended, these varieties are principally " influenced by climate, seasons and constitution, upon the disease, in different stages and degrees of it;" there will, in the curative indications, be considered two general states, or conditions of the disease; and under each be comprehended such varieties, as require particular methods of treatment.

I. When the disease is accompanied with heat, and a strong action of the arterial system of vessels, denoting a *synochal* state.

II. When the disease assumes a weak action of the heart and arteries, with languor and coldness, indicating a *typhoid* state.

A. When this disease is accompanied with high degrees of heat, strong action of the arterial system, severe gripes and tenesmus;

bleeding is indicated. From much experience we are convinced, that this is a remedy of too much importance to be omitted. By immediately abstracting from the body a quantity of stimulus, by blood-letting, heat is reduced, and pain mitigated. Bleeding is a well known mean of subduing inflammation, which constitutes the disease. It is not always the case that inflammation of the intestines exhibits itself by a strong and full pulse. Inflammation of the stomach as well as bowels, is usually accompanied with small action of the arteries, or rather contracted and hard pulse, at the same time, with no remarkable increased heat on the skin. This circumstance seems to contra-indicate the use of the lancet. Its employment, notwithstanding these appearances, is often as necessary in dysentery with the last described symptoms, as in pneumonia, with pain and great heat. Severe dysenteric symptoms, at their commencement, have been known to have been removed by one copious bleeding; and we have the practice of most celebrated authors upon the subject to justify its recommendation.

B. Remedies employed after venesection, are such as operate directly upon the diseased organs, by expelling or counteracting the causes of derangement. They are cathartics and emetics. The most violent forms of dysentery require the most prompt evacuations by the bowels, at the first attack of disease. Cathartics should be administered in full doses, so as to promote quick and thorough operations. From that class of medicine, which accelerates the peristaltic motion of the intestines, we select those articles, which purge effectually, with the least irritation, and occasion little or no gripings, viz. sulphate of soda, (glaubers salts;) sulphate of potash, (vitriolated tartar;) oil of castor. Submuriate of quicksilver, (calomel) is also employed in full doses for a cathartic. Jalap and calomel combined, is a favorite cathartic with some physicians on robust patients. Cathartics are to be employed, until the urgent symptoms of inflammation are abated. In idiopathic dysentery, little besides cathartics is necessary; for the disease is overcome in robust habits, as soon as the bowels are evacuated; when the appetite returns without any excitements. But after full evacuations,

the disease continuing, calomel, with or without opium, as symptoms demand, are administered; and in obstinate cases, are continued until a sore mouth, or gentle ptyalism is induced. It has
been frequently noticed, that as soon as the last effect has been
produced, the disease removes, or is mitigated. Ulcerations or
abrasions having supervened, experience has proved, that calomel is a doubtful medicine. Our practice in the army, demonstrated the correctness of the preceding observation.

c. Emetics are indicated, in cases where nausea and vomiting
exist, during the commencement of this disease. Tartrite of
antimony, (tartris antimon.) and ipecacuanha are severally or
jointly administered. The first of these emetics, in cases where
the patient is robust; the last, where delicate. Emetics not
only evacuate offending materials from the stomach, but promote
the secretions in general, particularly those of the liver and skin.
It has not escaped the observations of physicians, whenever a
full flow of bile follows the use of emetics or cathartics, the violent symptoms of this disease abate. A gentle perspiration succeeding any means employed, is considered a salutary symptom.

D. In cases where there is deficiency of bile, evidenced by
the absence of yellownes in the evacuations, by cardialgia, acid
eructations, and sensations of heat in the stomach; the following neutralizers of acids, magnesia, chalk, and lime-water, have
been employed, and not without benefit; but it has been experienced, that the weaker correctors of acidities are ineffectual
in all cases; and physicians of late are more in the use of alkalies, soda and potassa. Alkalies, it is to be observed, should be
employed in very diluted states, because when unneutralized,
they aggravate, by their stimulating properties, the inflammation
and pain in the bowels, when administered in quantity, greater
than necessary to neutralize the existent acidities. Doses are to
be regulated by effects produced.

E. Gripes and tenesmus, the most urgent symptoms of the disease, seem to demand the employment of anodynes. In the
use of these, much caution is to be exercised; and we should
be under some restriction in their administration. Although
the violence of the above symptoms, is, for a time, mitigated by

opium, yet, evacuations of the alimentary canal previous to their employment, are enjoined. By experience, we are convinced, that as soon as the pacific effects of opium cease, (anodynes having been employed, previous to suitable evacuations,) the gripes and tenesmus occur, and often with increased force, from the retention and consequent accumulation of the offending agents within the alimentary tube. The intestines, however, having been well evacuated, or the vitiating materials therein corrected, by the several means above recommended, opium becomes an indispensable remedy.

The beneficial effects of opium, in the synochal state of dysentery, are sometimes increased by calomel in small doses. By their joint operation, a kind of neutral effect is produced. The cathartic property of one obviates the restriction occasioned by the other ; so as while pain and tenesmus are mitigated by the anodyne effects of opium, the peristaltic action of the intestines is preserved by the calomel.

II. When the disease assumes a weak action of the heart and arteries with languor and coldness, indicating a typhoid state.

A. In this state, bleeding, either at the commencement, or in a more advanced stage of the disease, is unnecessary. Injurious consequences may follow its employment.

B. Cathartics, however, are indicated, for the same intentions as in the synochal, especially, where previous evacuations have not been made. Those cathartics already enumerated, as proper in the synochal state of the disease, may be employed here, where the vigour of the system, and strength of the stomach will admit of their use. But here, as no specific directions can be pointed out for every case, the judgment of the prescribing physician must dictate. As this state however is often accompanied with extreme debility and irritability of the stomach, inasmuch as it frequently rejects every article received; no prescription fulfils the intention of an evacuant so kindly, as a solution of manna, and cream of tartar, (super tartrite of potash,) or soluble tartar, (tartrite of potash,) administered at short intervals, i   ones which will not excite vomiting, until the proposed end is effected. No cathartic, in cases of nausea or vomit-

38

ing, is less offensive to the stomach; while it may with safety
be received in quantity sufficient to prove operative, even in cases of extreme debility.

c. Emetics of ipecacuanha are occasionally employed in this
state, as well as in the synochal; the doses should be regulated,
so as to produce one or two ejections at a time; and if necessary, may be repeated every day, or every second day. We
choose the morning for their administration, while the patient is
in bed. A smaller dose will answer the intention of an emetic,
at that time, in consequence of increase of sensorial power during sleep. (See DARWIN.) Emetics prove more diaphoretic,
and determine the material of perspiration to the skin most effectually, while the patient is in bed.

D. Alkalies in diluted states are employed in this state of
dysentery. To render them more agreeable to the palate,
and accommodating to the nauseated stomach, (for nausea, generally, accompanies the typhoid state of dysentery,) they are
joined to weak aromatics and bitters in decoction, or infusion;
viz. serp. virgin. (aristolochia serpentaria;) colombo. By these
means, we artificially furnish the intestines with the soda and
the bitter of bile.

E. Blisters are found beneficial in the typhoid state of dysentery. In the synochal, they are seldom necessary. In cases
of most obstinate pain, by making a derivation from the diseased
viscera, or by their counter-stimulus, they remove spasm, and
avert danger. When applied in cases of debility upon the epigastric, or umbilical regions, they not only mitigate pain, but
check nausea and vomiting. In states of languor, and where
coldness has supervened, their application upon the extremities
are important; while the daily repetition of one is beneficial to
excite the torpid system, and support the powers of life, sinking
under the weight of disease.

F. Opium has been, and is, at this time, on account of its restrictive powers, employed as the principal remedy for the cure
of dysentery by some physicians. It is our opinion, we should
be under restrictions even in a typhoid state of the disease, as
to its employment. Previous to which, evacuations are neces--

ary; while sometimes after its anodyne effects are over, a repetition of eccoprotics is demanded. In many cases opium becomes important, by procuring ease and sleep; and seems to invigorate the body worn out by tenesmus.

G. The tepid bath has been advantageously employed in some states of dysentery. It admirably co-operates with opium to remove spasm and pain. The bath relaxes the vessels upon the surface, which, by association with the intestines, mitigates griping pains within them. It also equalises, by its diffusive effects, the excitement throughout the animal system.

H. Mucilages, prepared from the farinacea, the gums and woods, are auxiliaries in the cure of every condition of dysentery. In severe cases, at the commencement of the disease, these soft articles may be taken in large quantities. From a vast variety at command, the judicious physician has an opportunity to make his selection.

I. Enemas, prepared with the mucilages, are often employed with much advantage, in cases of extreme irritability of the intestines. Where tenesmus is a very distressing symptom, we add laudanum to these mucilaginous enemas.

K. After evacuations have been employed, and pain and inflammation overcome by the various means above mentioned; and where the dyspeptic symptoms shew the inactive condition of the stomach and other organs, subservient to digestion; physicians have employed the cortex peruvianus, (chinchona,) astringents and bitters. We are not however convinced from experience, a preference is to be given to any one of these classes of medicine; which, by authors, have been supposed specific remedies in dysentery. Astringents and bitters may be of use under some circumstances. In whatever manner these medicines act, to give tone to the stomach and intestines, when in a condition to receive them; they should be cautiously employed, on account of the increased irritability of the alimentary canal in this disease. Where stimulants are demanded to support the action of the system of vessels, in the last and sinking stage of this disease, we administer wine in small doses, but frequently and with moderation; adapting the quantity to the state of debility, and excitability.

l. Diarrhœa and lienteria sometimes assume the place of dysentery.* In these cases, more dependence is to be placed upon opium and ipecacuanha combined, than upon astringents and bitters. Small and repeated doses of ipecacuanha, so as to excite vomiting, are found useful: a small emetic every twenty-four hours, for a few days. Anodynes, frequently repeated in small doses, are preferable to full doses, at long intervals.

m. In the apthous state of dysentery, we recommend the trial of blood-root, (sanguinaria canadense;) also, marsh rosemary, (Statice Limonium.) From the above medicine we have experienced benefit. They are generally employed in decoction, or infusion. In one case, where from soreness of the mouth, fauces and throat, swallowing was difficult; and from extreme irritability of the stomach, it rejected most articles; a tea-spoonful of olive oil was administered every fifteen minutes for twenty-four hours, and after, at intervals somewhat longer, in larger quantity; and was thus continued several days. This, with some soft nutriment, was supposed to be a mean of preserving life, and finally of restoring the patient to health.

n. In cases, where blood unmixed is evacuated in profusion, opium, bark and wine are among the principal remedies. This state of disease is not accompanied with pain; wherefore, abrasions are not here suspected. The liver is believed the source from which the blood flows. In these cases of active intestinal hemorrhages, the mineral astringents have been employed with much success; acetite of lead, (acetas plumbi;) vitriol of zinc, (sulphas zinci.) As it is highly probable, that these discharges of blood are from the liver, would a blister upon the region of this viscus be of service, to remove its torpidity?

DIETETIC MANAGEMENT.

In dysentery, the diet is to be regulated by the state of the disease. In all cases, the nutriment should consist principally of the farinaceous preparations; viz. rice, sago, salep, gruels prepared from the flour of the various species of corn, &c. So dispos-

* In the practice of the army, we experienced dysenteric symptoms, as tormenting gripes, and tenesmus to succeed diarrhœas.

ed is the alimentary canal to favor the putrefactive process within it, on account of the deficiency of bile and gastric liquors,
as well as excessive inflammation; animal nutriment is to be
prohibited the patient. After the disease is mitigated or removed, and appetite restored, a vegetable diet with milk should
be continued during a state of convalescency. Relapses have
been known to succeed an indulgence of animal nutriment,
even in a liquid form.*

Where stimulants higher in degree than simple vegetable nutriment are demanded to support the powers of life, wine is the
most appropriate. In all states of these disorders of the bowels, simplicity of diet is to be studied; the less compounded and
multiplied the regimen, the greater success may be expected.§

PRACTICAL REMARKS AND OBSERVATIONS.

1st. Physicians, conversant with dysentery, may have observed at the first onset of the disease, where there is great heat
and strength, the doses of cathartics are required to be larger,
than in most other diseases. By early and timely evacuations, the feculent, corruptible contents of the intestinal canal
are discharged before its coats are extremely diseased, and the
constitution weakened. The more thorough the cathartic operations in the commencement of the disease are, the less frequent the diseased tenesmal efforts, and less severe the gripes.
There are, after full dejections, always longer intermissions of
pain.

2nd. The morbid action of the intestines should not be mistaken for the operation of purgatives. The declarations of ignorant nurses are not to be depended upon, respecting evacuations from the bowels. Physicians, after the exhibition of ca-

* Among the soldiers on the frontiers, no article of diet agreed with the
sick, under diarrhœa, and dysenteric symptoms, so well as milk, and its
preparations in the form of porridge.

§ Army patients, with chronic diarrhœa, were supported a long time,
with diluted brandy, and opium occasionally; in addition to the above soft
nutriment.

thartics, should examine the stools to satisfy themselves, whether a cathartic has performed its office.

3d. The most drastic purges are not best adapted to the inflamed state of the inner coats of the intestines in dysentery. Irritating purges are not retained upon the stomach in many cases; and if they are retained, the effects of their stimulating properties continue a greater length of time upon the intestines, than neutral purging salts, or oil of castor; which operate quick and with little pain. In diarrhœa and lienteria, rhubarb, (rheum) in small doses, combined with magnesia, or chalk, has been administered by physicians, upon supposition that in addition to its cathartic property, it possesses considerable restrictive powers, noticed by the costive state which succeeds its cathartic operation.

4th. Antimonial emetics should be confined to patients of robust habits, while the disease is accompanied with heat and high inflammation. The active antimonial preparations operate severely upon the intestines, under high states of excitability from inflammation, or under states of debility. The glass of antimony, (oxidum antimonii cum sulphure virtrificatum) should be employed with much caution. This last antimonial preparation had acquired much of its reputation in the cure of dysentery, among that class of men, whose systems had become firm, and fibres rigid by hardships long endured. Among patients of every description and age, it should not be employed. " After the cerated glass of antimony had been introduced into practice, its reputation spread in Europe; but from the unguarded manner of giving it, while the patient was exposed, it was always dangerous, and sunk into discredit." The last observation was quoted from PRINGLE's diseases of the army.* HILLORY observes, " though it may be a good medicine when properly timed; yet, as it is frequently and promiscuously given in this disease, and under all circumstances, it cannot succeed." Doctor MOSELEY says, " he gave to a soldier three grains of glass of an-

---

* We have had occasion to protest against the employment of antimonials, in the field practice of our armies.

timony, finely powdered, made into a pill, in the worst condition of dysentery, with blood running from him, as an hemorrhage from a wound; it operated upwards and downwards; a violent sweat ensued; which was kept up by warm herb teas, and small doses of laudanum; which last is given with safety while the patient is sweating; even the first stool after sweating began, has been less bloody; the third and fourth scarcely tinged." Such he says is the power of revulsion. Doctor CULLEN employs tartrite of antimony, (tartris antimonii) in small doses; and observes, " its beneficial effects are mostly to be seen, when it operates by stool." If the principal benefit, expected from its employment, is its cathartic operation, it should with other active antimonials give place to those purges, whose salutary effects are more certain, and danger less doubtful.

5th. Ipecacuanha has been employed either as an emetic, or cathartic, from most ancient time down to the present, in the diseases of the bowels. Its superior efficacy was observed by PISO; and " where the evacuations were mixed with blood," he resorted to this medicine " as a sacred anker, than which nothing was more safe and effectual." He administered this drug in all fluxes, after the following prescription. Two drams of ipecacuanha were directed in four ounces of water; one ounce of which was frequently given for a dose, and daily repeated, until the disease was overcome. HUXHAM began the cure of this disease, most generally, by bleeding and ipecacuanha. TISSOT says, that tartrite of antimony will sometimes cure; but that an emetic of ipecacuanha is not less efficacious; and has been esteemed a certain specific in dysentery. BROCKLESBY, on diseases of the army, says, " a combination of two grains of opium, with three of ipecacuanha, made into a pill, was highly beneficial." PRINGLE also attests to the efficacy of this medicine administered, so as to operate as a cathartic; for which intention, he administered five grains every hour to his patients, until the desired operation was produced.*

---

* No article of the materia medica proved equally beneficial and safe, in chronic dysentery, and diarrhœa, as they appeared in our armies on the

6th. Astringents have been employed in dysentery, upon an erroneous opinion, that the frequent inclination to stool is the consequence of immoderate action of the intestines, the effects of debility; and that they required tonics and astringents to restrain profuse discharges. Premature administrations of this class of medicine, we are confident, have been productive of danger; as the fecal materials are thereby confined, and inflammation increased, inducing an increased tendency to gangrene and mortification.* In the convalescent state succeeding dysentery, and where tonics may with safety be employed, we have not succeeded as well with chinchona, as other articles of this class of medicine.

Physicians in the United States, we are warranted to notice, have not experienced the same efficacy from the bark, which British writers have ascribed to it; and have been disappointed in it, when administered agreeably to their practice, in apparently similar states of disease. Can this be accounted for upon any principle, but the known fact, that the poorer inhabitants of Europe, among whom diseases are most prevalent when they are epidemic, are generally supported with food less nutritious, than the Americans? The first, with their lax fibres, assume, when attacked with febrile diseases, that typhoid form, which requires tonics and stimulants; which experience proves to be inadmissible, in states of disease, apparently similar, among the well fed inhabitants of the United States. And where astringents and bitters are required, the indigenous productions of our own soil being fresh, are not less efficacious than exotics,

northern frontiers, as a combination of ipecacuanha and opium, in the form of Dover's powder. This has been before noticed, in the preceding Sketches, to which the reader is referred.

* The fatal effects of astringents during the war were often demonstrated; especially, when evacuations were suddenly checked by their use, when men were exposed to cold and moisture. These effects were most conspicuous, after the employment of acetite of lead. Cases in the foregoing Sketches are evidence convincing, without resorting to argumentative elucidation, to shew the manner, by which the injurious effects were produced.

found in the stores of druggists, subject to damage and corruption, by which their virtues are either destroyed or impaired.

7th. Diffusive stimulants perhaps, are in more general use among the inhabitants, than any article of the materia medica, when they are first seized with these complaints of the bowels. In all complaints of this description, ardent spirits are first resorted to by the ignorant; these potent stimulants are also directed by those who profess to be wise. We cannot deny, a disease caused by an extremely high degree of morbid exciting powers, may be subdued by active stimulants. But this favorable event is too seldom, to warrant our indiscriminate recommendation of them. The ingenious speculations of BROWN, in some measure, introduced the high stimulant plan of *attempting to cure diseases*, to the notice of physicians. His bold unqualified assertion, that ninety-eight out of an hundred cases, required stimulants, is not only imposing and pleasing to us, circumscribed as our knowledge of the states of diseases is, but is a subterfuge for ignorance; because if stimulants were prescribed in every case, were the position true, the prescribing physician could not err but twice, in one hundred cases. It had been believed, the stimulant plan recommended by BROWN, was going out of practice.*

SYDENHAM, however, has left on record, he cured at one period, dysentery by opium. In this instance, the disease appeared probably, more under the form of diarrhœa or lienteria, than when the disease was considered by him, as the fever of the season, turned in upon the bowels; in which he urged the necessity of evacuating the alimentary canal, previous to the employment of stimulants or anodynes. In chronic complaints of the bowels, in army practice, opium was indispensable, as well as ardent spirits diluted, but in moderate quantity.

* It has lately been revived in the New-England States, to a degree which is astonishing. The glass doses of BROWN, in consequence of want of success, have been by *the wise Æsculapeans*, increased to pint doses. Still with all this improvement, death closed the scene. The physicians, although fairly beaten, acquired high degrees of honor, by their perseverance, and courageously fighting their foe, to the last breath.

39

8th. MOSELEY believed, the matter of perspiration, thrown upon the intestines, in consequence of obstruction on the surface of the body, is the cause of dysentery; and conceived by returning it back to the skin, its natural channel, the disease is readily removed. After bleeding, and evacuations by emetics and cathartics, he depended on sudorifics to complete the cure. With this intention "laudanum and antimonial wine" were recommended, "as a pleasant, and certain diaphoretic." JAMES' powder, he says, is admirably calculated to answer the above intention. If the disease continues obstinate, repeated vomits of ipecacuanha are given, to divert the blood from the intestines, and force it to the surface of the body. Let it be here observed, that however correct MOSELEY'S practice might be, yet it does not follow, that obstructed perspiration is the cause of dysentery. And inasmuch as an evacuation from one part will remove inflammation from one remote by revulsion, or by absorption; such evacuation should be promoted, not however from a belief that obstructed perspiration is the cause, but an effect, which should be obviated, to expedite the cure of this disease. Dysenteric patients therefore, should not be exposed to currents of air, or cold, but confined in situations favorable to promote perspiration.

9th. "In chronic dysentery, and perverse diarrhœa, which may occur in practice; from errors, want of skillful advice and conveniences," MOSELEY gives a formula, composed of sulphate of zinc and alum, which may be found in his treatise on tropical diseases. The quantities of the vitriol and alum, are varied in the prescription, as their restrictive or evacuating properties are required.*

10th. Dysenteric patients, where their diseases are chronic, and obstinately resist common remedies, have been benefitted, if not cured by flannel waistcoats next the skin; and they become more important, when the disease continues into winter;

* This vitriolic preparation, was repeatedly tried in army and hospital practice, on the northern fro iers, without apparent benefit; still we have reason to believe, under some circumstances, it is a valuable medicine in these chronic diseases of the bowels.

when every mean should be employed, to support the action of the extreme vessels, by retaining the caloric of the body, and obviating its evaporation upon the surface.

11th. A change of climate becomes necessary sometimes, to cure chronic dysenteries and diarrhœas. Invalids in the West-Indies, have been frequently advised to remove to the eastern states of America, to re-establish health. It has been observed, when these convalescents do not arrive, until the setting in of frost in autumn, their complaints deteriorate, or continue through the cold of winter, until the warmth of summer commences. As our cold latitudes prevent the necessary action upon the skin, and a general healthy excitement, warmer latitudes are to be preferred.

12th. When diarrhœas become chronic in our climate, and obstinately resist remedies, until autumn commences; the patients have been benefitted by a change, either to southern latitudes of the United States, or the West-Indies.

13th. Too much attention cannot be paid to cleanliness in all diseases, more especially in this, which, from its nature, is peculiarly offensive. Excrementitious materials, should be immediately removed from the sick room. When it is apprehended that a prevalent disease might have originated, or been aggravated by materials in a state of putrefaction, the offensive articles should be immediately removed from the vicinity of dwellings, or covered with earth; and if from neglect of domestic ablutions and purifications, "recourse should be had to means well known to every wash-woman, but too little practised by a large proportion of mankind; viz. a liberal use of water, soap and lime."

CONCLUSION.

From the earliest ages of antiquity, physicians have been searching after specifics to cure all diseases. Some have flattered thems. 'ves, every disease, to which the human body is liable, has either upon the surface of the globe, or concealed within its bowels, an antidote; while others have believed, there existed under some form, an universal medicine; which, as with a charm, possessed the wonderful power, not only of removing

infirmities accompanying diseases, but the imbecilities peculiar
to old age.

That medical enthusiasts, and pretenders of the healing art,
should have frequently imposed upon the credulous their specifics, for the cure of diseases, which experience proves to be a de-
ception, is not a passing strange event; but, that mankind, not
satisfied with having paid one tax on account of their credulity,
should, at this more enlightened period of the arts and sciences,
suffer many to be extorted by artful impostors, is truly wonderful.

The name of a disease, by the scientific physician, is less attended to, while making his prescriptions, than the state; while
experience evinces, that a specific does scarcely exist; and
a medicine, possessing the powers to cure all diseases, is a mere
fancy of an extravagant imagination.

The various states of excitability, to which the human system
is subjected, in consequence of the variableness in the seasons,
of age and temperament, evince this incontrovertible truth, that
the same exciting powers, are not adapted to every existing
state of disease. A general knowledge of the above physiolog-
ical fact, may prevent impositions from those, who deal in specifics and catholicons; as well as ensure a more judicious practice, from the honestly disposed physician.

WINTER EPIDEMIC OF 1815--16.

An epidemic peripneumonia notha prevailed during part of the month of February, March, and into April, in the town of Sharon, County of Norfolk, twenty miles southerly from Boston; where in the course of ten days, eighteen persons out of the first twenty-four cases of the disease died. In consequence of the alarm given by this uncommon mortality, I was invited to attend the sick. During my stay of sixteen days in the town, I visited between sixty and seventy patients, who were attacked with this malady; of whom three died, one of eighty-two, one of seventy-two, and one of sixty-two years of age. The following extract of a letter which appeared in the Boston Patriot, and Daily Advertiser, is expressive of the opinion, which the inhabitants of the town of Sharon possessed, respecting the practice which was adopted by myself, in that complaint.

"Through the medium of your paper, we wish to express our full satisfaction of Doctor Mann's practice; believing as we do, that he is as well qualified to combat the mortal effects of this disease, as any physician within the circle of our knowledge."

"It is our wish, he would lay before the public, the nature of this disease, which has appeared to confound and distract many; while his method of practice, different in many respects from what had been pursued, might be a mean of saving many valuable lives."

(Signed)

ENOCH HEWINS, Jun.
JOHN MORSE,
BENJAMIN RAYNOLDS,
JOHN SAVELS,
OLIVER WILLIAMS,
JONATHAN COBB,
RANSLE JONES,
TYLER PITTEE,

} *Selectmen of Sharon*

LEWIS MORSE,
AARON FISHER,
JOSEPH MORSE,
ELIJAH HEWINS, Jun.

In the same paper, notice was given, that in compliance with the request of the gentlemen of the town of Sharon, it was my intention to give to the public, a statement of the prevalent epidemic, as it appeared at that place, under its various forms, with the most successful method of practice pursued. After exhibiting my general practice, it was observed, I had never seen the *peripneumonia notha,* as an epidemic in this section of New-England, until I saw the disease at *Sharon;* that sporadic cases of this disease sometimes occur on the aged and infirm, during periods of pneumonic disorders; that about fifty years ago, a similar disease, which proved very mortal, appeared in the upper towns of Norfolk, and adjacent towns in the county of Bristol; and that many physicians have seemed to run wild, with appearances of new diseases.

Hence, we find diseases at the present day, described under new names; which are calculated to seduce the young practitioner, from a correct and established practice. It is true, that improvements have been made in the science of medicine; but it requires a discriminating mind, and an extensive knowledge of ancient as well as modern authors, so to apply these improvements, as to be able to meet diseases, in all their varying shapes, which they assume in the routine of years.

A student of the present day, may make himself well acquainted with the prevailing diseases of his time, by a little reading, and an extensive practice under a judicious physician; but without an extensive knowledge of books, can he be prepared to prescribe with the best effects, to a disease, the form of which he has never seen, and of which he has little or no knowledge, by the aid of medical books?

For instance, the spotted fever, when it first appeared, was considered a novel disease. It is not a new disease under the sun. Various remedies were prescribed, by the most judicious, before a permanent efficient practice was adopted. After the spotted fever had its mortal race a few years, at its heel, appeared the *peripneumonia notha,* no less formidable in various places on the northern frontiers, during the winters of 1812–13–14, not only among the troops, but with *equal mortality* over an extensive district of country among the citizens, in the states of New-York, Connecticut, Massachusetts, Vermont and New-Hampshire; and where these two formidable disorders were frequently confounded with each other.—From the sudden deaths which occurred, and the general fatal tendency of the last disease, physicians conceived it was *typhoid*, or a disease of debility; whence ardent spirits and wine were resorted to as remedies. Indeed, when the *peripneumonia notha* first appeared at Burlington, Vermont, and its vicinty, in 1812–13, it was viewed and treated by some, as that form of disease called *spotted fever* had been. By the last name, the *pneumonic epidemic* of the last winter, in some parts of the counties of Norfolk and Bristol, has been called; especially where it has proved *mortal*; for every mortal disease, whether necessarily mortal from its nature, or bad management, must have attached to it some *terrific* name; and since *spotted fever* has become a fashionable frightful disease, the *old* and more common *terrific* term *malignant* is laid up for future use; but how soon it may again be ordered into service, time, which changes the fashion of *names*, as well as things, will only disclose.

This same *peripneumonia notha*, has also attached to it in some places, the additional *terrible* name *cold plague*; in consequence of a torpor and coldness, which accompanies its first attack. Thus this disease commenced its first onset, in *Attleborough, Mansfield, Wrentham, Sharon*, &c.

Thus we perceive, a *formidable name*, in many instances, instrumental of introducing an incorrect practice, to the no small discredit of the medical profession; and this will ever be the case, while physicians administer to *names*, rather than the *symptoms* and *states* of disease.

In some places, profuse sweatings have been resorted to, in the first attack of this disease. If any have been so fortunate as to pass through this mode of practice, in addition to the weight of disease, they have abundant reason to bless their strength of constitution, not their prescribing physicians. I have the fullest evidence to convince myself, that many have succumbed under this absurd practice. Some probably have survived this violent process, as well as the more stimulating practice of ardent spirits, by *pints* and *quarts;* their number however, are too few to induce a belief, that these irregular means, are the most eligible remedies.

As this disease is nearly allied to the more common disease, denominated pleurisy; bleeding, was, in some instances, indiscriminately resorted to, at its first attack, in connection with stimulants; but as death too frequently followed this irregular practice, it was rejected as a deadly practice, *in toto.* Almost every potent remedy has had its day of trial, in this epidemic; and in their turn, have been indiscriminately condemned. Whereas, many of those, excepting profuse sweatings, and ardent spirits, may be not only suitable, but necessary, in some of the forms of this disease; while the success of their different administrations, depends altogether upon the ages, constitutions, temperaments, and habits of the patients.

At *Sharon,* the *peripneumonia notha* made its first attack, with symptoms of uncommon coldness and torpor, which pervaded the whole system, without those strong rigors observed in pleurisy, and intermittent fever; the heat of the body at the same time, to the touch, much below the standard of health. During the state of torpor, an oppressed respiration supervened, accompanied with pain in one side, which increased, as the paroxism of fever came on. The heat of the body during the febrile stage, was never much above the standard of health; sometimes the heat did not appear to be higher in degree than natural. The pulse during the cold stage, was very small; and somewhat fuller than natural, during the hot stage; but not what might be denominated a hard full pulse, except in two or three instances, in very robust constitutions. There was a remarkable pale pink coloured suffusion over the whole face, distinct from the usual febrile blush in the cheeks; the appearance was similar to the sudden flush colour, produced by sitting before a fire, after having been exposed to cold. This appearance was most conspicuous on persons having fair and light complexions. This was accompanied with a bloated countenance, which gave to the spare and pale-faced patient, additional beauty to the general features. This rouge-like appearance, was less conspicuous on the body, than the face. A cough supervened, after the first twenty-four hours, in some instances; and when it was accompanied with an expectoration, the pain in the side abated; but if no expectoration accompanied the cough, all the dangerous symptoms were aggravated. The expectoration was different, according to the degrees of danger. The matter expectorated, did not appear like common mucus; but more similar to lymph, intimately tinged or tinctured with blood, varying its hue in different subjects. Sometimes the expectoration was ash-coloured, or dark brown; in a few cases, it was a simple phlegm. The tongue, the first twenty-four hours, assumed a very foul appearance, from a thick yellow fur, to a dark brown colour. The dark coloured tongues, were dry, hard, and rough; and on the second day, appeared like the dark furred tongues of those, who have been sick with typhous fever a fortnight; when, after the fur separated, or sloughed off, the tongue appeared of strawberry, or cranberry red, as did the fauces. It is to be noticed, that during the cold stage, the patients suffered from pain throughout the muscles of the body, in one case similar to rheumatism. In four or five instances, this epidemic made its assault upon the head; which bleeding immediately relieved; upon enquiry, I found there was here no complaint whatever within the chest. It was then prognosticated, that in twenty-four hours, more or less disease would exhibit itself on the lungs. This prediction, which was presumed upon former experience, on the northern frontiers, was fulfilled in every instance where made; while the pneumonic symptoms which followed, were not eventually less severe, than in those cases, where the first symptoms of disease shewed themselves, within the breast.

There were *three* among seventy or more sick, not marked with characteristic symptoms of the epidemic, which assumed the form of genuine *erysipelas*; where the inflammation, in one instance, pervaded successively every part of the body. These forms of disease, were unaccompanied with any pneumonic affection; but required the general remedies employed in that complaint.

This disease was not confined to any age; upon those over

40

fifty years, it was most severe; it appeared on those under ten years of age, as a common pneumonia. A similar disease prevailed in some of the neighbouring towns, during the winter months; and in the town of *Attleborough*, distant fifteen miles from *Sharon;* more than one hundred died with this epidemic, in the course of three months.

The weather during the past winter was very changeable. After a very cold period in the month of January, and during part of the month of February, the transition from cold to very warm, was sudden. This month anticipated spring, so as to dissolve the ice in the fresh ponds in the country. The change again was so great in the month of March, from very pleasant to severe cold, that these ponds were again frozen; and during the last month, the daily transitions of weather were great; and these sudden variations continued into May. These transitions are believed to have been one cause of this epidemic. To search for remote predisponent causes, floating on the wings of the wind, is like building castles in the air. Atmospheric influences, independent of hot and dry, cold and wet, are out of the bounds of our circumscribed knowledge; and were we able to comprehend their nature, could we by any means control their powers, so as to obviate their effects upon the human constitution?

While the animal creation is fortified by nature, against the varying seasons, and more sudden transitions of weather; man is endowed with reason to direct him, how to avoid their deleterious effects. This first gift of heaven will not be improved to secure his health, while he erroneously believes, that occult agents are the sole causes of disease. Natural evil is so intimately connected with moral, to obviate the *first*, man should shun the *last*. No species of irregularity, predisposes the body to disease, in so high degrees, as an intemperate use of ardent spirits; while, during periods of epidemic diseases, these exciting liquors are swallowed by those ignorant of their dangerous tendency, in still greater profusion, as a mean to obviate those very diseases, which they often generate, or excite to states of excessive danger. One of the most effectual means, to secure the body against all our winter epidemics, is warm clothing; and could the inhabitants of New-England, but be made sensible, that ardent spirits do not protect the body from diseases of any kind; and would they adopt a firm resolution, to drink none of these stimulating liquors, and place the value usually consumed, in woollen or flannel garments upon their bodies, they would, when they settle their annual accounts, find themselves not only richer in the means to render themselves happy, but abounding in health; the greatest blessing which man can possess on earth.

Vicious habits once confirmed, are with difficulty overcome; but however bad, they may be conquered by persevering resolution. Those, who have been in the intemperate use of ardent spirits, experience a sinking sensation at the stomach, when they abstain from these liquors; which discourages them in their first attempts to reform. The stimulating effects of ardent spirits, are of short duration; while the debility induced, renders the subjects of intemperance not less, but more susceptive of cold.

To cure intemperance, the patient may advantageously drink sweetened water, charged with ginger or red pepper; in the proportion of a table-spoonful of the first, or a tea-spoonful of the last, to a pint of water. When the above liquor is drank to resist cold, it should be taken into the stomach milk warm; and where it is advised to old inebriates, the water should be as highly impregnated with the pepper, as can be borne on the stomach.

Much experience has convinced me, that nothing fortifies the body to endure severe cold so long, as strong coffee, with a small quantity of animal food. The writer of this, has repeatedly rode on horseback fifty miles, in a cold winter's day, without taking into his stomach any stimulating article, except hot coffee, and a piece of bread and meat. With this stimulus alone, he was rendered capable of enduring the severest cold of a northern climate, three hours, with little inconvenience. Where circumstances do not admit of the benefit of coffee beverage, the ginger and pepper drink may be equally beneficial, taken with some animal nutriment; and perhaps more useful than coffee, to those habituated to the stimulus of ardent spirits.

Among the means most effective, to secure the body from attacks of infectious diseases, are cleanliness, cheerfulness, and a
soft nutritious diet. Fear, despondency, fatigue, and long watchings, co-operate with hurtful agents, to produce disease. When
a violent disease assails one member of a family, and others in
the same dwelling are taken down, it is often apprehended the
disease is contagious. The sick are shunned by friends, and
assistance is with difficulty procured. Hence, during epidemics,
the diseased, who might have been preserved by suitable means,
perish; while the general and local causes of the disease, as putrid effluvia, transitions of weather, &c. co-operate with the fac-
titious, to induce on each individual, a similar disease. I once
predicted, that a family would be invaded by disease. The
precaution was suggested, to induce a removal of filth, which
incommoded their habitation, during the hot season. Previous
to the expiration of four weeks, my prognostication was verified,
by the appearance of a typhous fever, which seized successively
the whole family. In this instance, as in similar occurrences,
a belief existed, that the fever was contagious, and communicated from one to others. The truth was, as all were subjected
to the generating cause of the disease, the surrounding filth, so
all were infected.

During periods of epidemic disorders, every irregularity, capable of exciting disorder in the system, will produce a disease,
correspondent with that form of fever most prevalent. This of
itself is evidence, that during these states, more or less predisposition to disease, exists within the human system, even when
a person appears in perfect health. A transition from high
states of health, to severe disease, is not unfrequent, sometimes
very sudden; and a disease which might have been light, produced by mere atmospheric influence, may become, by additional exciting causes, extremely dangerous. The scourge of
epidemics may, in some degree, be prevented, by protecting the
body from cold, by woollen garments next the skin; by a rigid
temperance in eating and drinking; by avoiding excessive fatigues and watchings, and contaminated air, generated in small
close rooms, by an assemblage of people; and after respiring

fonger, than to restore natural heat. The cure depended upon assiduous administration of the antiphlogistic regimen; evacuants, expectorants and diaphoretics, with the aid of blisters.

Bleeding was considered among the first remedies; not because it was demanded in all cases, but the first in order where indicated. It could not be dispensed with in many cases, but should in no instance be employed, until natural heat is restored; and then repeated small bleedings were preferred to one or two large. If we were to be governed by professional rules, the pulse seldom indicated the employment of the lancet. It was pain and laborious respiration which directed its use; while the practice was warranted by repeated and acknowledged succe. , which followed blood-letting. In most obstinate cases, it was employed two, three and four times in twenty-four hours. A practice similar, was attended with the best effects, during the winters 1812-13-14, on the northern frontiers. It is however to be observed, fewer cases required bleeding at *Sharon* and *Rochester*, than in the army, and the reason is obvious. In hospital practice, its beneficial effects were more evident; the patients were continually under the eye of the surgeons, who improved the import t moment, when bleeding was most necessary. In country practice, where patients cannot receive a visit only once in twenty-four hours, the favorable period for bleeding, or its repetition was frequently lost.

At *Sharon*, out of sixty cases, seven were bled; those who were bled, recovered. Three who were advanced in years, who were not bled, died. At *Rochester*, twenty out of near seventy cases, which came under my observation, were bled; three of whom died. One of whom was bled eight ounces, and within twenty-four hours, took one hundred grains of calomel, one hundred grains of jalap, two ounces of castor oil, and four ounces of sulphate of soda, all of which produced only two small evacuations. In this case, the lancet was timidly employed. The man was very robust; previous to the disease, for a length of time, he had been in the daily habit of drinking a pint or more of ardent spirits. This man died suffocated, while walking his room. The two others, it was believed, counteracted the beneficial ef fects of remedies, by an habitual employment of opium; from the use of which, they would not be restrained.

It was most evident, the pulse became fuller, and heat of the body increased after the first bleedings, when difficult respiration abated. If this most dreaded symptom was not overcome by the third, fourth or fifth day, the patient died, suffocated; in strength, not in a typhous state of fever, as by many has been apprehended.

The internal remedies upon which most dependence was placed were calomel and antimonials. These were repeated in doses, every two or three hours, so as to prove cathartic within the first twenty-four hours; and if not effected in the above time, a full cathartic of calomel and jalap, twenty grains each was administered, which was sometimes repeated. From one to five grains of calomel, and from $\frac{1}{4}$ to $\frac{1}{8}$ of tartrite of antimony were continued at short intervals, until a resolution of fever was effected. The commencement of which was known by a free expectoration, and a gentle diaphoresis. In robust habits, drastic purges were occasionally repeated; in less robust, cathartics of sulphate of soda, or castor oil, fulfilled the intention. Sometimes ipecacuanha was combined with calomel in small doses, instead of the antimony; especially when disposed to pass off by the bowels.

In most severe cases, calomel was believed of so much importance, that we were certain to effect a cure, when a sore mouth was produced by its use.

Emetics were not administered until after bleeding (where necessary,) and cathartics had been employed; especially where the head or breast were affected with severe pain. After expectoration had supervened, and from any cause it stopped, small emetics of ipecacuanha were found beneficial, while their repetition was necessary. This seldom failed to reproduce expectoration. In apthous state of fever, ipecacuanha, blood-root, and seneka in small repeated doses, were employed with advantage.

Extensive blisters on the chest, were of the highest importance, from the commencement of the disease. These, in obstinate cases, were daily renewed with benefit; blister succeeding blister on the side and breast, until pain was removed.

Stimulants of ardent spirits or vinous liquors, were of no benefit in the course of the fever, nor even during convalescency. The only stimulus employed in the convalescent state, was a mixture of spirits of nitre dulcified, and water of volatile ammonia, in such proportions as the volatile predominated. A teaspoonful of this compound, proved a cordial and expectorant, at the termination of the disease, administered once in three or four hours; as did also a mixture of equal parts of camphorated tincture of opium and antimonial wine, where a cough was troublesome.

Opium was of no use to subdue pain in the disease; it was found injurious until fever was overcome; combined sometimes either with calomel or ipecacuanha, at the close of fever to allay cough, it was advantageous.

Relapses have succeeded the use of ardent spirits during the state of convalescency. These stimulants, in every instance where employed under my observation, have checked that expectoration from the lungs, which is so necessary to complete a resolution of the disease, and which was considered the natural cure of that formidable epidemic. Many have died under a stimulating regimen, which had been adopted at the commencement of the disease, or been introduced during its more advanced stage; under a presumption, the disease was typhous, or had a tendency to that state. Whereas, when the disease was overcome by the antiphlogistic practice, the appetite returned without the aid of excitements. The natural stimulants of life only were necessary, to restore health and give strength.

41